Praise for *The Ride Together*

"[E]xtends out of the page and pulls you in. Still, it's David who sets the family apart. . . . He's a vivid character—a mystery that we want to solve but never can."

—Andrew Arnold, *Time*

"Unsentimental and unorthodox . . . a candid, funny, and nuanced portrait." —*City Paper*

"Beautiful. . . . a hard, honest, and poignant look at how family works. A powerful story, told with tolerance, in pictures and in words."

—Patricia MacLachlan, Newbery Award winner, *Sarah, Plain and Tall*

"A funny and no-punches-pulled account of family life when one member is very different from most people, yet no less interesting and no less loved. . . . What sets this book apart is its genuinely moving sentiment that never devolves into cheap sentimentality."

—*The Hartford Courant* (CT)

"Fascinating reading. The vivid portrait of David—a loving, joyous, dignified, and creative person—demonstrates the potential and the humanity of all people with disabilities."

—Steven M. Eidelman, Executive Director of the Arc of the United States

"[A] deeply affecting joint memoir . . . Judy [writes] with a spare elegance that makes one hope to see a novel from her some day. . . . Paul's similarly economical drawing style answers in ebullience and even glee his sister's greater emotional intensity; he lets us see that his brother, although he behaves peculiarly, is fully lovable as well as bewildering and sometimes heartbreaking. —*Booklist*

"A remarkable book. . . . strongly recommended for all public libraries and academic libraries . . . as well as for book groups that wish to include a graphic novel."

—*Library Journal*

"A fascinating look at the ways in which prose and comics work to tell the same story."

—*Ninth Art*

"Judy and Paul tell not just of heart wrench and worry, but of the anger, frustration, indignity, and bewilderment David imposes upon their lives. Yet, through it all, they really love the alien visitor who is their brother!" —*The Arc News*

"It was so exciting to read a really good book that tells people the way it actually is. We all have experienced these moments. I couldn't stop reading it." —Liz Roth, parent

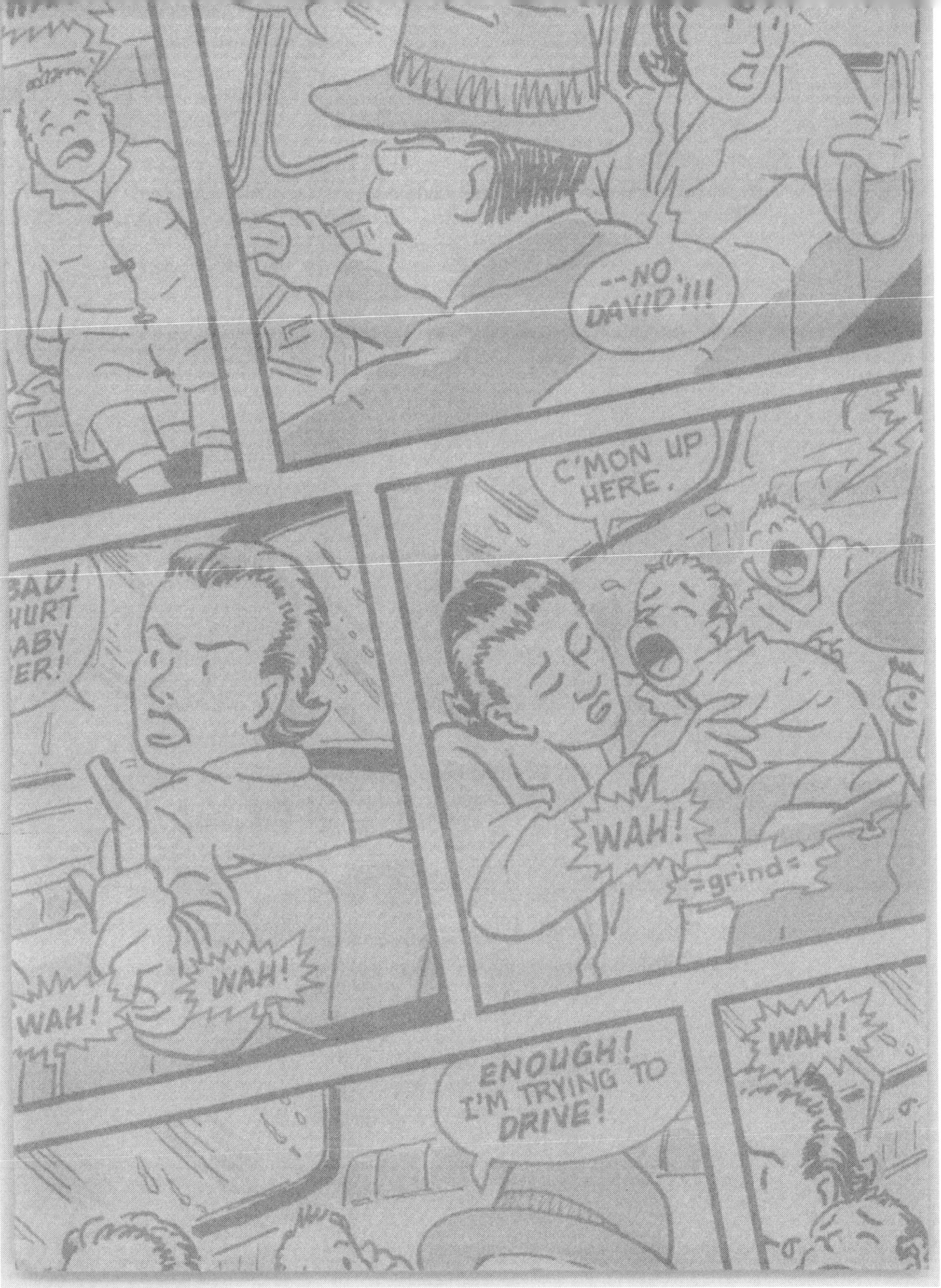
--NO, DAVID!!!
C'MON UP HERE.
BAD! HURT ABY ER!
WAH!
=grind=
WAH!
WAH!
ENOUGH! I'M TRYING TO DRIVE!
WAH!

THE RIDE TOGETHER

A Brother and Sister's Memoir of Autism in the Family

Text Chapters by Judy Karasik

Comics Chapters by Paul Karasik

WSP

WASHINGTON SQUARE PRESS
New York London Toronto Sydney

WASHINGTON SQUARE PRESS
1230 Avenue of the Americas
New York, NY 10020

ISBN: 978-0-7434-2337-3

First Washington Square Press trade paperback edition September 2004

10 9 8 7 6 5 4 3 2 1

WASHINGTON SQUARE PRESS and colophon are
registered trademarks of Simon & Schuster, Inc.

Manufactured in the United States of America

For information regarding special discounts for bulk purchases, please contact
Simon & Schuster Special Sales at 1-800-456-6798 or business@simonandschuster.com

THE RIDE TOGETHER

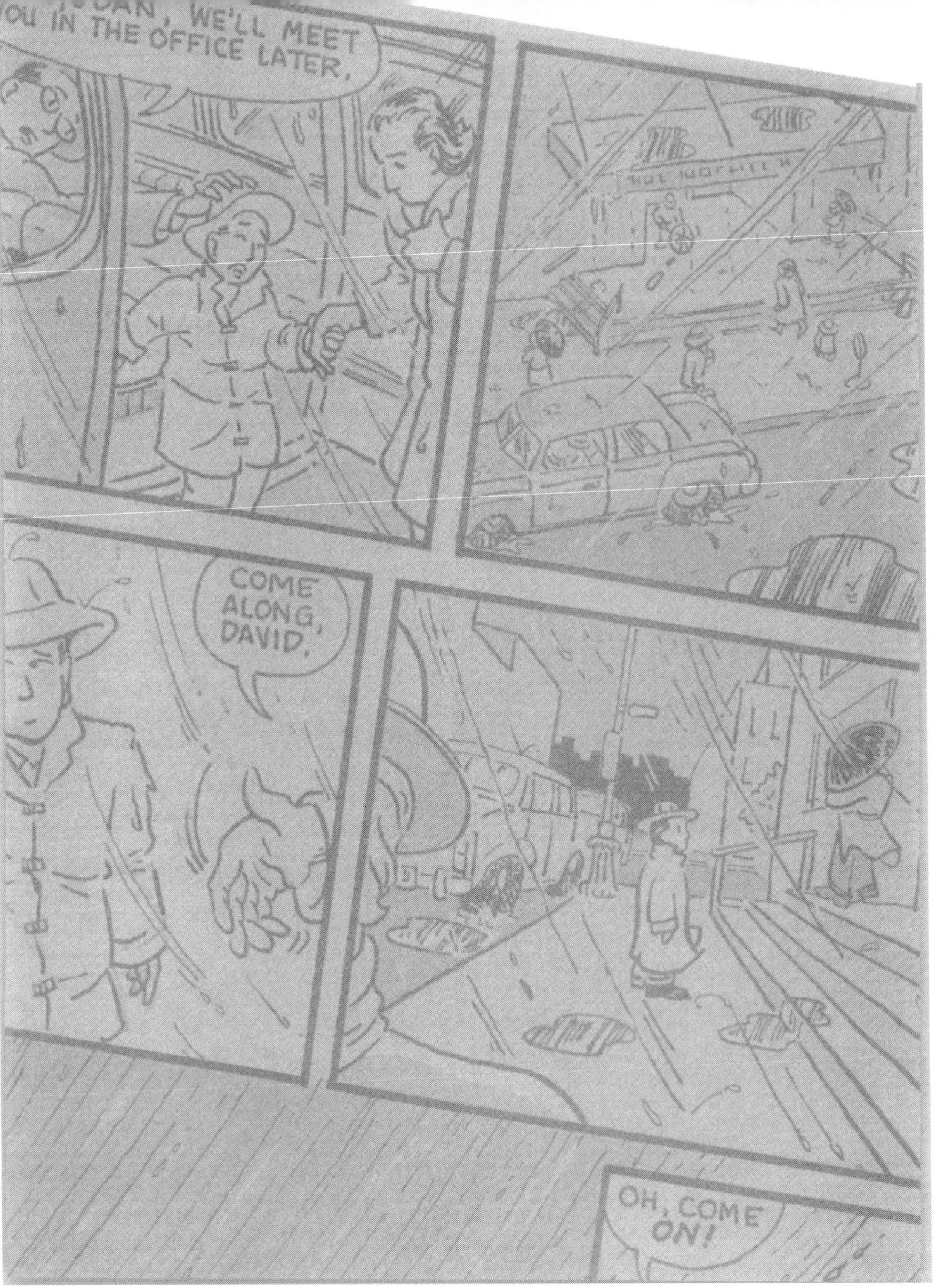

JOAN, WE'LL MEET YOU IN THE OFFICE LATER.
COME ALONG, DAVID.
OH, COME ON!

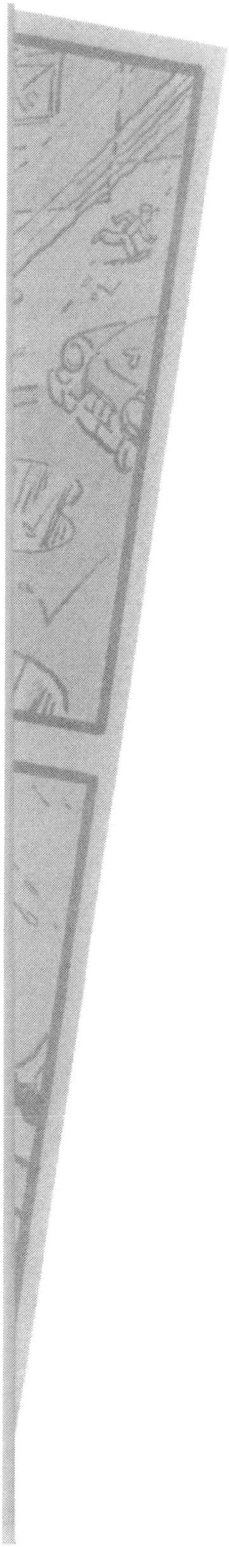

CONTENTS

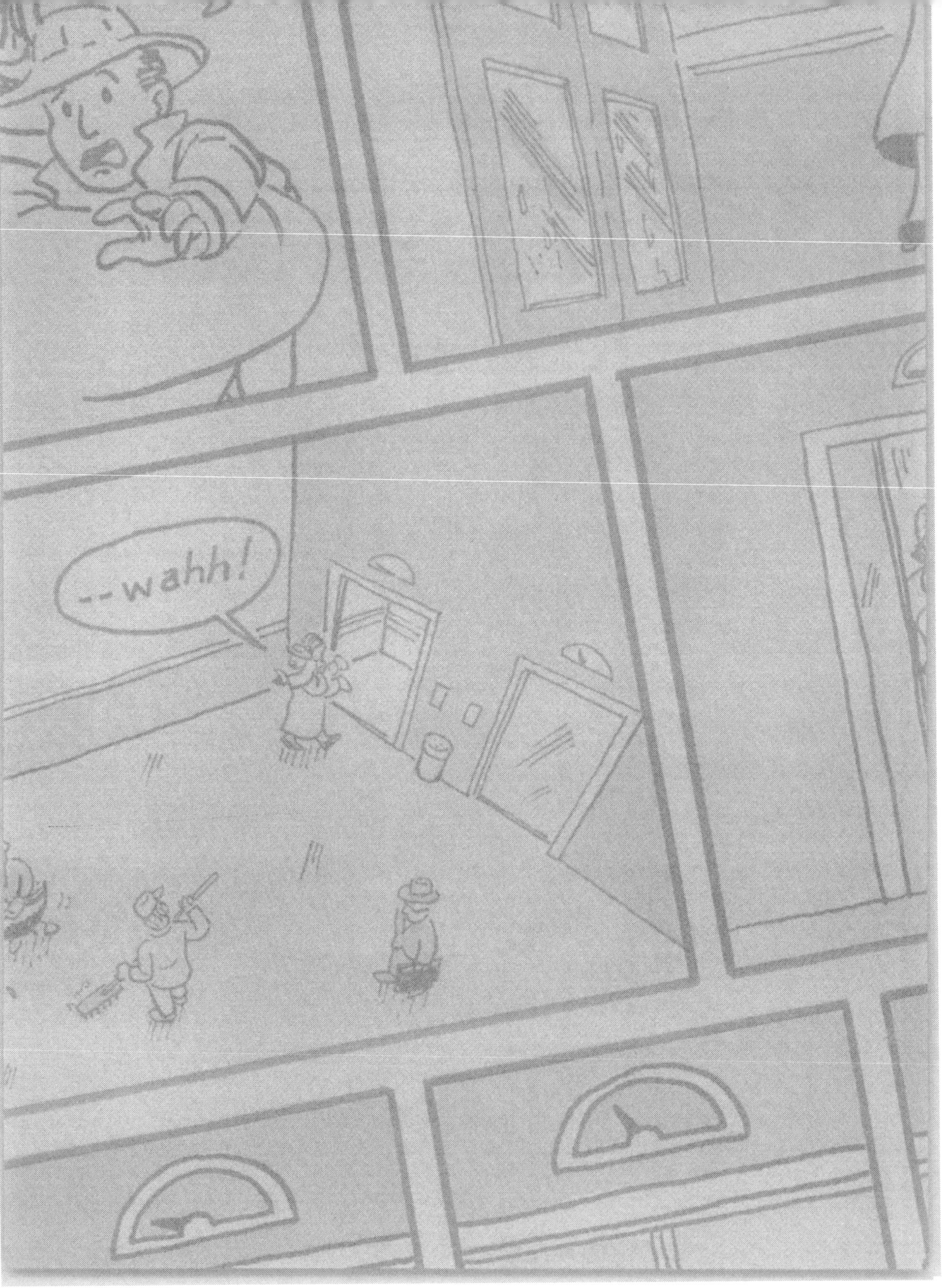
--wahh!

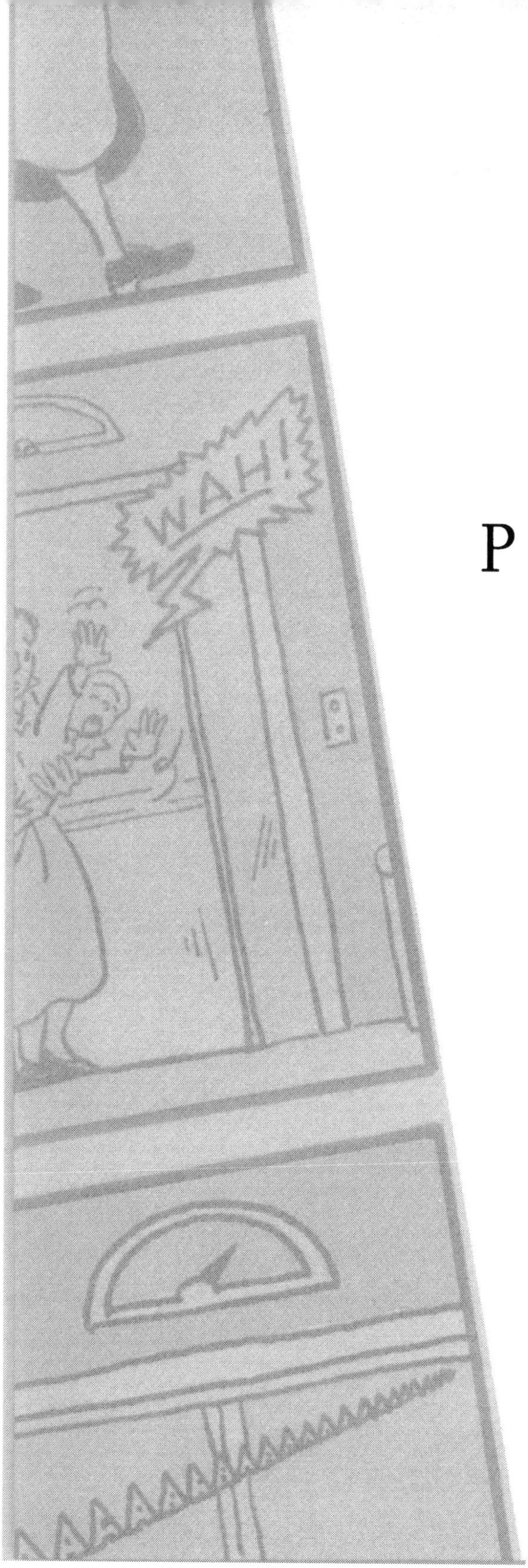
WAH!

PART ONE

1995

1 *Family*

We looked like a cup of human fruit cocktail dumped onto the top of the house, each piece different but all out of the same can: Mom, David in his pajamas, Michael and his wife, Paul and his wife, various children, and me. Everyone present and accounted for, as Pop would have said—and come to think of it, he was probably up there too, like the ghost in *Hamlet*, the late King Monroe wandering the castle parapet.

We were together there for one last time, up on the roof, as though sitting on top of the old house would make it easier for the family to remember everything that had happened there. After thirty-eight years we were leaving; the place was sold and Mom was moving on to something smaller.

Each of us had climbed a rickety ladder in the attic; the ladder rose straight to hook onto a metal bar under the trapdoor. One by one, we'd emerged through the trapdoor onto the widow's walk, a square platform surrounded by a wooden guardrail, right in the center and at the very top of the roof, up high, above three tall stories.

This was the first time our oldest brother, David, had ever been on the roof. Although we had lived in the house for nearly forty years, over all this time nobody had thought to take him up, creating one of those gaps in ordinary experience that are scattered throughout the life of a person with autism.

We gazed toward the other houses on Lenox Street, visible through wind-shifting leaves, like ocean boulders appearing and disappearing with the waves. It was a late afternoon in April of 1995, in spring, that pale, open, sweet time of year when new and unexpected things seem about to occur. This did not make me happy.

I was forty-one years old and unlike Michael and Paul, I was single. I was terrified of what the future would hold. The house was where it had all happened. The house was where we had gathered, where we had been children, where we had grown up, where grandparents and other relatives and friends had come to live, some of them for years, with our strange, proud, ordinary family, in the country inside our house. This was the place we had returned to and left again, reminding ourselves of who we were. The house had kept our faith, but now it couldn't protect me. If it were gone, what would remind Michael and Paul of who we were, how we lived our lives?

I saw myself holding my brother David's hand, leading him through his days, big emptiness all around me.

We had a couple of bottles of good champagne. While Paul's two teenage stepdaughters, Gia and Cleo, watched, I showed first Henry, Michael's three-year-old son, then Nora, Paul's five-year-old daughter, how you gently ease the cork out of a champagne bottle, and the great noise it makes, and how the cork flies, shot out of the thick cannon of the bottle's neck.

"I used to come up here and see whales," I told Henry. "Sometimes I would come up and instead of trees and streets, there would be an ocean filled with fish and whales." And our big rock on Lenox Street became a schooner and we could sail away, we could voyage forever in the beautiful day, into the starry night.

I was drunk on champagne and all I wanted to do was make trouble. "Mom," I said, innocent-like, "you know, I used to come up here and go out onto the roof. Just walked out on the roof. Not like you and Pop—you used a rope. I just walked out."

For many years, until Joan and Monroe were both well into their sixties, my parents had cleaned the gutters of the house together. My mother tied a rope around my father's waist, looping it several times around the posts of the widow's walk, belaying Pop as he inched out down the roof, which sloped at a steep pitch in all four directions, scooped out the crud from the gutters, and carefully threw the debris down onto the lawn.

"Well," my mother commented, "what we did probably wasn't all that safe, either, when you get right down to it."

"It was nuts, Mom," Michael commented cheerfully. "You should have hired people, like all the neighbors do. People younger, stronger, and stupider. The whole idea was nuts."

"I didn't use a rope," I said, twisting the conversation back to me. "Just went over the rail and down the side of that dormer. I sat on my rear end and scooted all the way to the front of the dormer. There's a little sloping piece of the roof in front of the dormer."

Nobody said anything. My sisters-in-law were looking at their children. None of them could believe I would put an idea like this in the minds of these children.

There's no talking to people when they get like that, no explaining.

I remembered it so clearly: the neighborhood laid out like a diagram in front of me, with a clarity and definition that it lacked at all other times, and, securely stowed right below me, every single one of the people I knew the best.

I don't think there was a moment in my life when I'd felt safer.

Family

Then someone made a joke, and Paul changed the subject, and all of a sudden the champagne was finished and we all went downstairs, perhaps a little more carefully than we had gone up, for a last supper of leftovers.

Brothers, wives, children, Mom, and me, everybody pulled food out of the refrigerator. David pulled out a plate of smoked turkey and took it out to the table. Michael had smoked it perfectly, which took hours of tending to do.

We all went out to the porch and sat around the folding table that our mother had modified thirty-four years before, a tidy Joan-like design that used only two small blocks of wood and two hooks and eyes to make it the right height to eat at, sitting on the hickory and oak chairs that came from Mr. Dietz's shop in New Paris, Pennsylvania. Our father had always explained the design of the chairs to every new guest: the oak slat backs had been bent in such a way that they fit the small of your back comfortably no matter what size you were. After the explanation he would smile and get back to work, spinning ice in the martini glasses to chill them, then, with the final spin, shooting the ice over the porch railing into the bushes. We all believed that someday ice trees would grow from those cubes. Even that belief we were leaving behind.

David said grace and then we all started eating.

A few minutes into the meal, Michael noticed that David had an immense amount of smoked turkey on his plate and was eating and eating, slice after slice of the turkey. David eats fast and he can gulp his food. He can consume full plates in minutes, as though he absolutely needs to eat all of it, as though he intends to eat a lot and leave nothing behind. Michael got up quickly and went into the kitchen. I knew what he was thinking. He was thinking, Is this the last of my smoked turkey?

And from inside the house, soon, Michael cried, *"Stop him."*

We all knew what Michael meant.

Michael flew out of the house and grabbed the plate from in front of David, just as David reached for another piece. I was next to David. Michael's elbow grazed my face. When Michael gave the plate back to Dave, there were only a few pieces left.

Michael added the turkey to the great feast the rest of us drew from.

There was already plenty of food for everyone.

We all ate. David ate, but he was nervous. I was sitting next to him and I could see his nervousness. I could see him shake.

His plate fell away from him. It fell onto the porch floor and broke.

Some people pretended nothing had happened. Some people stopped and looked.

Someone said, "Oh, no!"

David ran into the house.

I bent down and picked up the pieces of plate. I picked up the slices of turkey. I pinched the small shards of china and placed them like needles on the slices of plate.

"Nobody with bare feet over here," I said. "Keep the children away."

Then David reappeared, with a broom and a dustpan.

"Let me help," I said to him. I knelt and held the dustpan as he swept up the shards.

"Good, Dave," I said. "Let me take that out."

Michael's wife, Ellen, brought David another plate.

I went into the kitchen and threw out bits and pieces of plate. Michael stood at the sink. Maybe he was collecting his thoughts.

"I'm not going to make a big deal out of this," I said, almost spitting out the words, "but I have to tell you that what you just did with David was completely out of line."

"Well," he shrugged, "I didn't want him to have all the turkey."

"It was *completely* out of line," I said.

He shrugged again. "Yeah," he said, "yeah, it was."

I decided to take a walk. I needed to calm myself.

Down Lenox Street, down the street where we had all grown up, in the days before Michael and Paul had wives and children and other allegiances.

I thought the walk would calm me, but I started to cry and couldn't stop. Now I saw the rest of my life. If this was Michael's capacity for cruelty, I could not let him take care of our brother. And Paul lived on an island, I thought, as though that said it all.

I made a lot of that broken plate. Electric current was zinging through me as I turned back toward the house and headed up the slope of the driveway.

All I needed was my bag and I could leave. I could go downtown to my apartment and leave them all. I walked through the kitchen, past Michael and Paul leaning against the counters, as silent as though they were hooked up to the sink and the refrigerator. I was still crying.

The bag was in the study; I jammed it on my shoulder to head out.

Paul and Michael were still in the kitchen, but suddenly it seemed everyone else had gone.

"I'm leaving, you guys," I said. "I don't want to spend another minute with you. Either one of you."

"Judy, what's bothering you?" asked Michael. I must admit he showed some courage. Michael knew what was coming. He and Paul knew what was coming, more than I did. Because it was their worst nightmare, one they'd spent a lot of off-duty brain time trying not to imagine. Paul had been in town since Thursday; this was Sunday. We were supposed to have a family meeting, one I had been asking for since Pop had died three years earlier. I knew they were both going to go home with their families. We would have no meeting. And they had the protection of families and I did not.

"What's bothering me? Forget it, Michael," I said, hoisting my bag over my shoulder.

"Do you want to talk about it, Judy?" asked Paul.

"No," I said, "No. I don't want to talk about it. And I *really* don't want to talk about it with either of you two. I will only get blamed and dismissed for being emotional. *Emotional?* There are some things you should be emotional about. And I won't be blamed for that."

"Let's talk," said Michael. "For heaven's sake, Judy, give us a chance."

"You?" I replied. "*You?* I don't think so."

I headed past the washer and dryer and out the back door and down the back steps and onto the driveway.

Paul and Michael followed.

"This isn't just about you," said Paul. "You want to make it that way. You want to be a martyr? We have feelings, too. You think we don't have feelings. Come on, Judy," he said, "let's talk."

I stopped. "You want to talk?" I screamed into the beautiful calm twilight of our last day as a family in Chevy Chase, Maryland, tears pouring down my face. I looked at them both. "Okay," I spluttered, "let's talk." I took a breath. "Okay," I said, "for starters, *What do you two plan to do about your brother when your mother dies?*"

That is where the conversation began.

In the photographs of that afternoon David sits, dressed in his pajamas, snuggled against a corner of the widow's walk railing, happily hugging his knees and smiling for the picture. He looks good. He is wearing black dress shoes with his pajamas.

Michael mentioned something else about David later. He told me that, at the time, for several months during David's periodic visits home he had noticed that David's compulsive behaviors had been more and more out of control; Michael believed that it was his role to watch out for David, pay attention to those behaviors, and keep them to a minimum. Maybe David's behaviors had to do with Pop's death, Michael had thought, with the changes in the family, with the move out of the old house.

When Michael said this to me, my reaction was that David wasn't the problem and keeping his so-called compulsive behaviors controlled wasn't the point.

But as it turned out, in some ways Michael and I were both right.

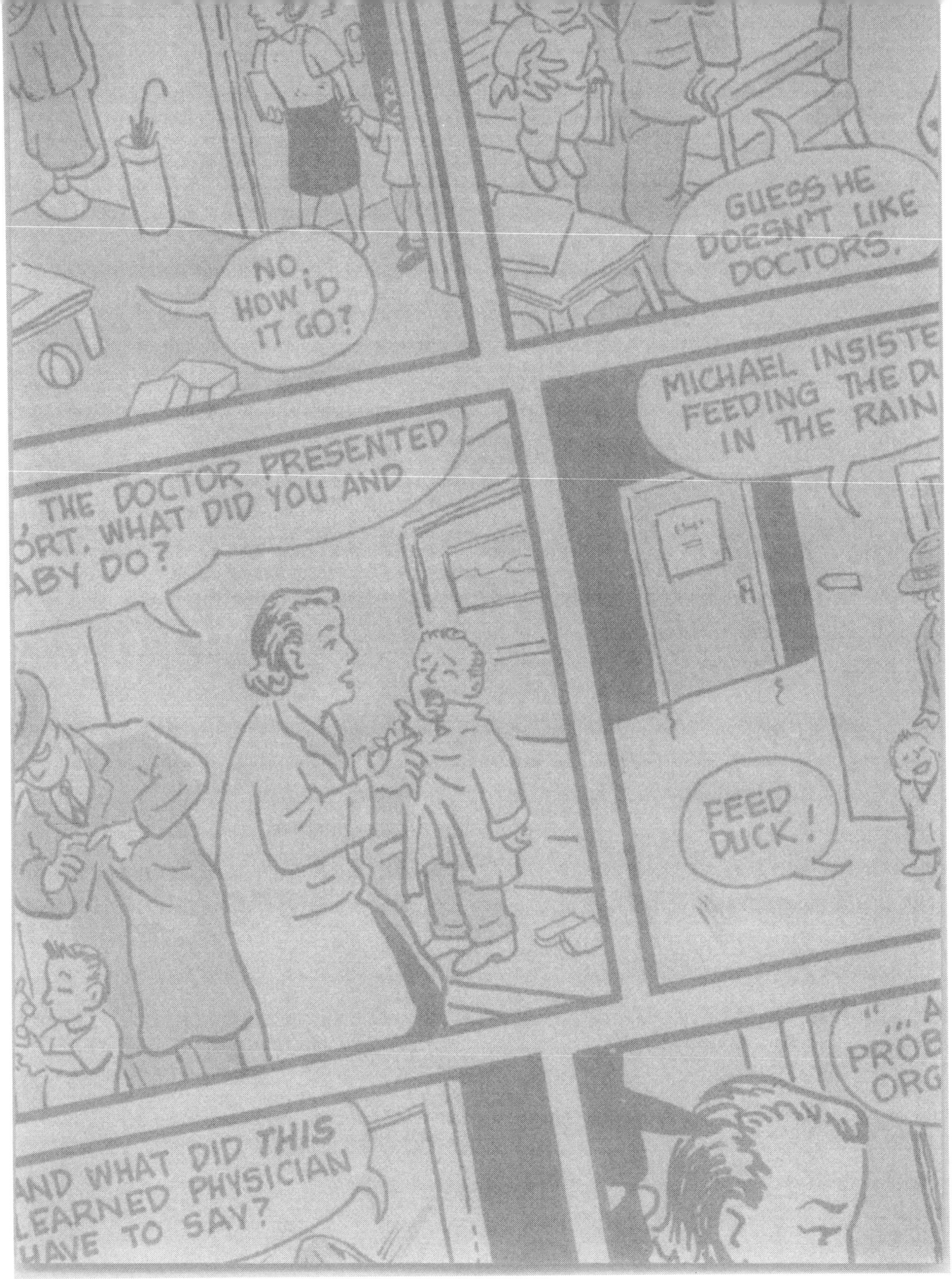

NO, HOW'D IT GO?
GUESS HE DOESN'T LIKE DOCTORS.
, THE DOCTOR PRESENTED
ORT. WHAT DID YOU AND
ABY DO?
MICHAEL INSISTE
FEEDING THE DU
IN THE RAIN
FEED DUCK!
AND WHAT DID THIS LEARNED PHYSICIAN HAVE TO SAY?
"... A
PROB
ORG

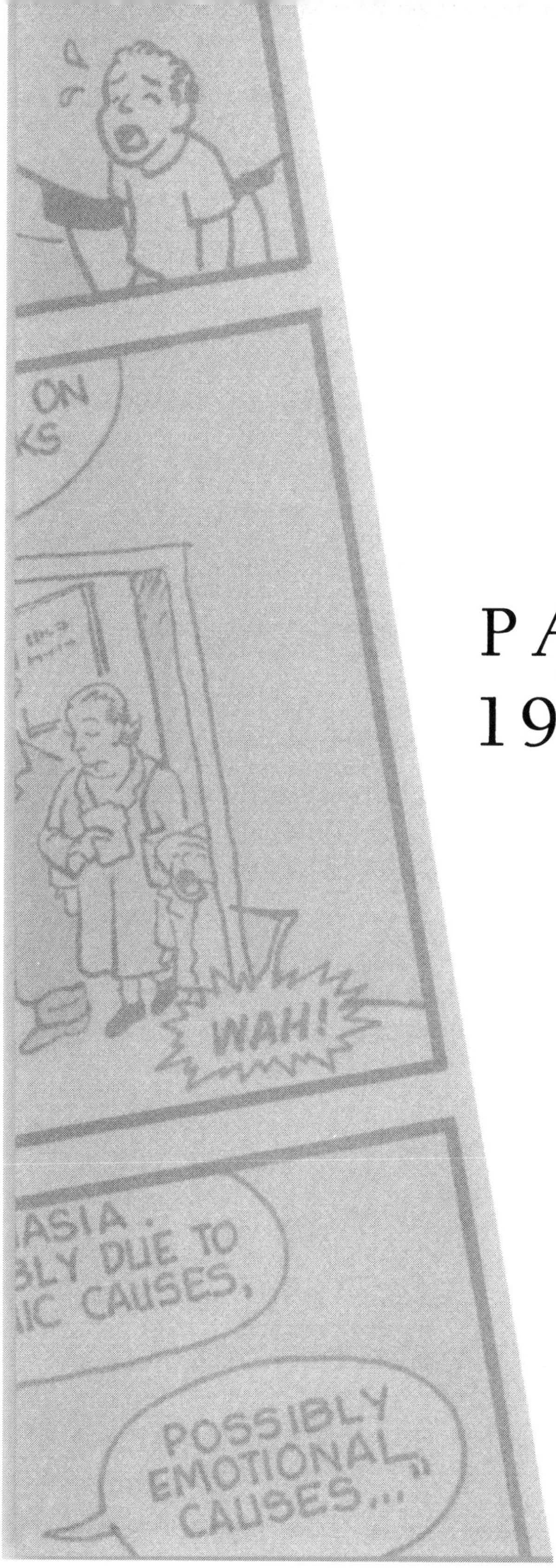
WAH!
POSSIBLY EMOTIONAL CAUSES...

PART TWO

1953—1966

2 *Diagnosis*

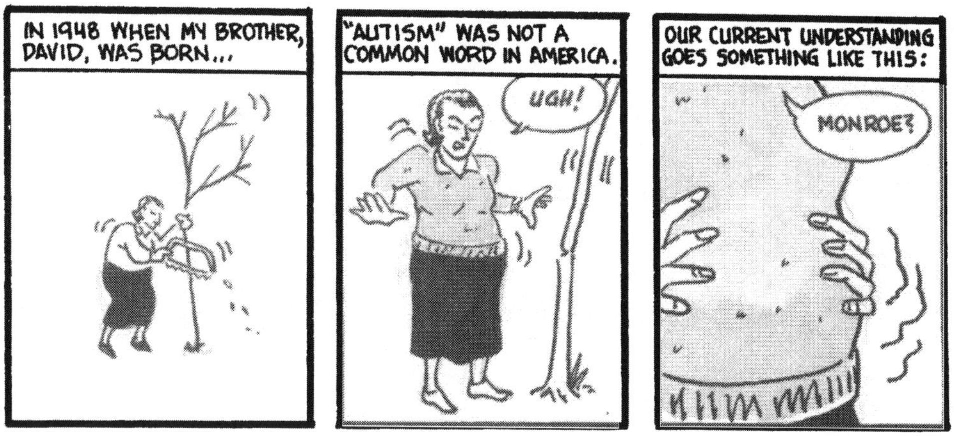
IN 1948 WHEN MY BROTHER, DAVID, WAS BORN...
"AUTISM" WAS NOT A COMMON WORD IN AMERICA.
UGH!
OUR CURRENT UNDERSTANDING GOES SOMETHING LIKE THIS:
MONROE?

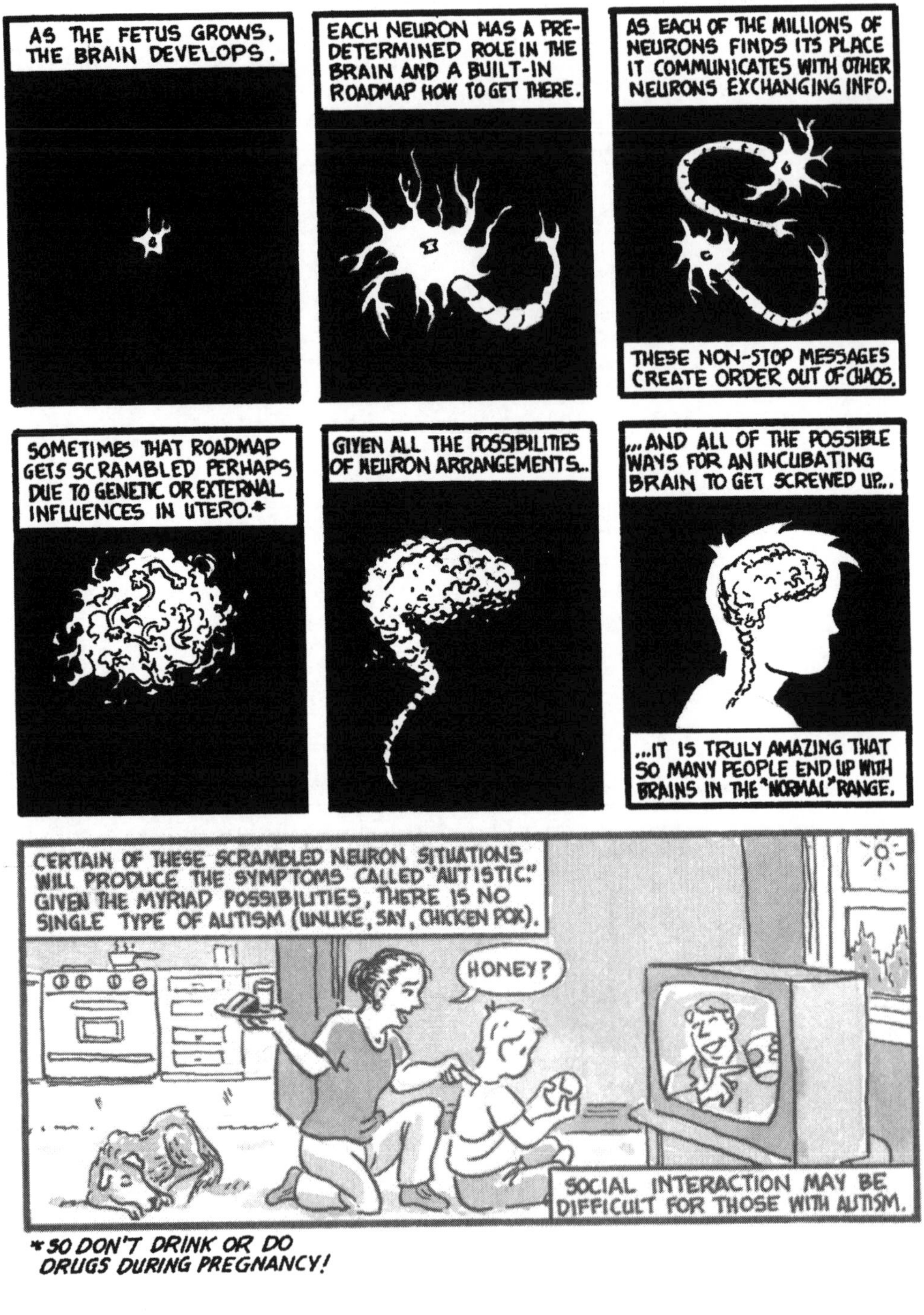
AS THE FETUS GROWS, THE BRAIN DEVELOPS.
EACH NEURON HAS A PRE-DETERMINED ROLE IN THE BRAIN AND A BUILT-IN ROADMAP HOW TO GET THERE.
AS EACH OF THE MILLIONS OF NEURONS FINDS ITS PLACE IT COMMUNICATES WITH OTHER NEURONS EXCHANGING INFO.
THESE NON-STOP MESSAGES CREATE ORDER OUT OF CHAOS.
SOMETIMES THAT ROADMAP GETS SCRAMBLED PERHAPS DUE TO GENETIC OR EXTERNAL INFLUENCES IN UTERO.*
GIVEN ALL THE POSSIBILITIES OF NEURON ARRANGEMENTS...
...AND ALL OF THE POSSIBLE WAYS FOR AN INCUBATING BRAIN TO GET SCREWED UP...
...IT IS TRULY AMAZING THAT SO MANY PEOPLE END UP WITH BRAINS IN THE "NORMAL" RANGE.
CERTAIN OF THESE SCRAMBLED NEURON SITUATIONS WILL PRODUCE THE SYMPTOMS CALLED "AUTISTIC." GIVEN THE MYRIAD POSSIBILITIES, THERE IS NO SINGLE TYPE OF AUTISM (UNLIKE, SAY, CHICKEN POX).
HONEY?
SOCIAL INTERACTION MAY BE DIFFICULT FOR THOSE WITH AUTISM.
*SO DON'T DRINK OR DO DRUGS DURING PREGNANCY!

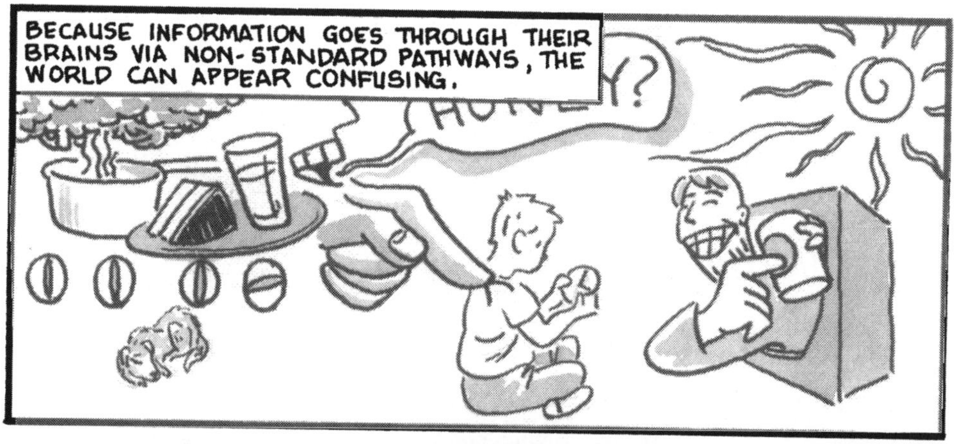
BECAUSE INFORMATION GOES THROUGH THEIR BRAINS VIA NON-STANDARD PATHWAYS, THE WORLD CAN APPEAR CONFUSING.

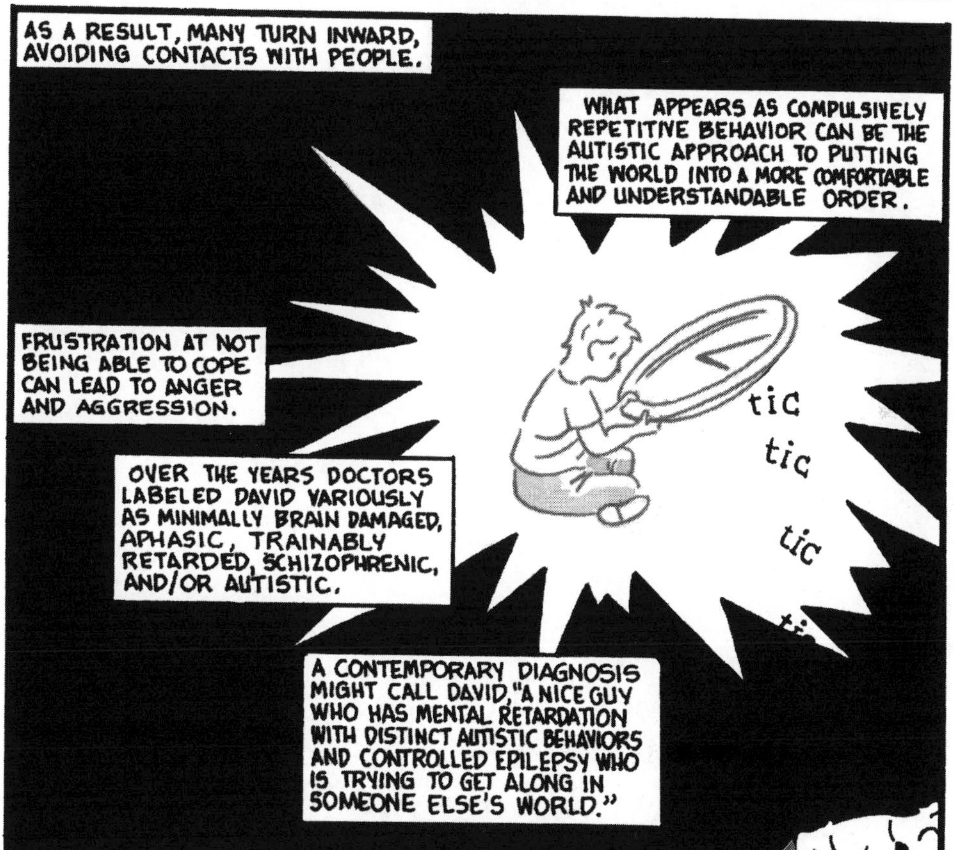
AS A RESULT, MANY TURN INWARD, AVOIDING CONTACTS WITH PEOPLE.
WHAT APPEARS AS COMPULSIVELY REPETITIVE BEHAVIOR CAN BE THE AUTISTIC APPROACH TO PUTTING THE WORLD INTO A MORE COMFORTABLE AND UNDERSTANDABLE ORDER.
FRUSTRATION AT NOT BEING ABLE TO COPE CAN LEAD TO ANGER AND AGGRESSION.
tic
tic
tic
OVER THE YEARS DOCTORS LABELED DAVID VARIOUSLY AS MINIMALLY BRAIN DAMAGED, APHASIC, TRAINABLY RETARDED, SCHIZOPHRENIC, AND/OR AUTISTIC.
A CONTEMPORARY DIAGNOSIS MIGHT CALL DAVID, "A NICE GUY WHO HAS MENTAL RETARDATION WITH DISTINCT AUTISTIC BEHAVIORS AND CONTROLLED EPILEPSY WHO IS TRYING TO GET ALONG IN SOMEONE ELSE'S WORLD."

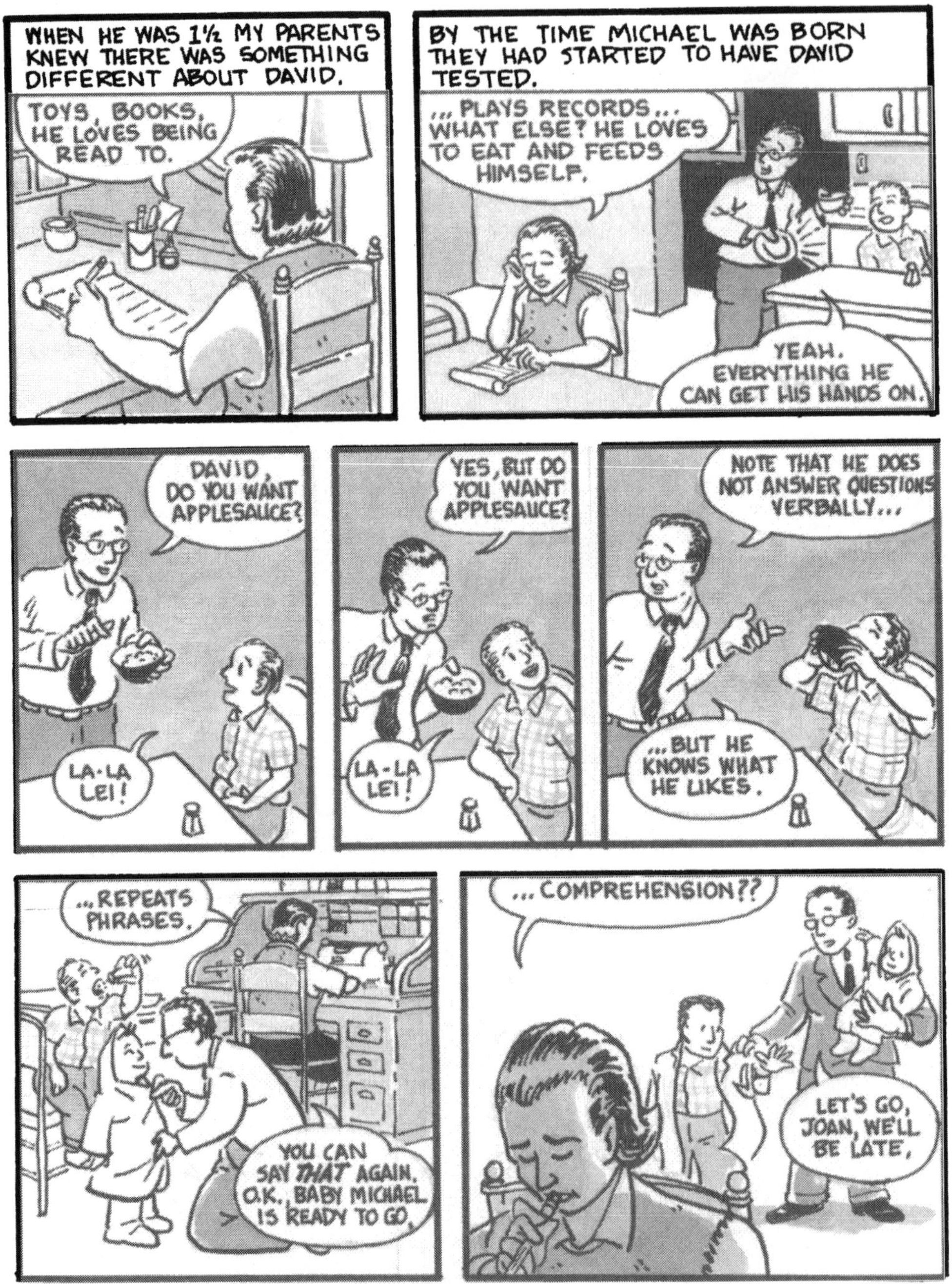
WHEN HE WAS 1½ MY PARENTS KNEW THERE WAS SOMETHING DIFFERENT ABOUT DAVID.
TOYS, BOOKS, HE LOVES BEING READ TO.
BY THE TIME MICHAEL WAS BORN THEY HAD STARTED TO HAVE DAVID TESTED.
... PLAYS RECORDS... WHAT ELSE? HE LOVES TO EAT AND FEEDS HIMSELF.
YEAH. EVERYTHING HE CAN GET HIS HANDS ON.
DAVID, DO YOU WANT APPLESAUCE?
LA-LA LEI!
YES, BUT DO YOU WANT APPLESAUCE?
LA-LA LEI!
NOTE THAT HE DOES NOT ANSWER QUESTIONS VERBALLY...
...BUT HE KNOWS WHAT HE LIKES.
...REPEATS PHRASES.
YOU CAN SAY THAT AGAIN. O.K. BABY MICHAEL IS READY TO GO.
...COMPREHENSION??
LET'S GO, JOAN, WE'LL BE LATE.

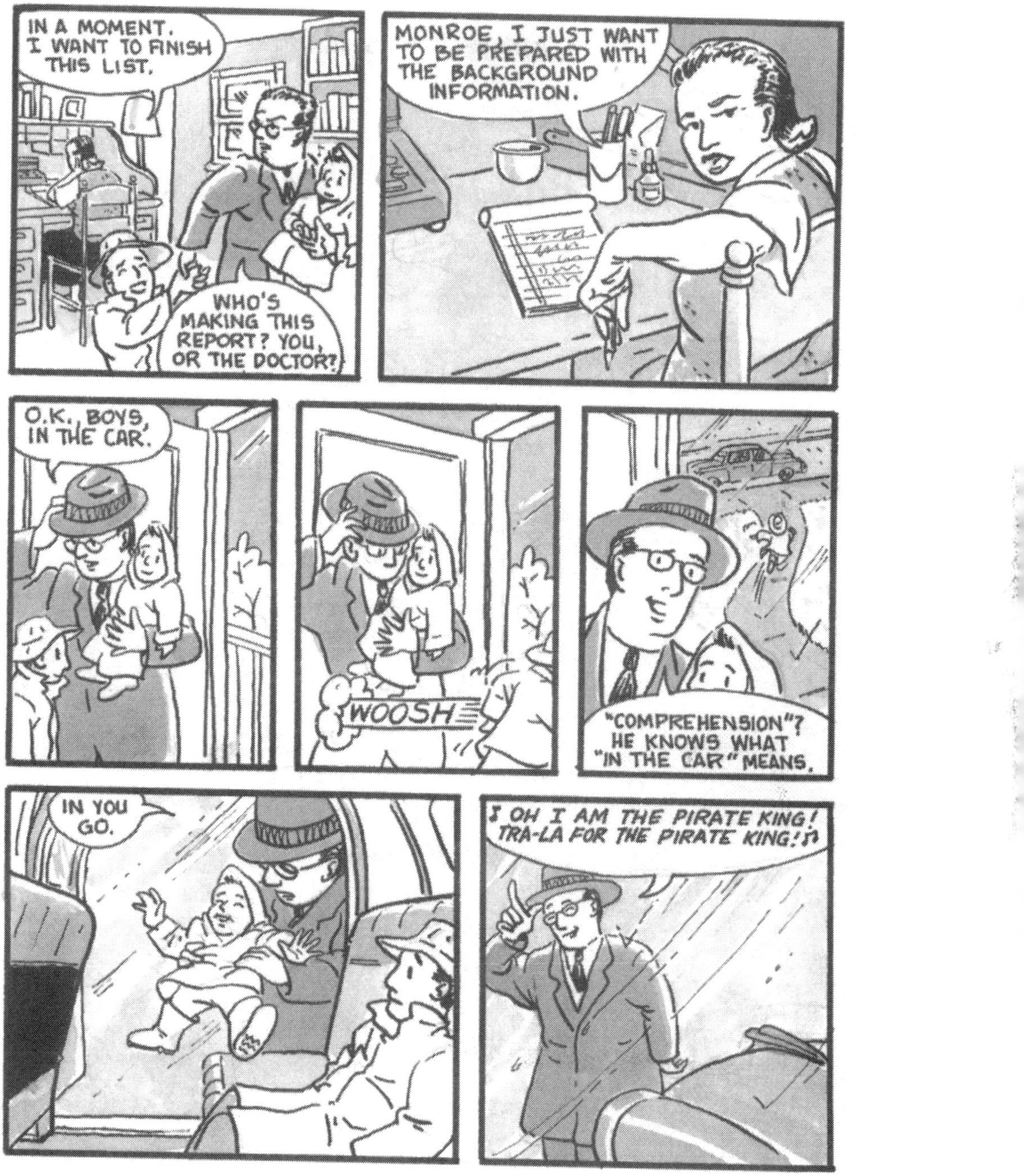
IN A MOMENT. I WANT TO FINISH THIS LIST.
WHO'S MAKING THIS REPORT? YOU, OR THE DOCTOR?
MONROE, I JUST WANT TO BE PREPARED WITH THE BACKGROUND INFORMATION.
O.K., BOYS, IN THE CAR.
WOOSH
"COMPREHENSION"? HE KNOWS WHAT "IN THE CAR" MEANS.
IN YOU GO.
♪ OH I AM THE PIRATE KING! TRA-LA FOR THE PIRATE KING! ♫

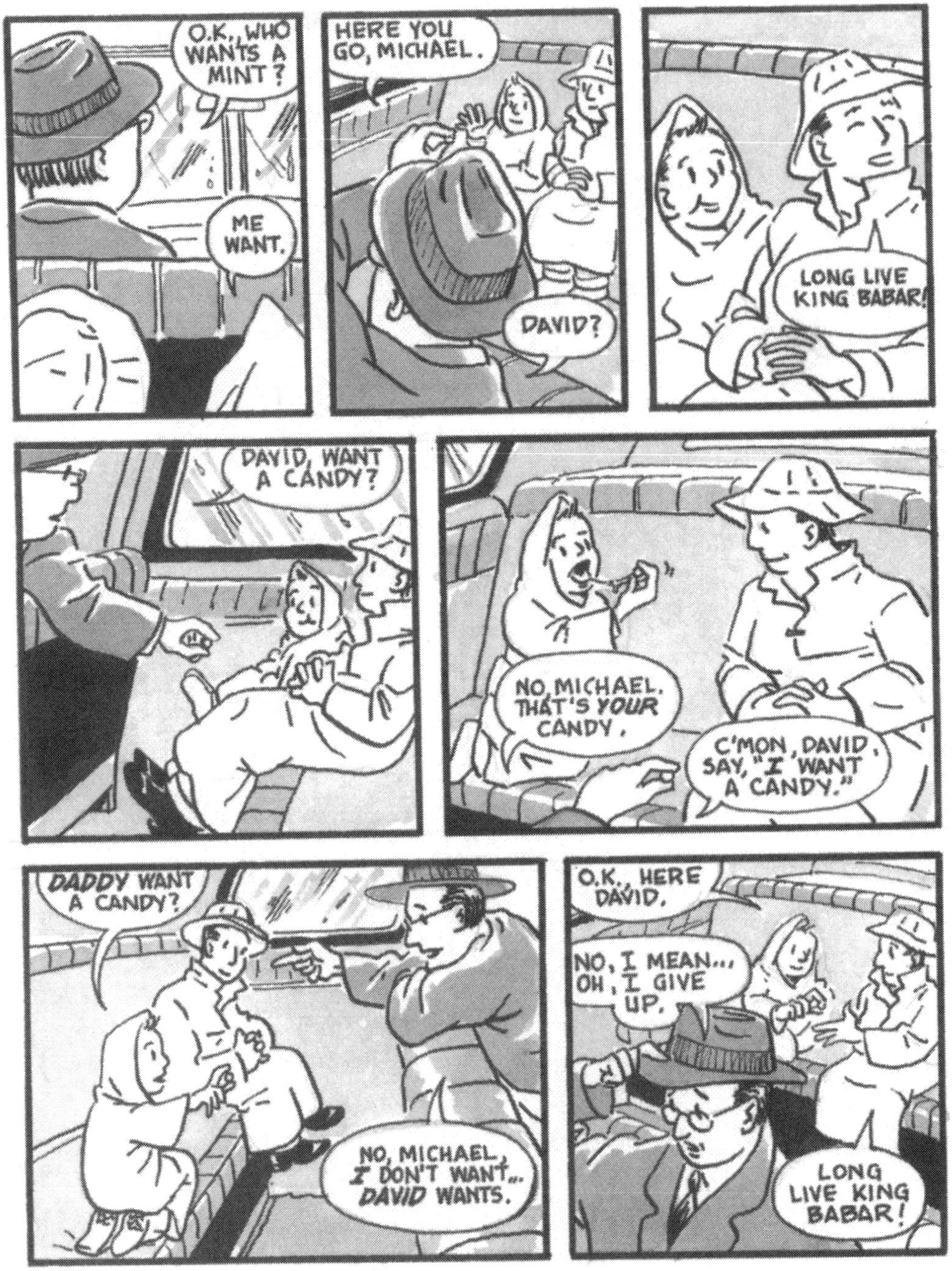
O.K., WHO WANTS A MINT?
ME WANT.
HERE YOU GO, MICHAEL.
DAVID?
LONG LIVE KING BABAR!
DAVID, WANT A CANDY?
NO, MICHAEL. THAT'S YOUR CANDY.
C'MON, DAVID, SAY, "I WANT A CANDY."
DADDY WANT A CANDY?
NO, MICHAEL. I DON'T WANT... DAVID WANTS.
O.K., HERE DAVID.
NO, I MEAN... OH, I GIVE UP.
LONG LIVE KING BABAR!

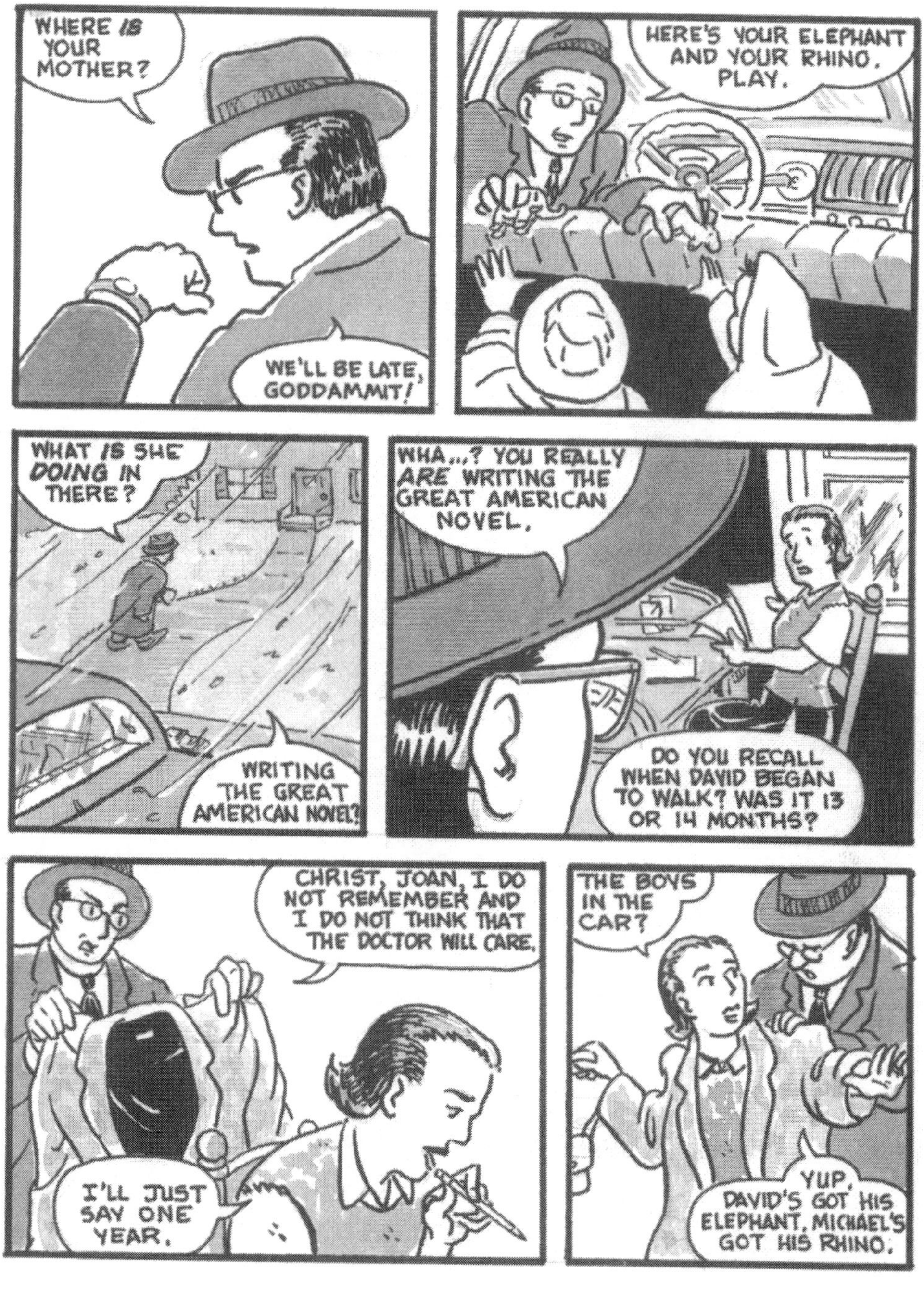
WHERE IS YOUR MOTHER?
WE'LL BE LATE, GODDAMMIT!
HERE'S YOUR ELEPHANT AND YOUR RHINO. PLAY.
WHAT IS SHE DOING IN THERE?
WRITING THE GREAT AMERICAN NOVEL?
WHA...? YOU REALLY ARE WRITING THE GREAT AMERICAN NOVEL.
DO YOU RECALL WHEN DAVID BEGAN TO WALK? WAS IT 13 OR 14 MONTHS?
CHRIST, JOAN, I DO NOT REMEMBER AND I DO NOT THINK THAT THE DOCTOR WILL CARE.
I'LL JUST SAY ONE YEAR.
THE BOYS IN THE CAR?
YUP, DAVID'S GOT HIS ELEPHANT, MICHAEL'S GOT HIS RHINO.

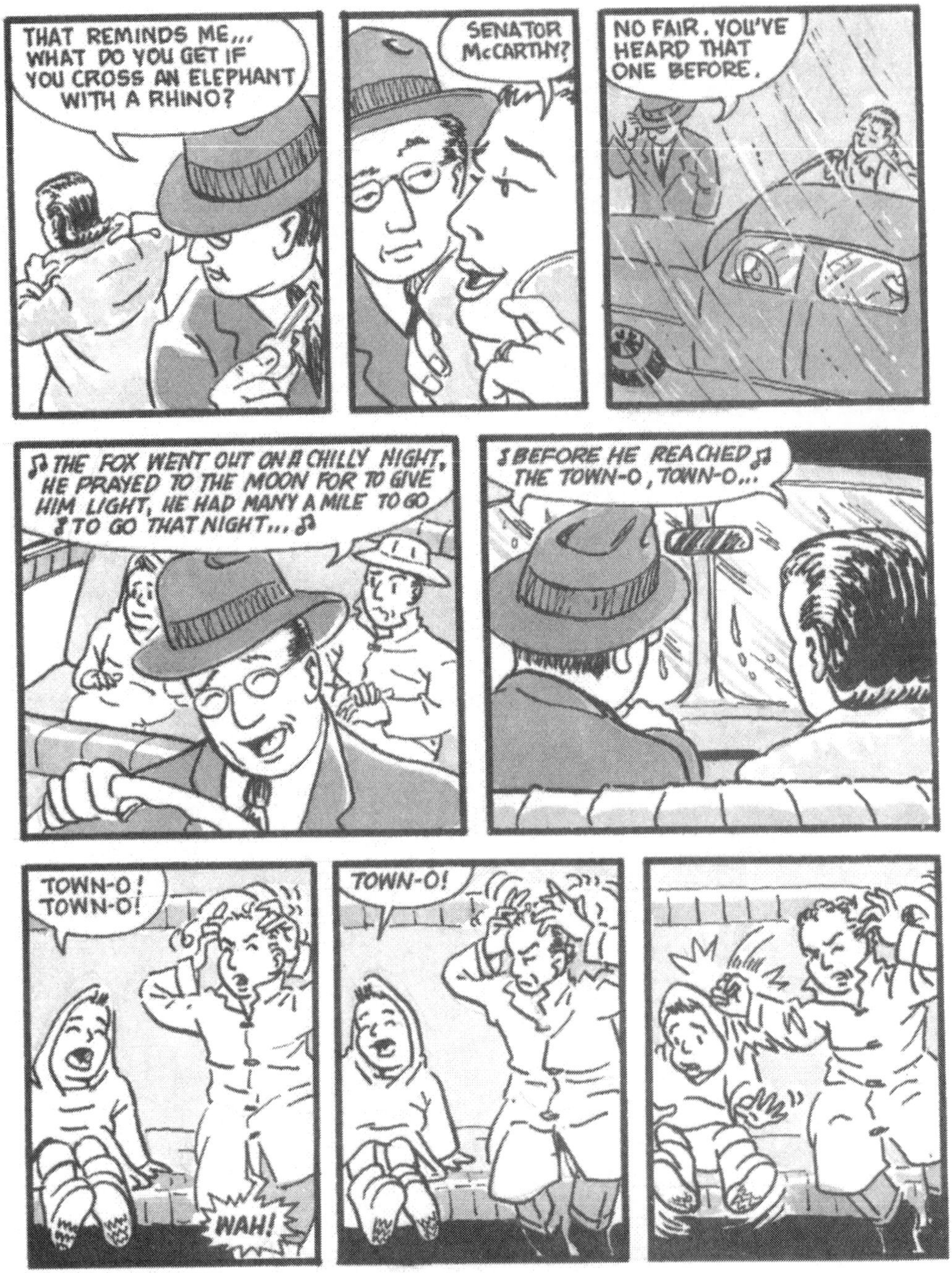
THAT REMINDS ME... WHAT DO YOU GET IF YOU CROSS AN ELEPHANT WITH A RHINO?
SENATOR McCARTHY?
NO FAIR. YOU'VE HEARD THAT ONE BEFORE.
♫ THE FOX WENT OUT ON A CHILLY NIGHT, HE PRAYED TO THE MOON FOR TO GIVE HIM LIGHT, HE HAD MANY A MILE TO GO ♪ TO GO THAT NIGHT... ♫
♪ BEFORE HE REACHED ♫ THE TOWN-O, TOWN-O...
TOWN-O! TOWN-O!
WAH!
TOWN-O!

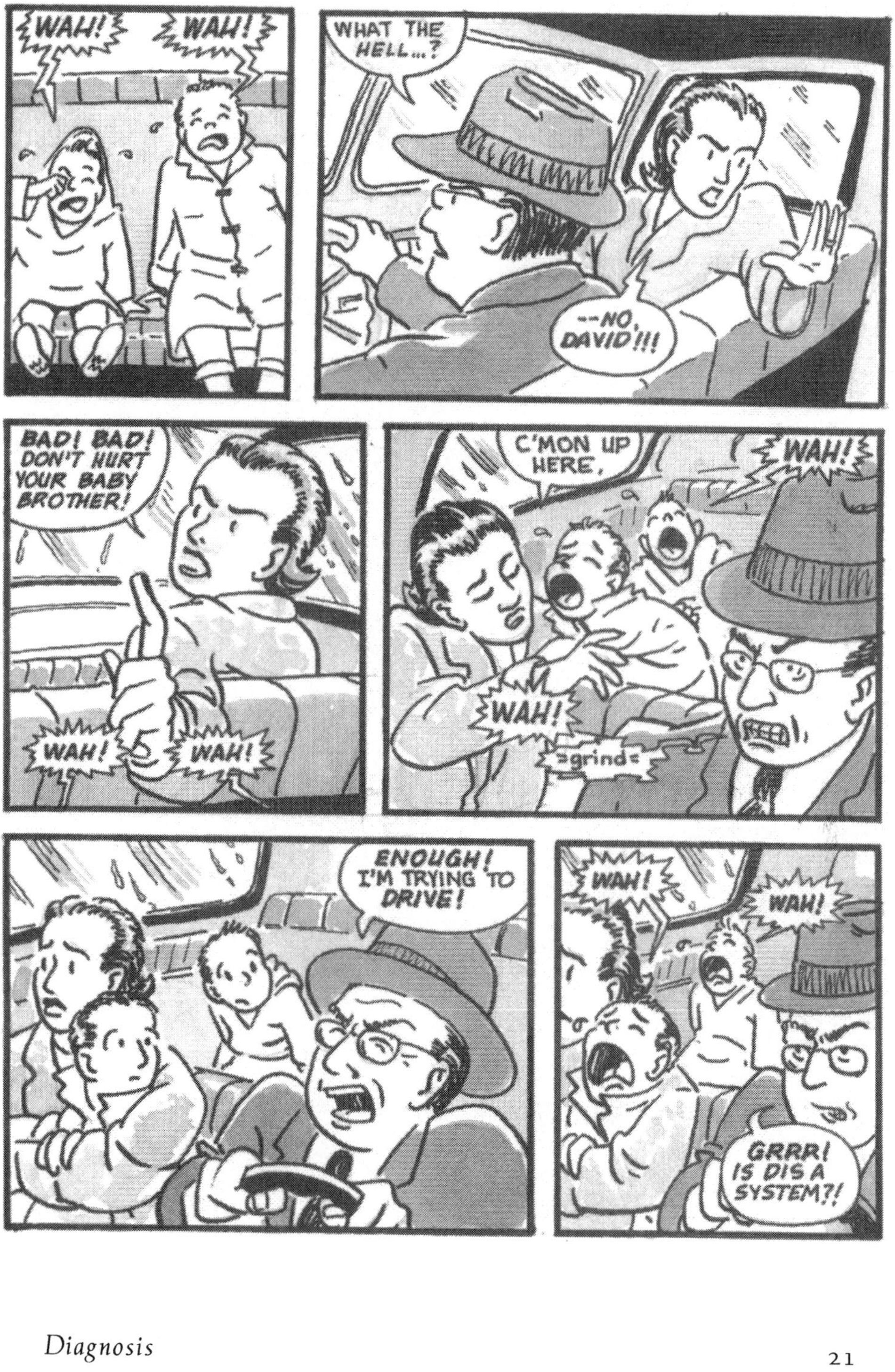
WAH!
WAH!
WHAT THE HELL...?
--NO, DAVID!!!
BAD! BAD! DON'T HURT YOUR BABY BROTHER!
WAH!
WAH!
C'MON UP HERE.
WAH!
WAH!
≈grind≈
ENOUGH! I'M TRYING TO DRIVE!
WAH!
WAH!
GRRR! IS DIS A SYSTEM?!

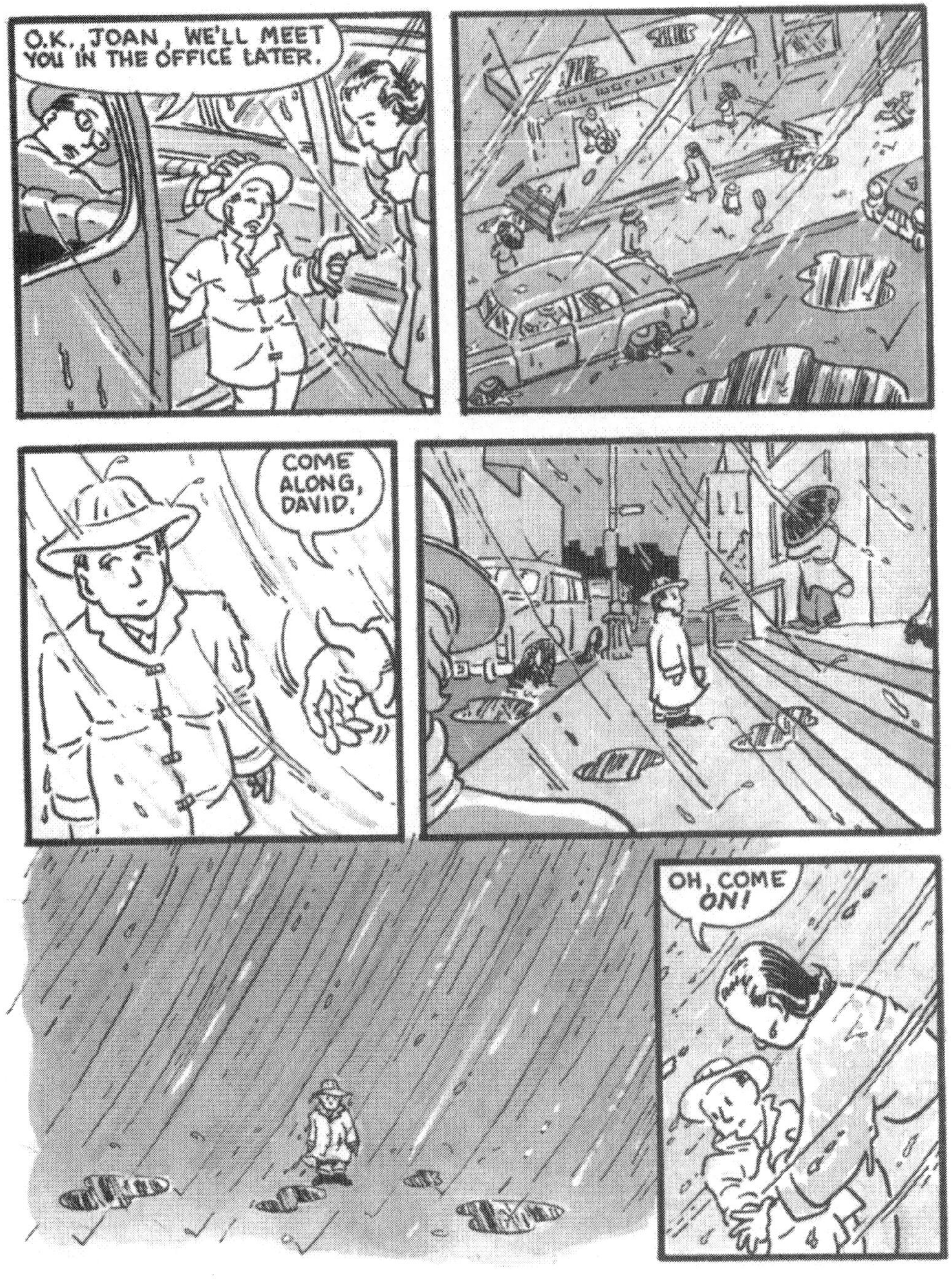
O.K., JOAN, WE'LL MEET YOU IN THE OFFICE LATER.
COME ALONG, DAVID.
OH, COME ON!

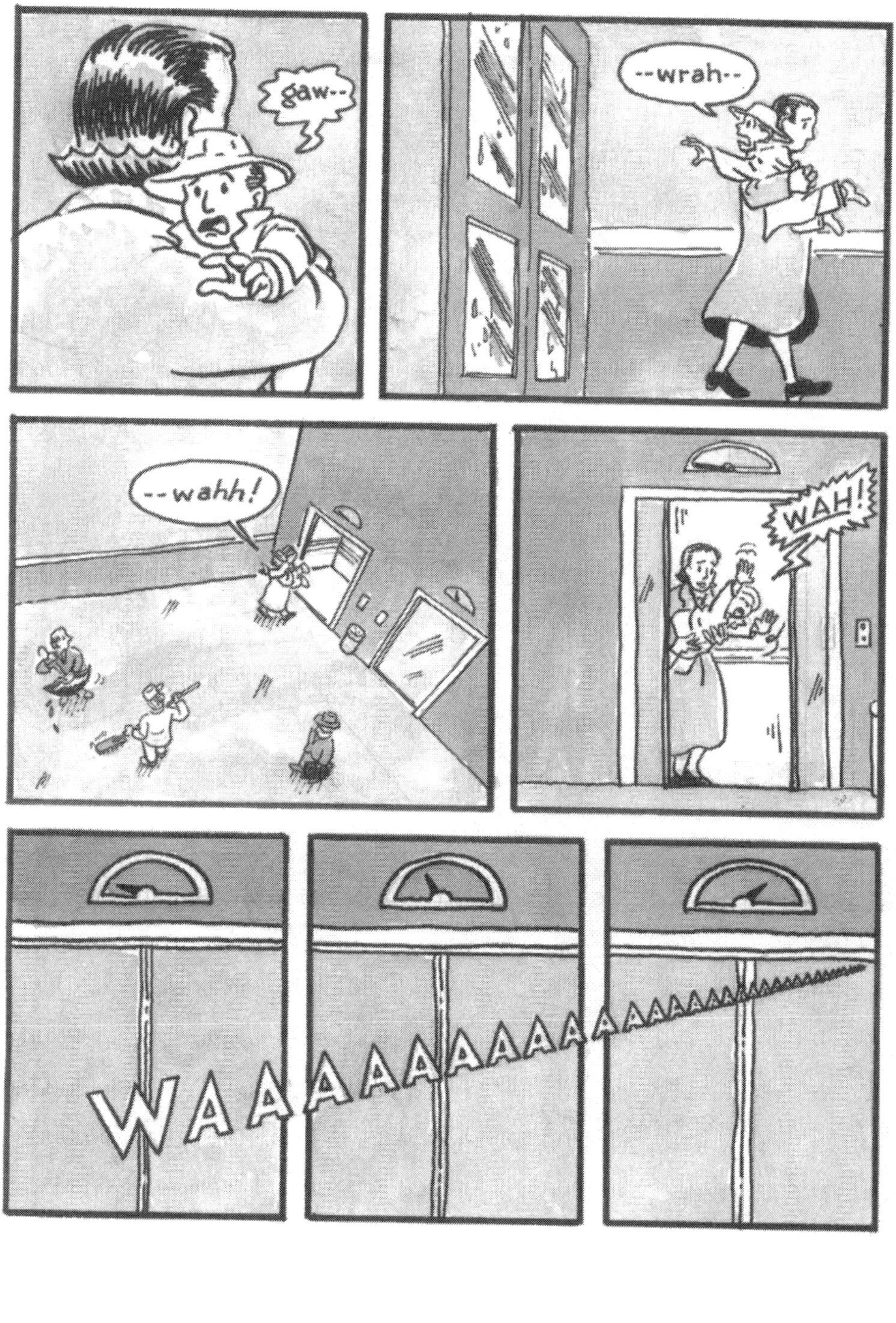
gaw--
--wrah--
--wahh!
WAH!
WAAAAAAAAAAAAAAAAAAAAAAAAAAAAAAA

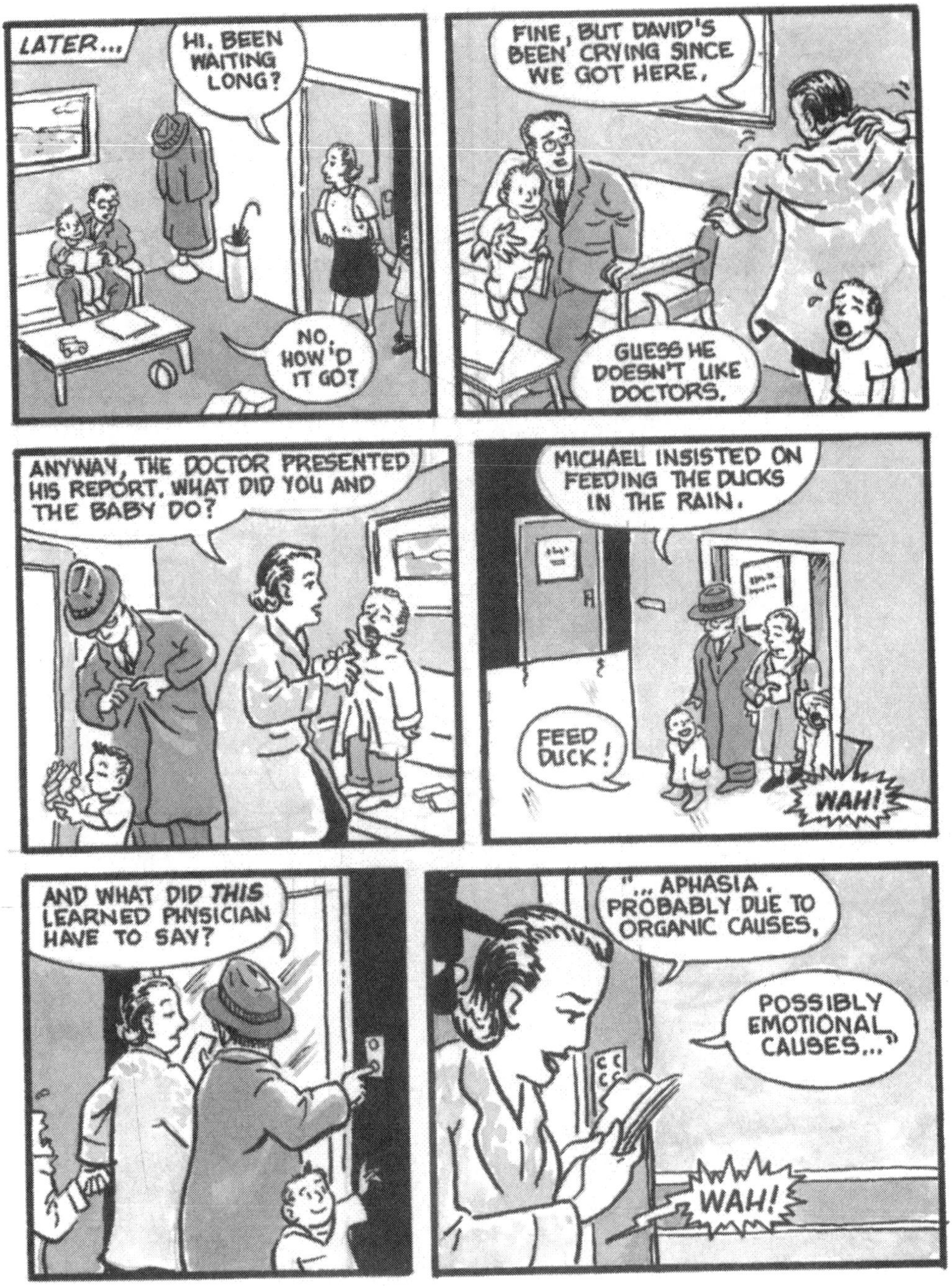
LATER...
HI. BEEN WAITING LONG?
NO. HOW'D IT GO?
FINE, BUT DAVID'S BEEN CRYING SINCE WE GOT HERE.
GUESS HE DOESN'T LIKE DOCTORS.
ANYWAY, THE DOCTOR PRESENTED HIS REPORT. WHAT DID YOU AND THE BABY DO?
MICHAEL INSISTED ON FEEDING THE DUCKS IN THE RAIN.
FEED DUCK!
WAH!
AND WHAT DID THIS LEARNED PHYSICIAN HAVE TO SAY?
"...APHASIA. PROBABLY DUE TO ORGANIC CAUSES.
POSSIBLY EMOTIONAL CAUSES..."
WAH!

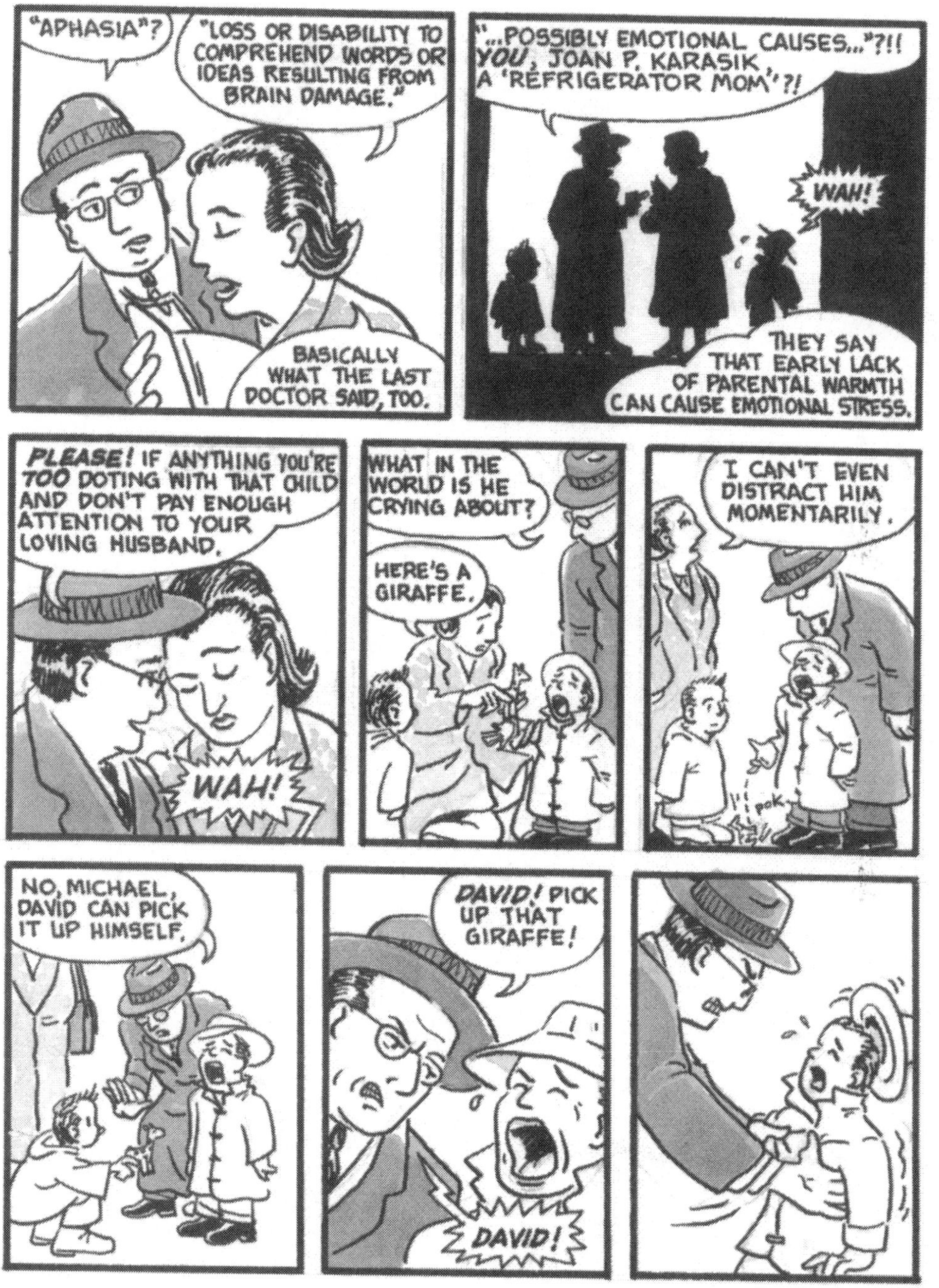
"APHASIA"?
"LOSS OR DISABILITY TO COMPREHEND WORDS OR IDEAS RESULTING FROM BRAIN DAMAGE."
BASICALLY WHAT THE LAST DOCTOR SAID, TOO.
"...POSSIBLY EMOTIONAL CAUSES..."?!! YOU, JOAN P. KARASIK, A 'REFRIGERATOR MOM'?!
WAH!
THEY SAY THAT EARLY LACK OF PARENTAL WARMTH CAN CAUSE EMOTIONAL STRESS.
PLEASE! IF ANYTHING YOU'RE TOO DOTING WITH THAT CHILD AND DON'T PAY ENOUGH ATTENTION TO YOUR LOVING HUSBAND.
WAH!
WHAT IN THE WORLD IS HE CRYING ABOUT?
HERE'S A GIRAFFE.
I CAN'T EVEN DISTRACT HIM MOMENTARILY.
pok
NO, MICHAEL, DAVID CAN PICK IT UP HIMSELF.
DAVID! PICK UP THAT GIRAFFE!
DAVID!

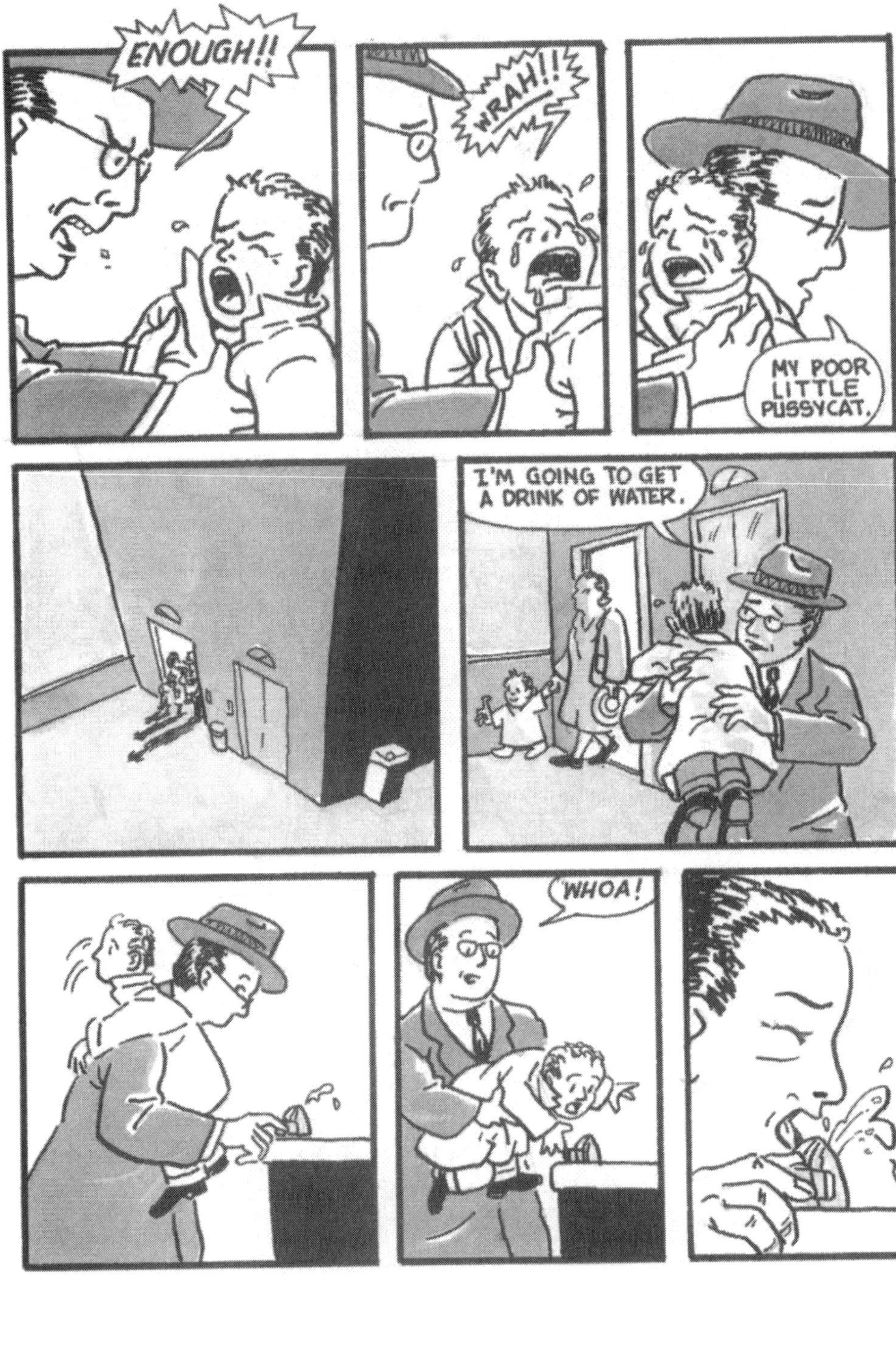
ENOUGH!!
WRAH!!
MY POOR LITTLE PUSSYCAT.
I'M GOING TO GET A DRINK OF WATER.
WHOA!

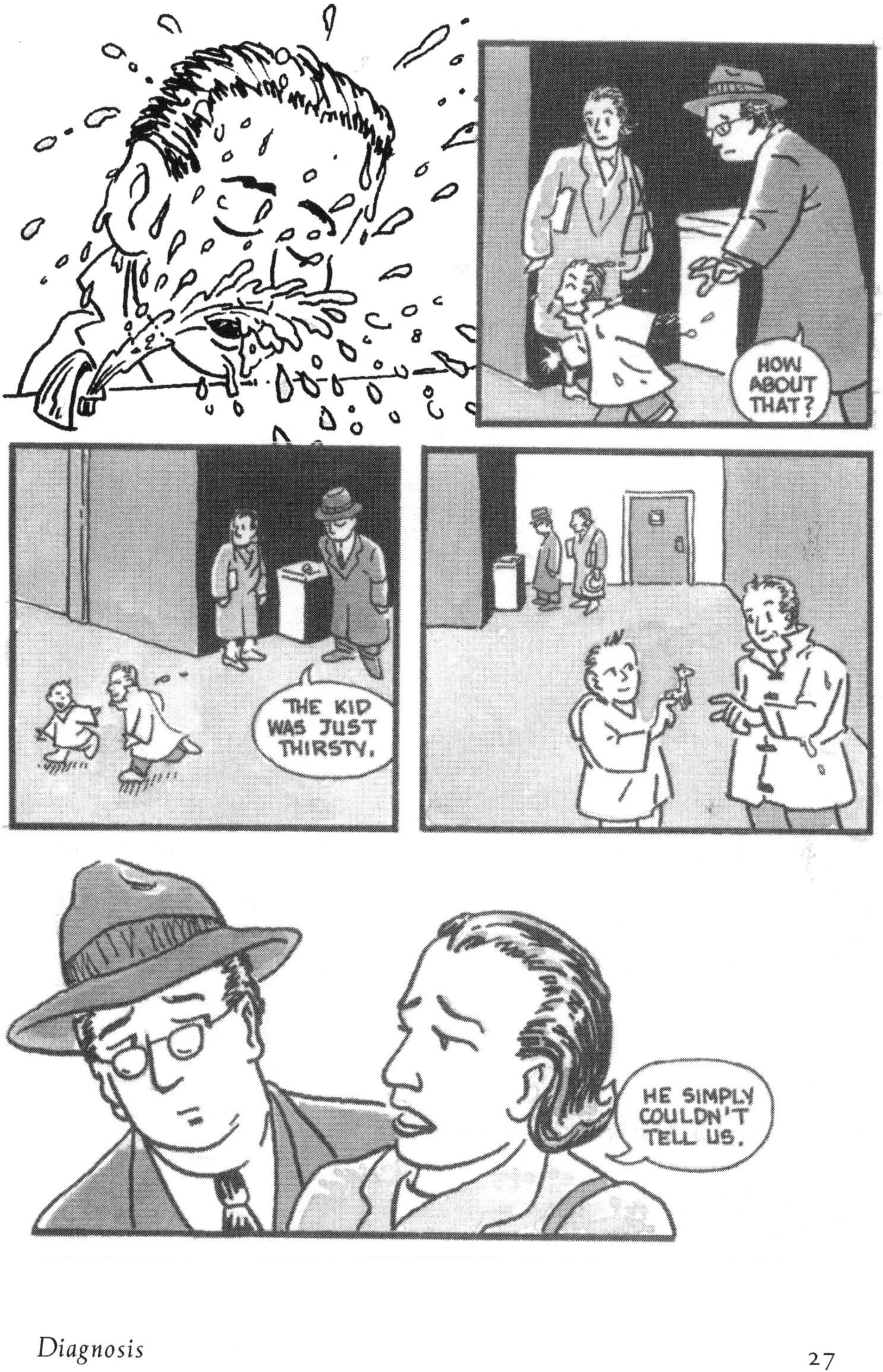
HOW ABOUT THAT?
THE KID WAS JUST THIRSTY.
HE SIMPLY COULDN'T TELL US.

3 Superman in the Living Room

I piled the used evening gowns in the dress-up chest and slammed the top down on the stew of pink net, coral sequin, purple lace, frog-green satin. Done. Crayons and pencils I threw into an empty shoe box. My dirty clothes, from next to my bed, from the bottom of the closet, from over the radiator, from the middle of the floor, I crammed into the bathroom hamper. Done. I stacked my big books in one pile and the skinny paperback school-book-club books in another, keeping out two copies of *TV Guide*, which belonged to David.

There. My room was clean. Now finally I could play, which meant that all the stuff would come right back out. This business of cleaning your room made no sense but I was starting to be a big kid, seven years old, and while being older of course was a fun thing in many ways, it also entailed additional obligatory goodness.

I carried the *TV Guides* into David's room and looked for the cardboard box where he kept his vast collection. *TV Guide* was an excellent source of information about many things, including what kinds of bathing suits grown-up women wore. I found the box under his bathrobe and as I dumped in the two issues I'd borrowed, it struck me that David never had to clean his room. Typical. Here I was wasting half the day moving things around and for what reason? And his stuff got to stay where he wanted it.

I couldn't be the only one who felt this was wrong. From behind Michael's door I heard the sound of Paul's four-year-old voice. No time like the present.

My younger brother was sitting down on the floor next to Michael's miniature steam engine. Michael, who was nine, was showing him the things the steam engine could do.

"Here's how you stop it," he said to Paul. "Watch how it slows down first."

"How come David never has to clean up his room?" I asked.

Michael opened up the door to the toy furnace and blew out the ghostly fire hovering over the small white bricks of solid fuel. He turned a lever, steam hissed out from the water tank, the shiny silver pistons reduced their pace, and the engine's wheel stopped its spinning.

"What are you talking about?" he asked.

"Look at the wheel slow down, Judy," said Paul, whose mind had remained on the steam engine.

"He gets special treatment," I said. "That's not right. It's not fair."

"Huh?" Michael asked, puzzled. "Oh yeah," he said, as his brain stretched around to include my way of seeing things. He pulled open the door to the furnace, lit another match, and reached in to reignite the cube.

"Well, Judy, David is David," Michael said. "You know who he is."

The fuel took. Trembling smoke-shaped flames chased one another along the brick's length.

"It's not fair," I said. "It's always like this. We get one set of rules but he gets another."

David didn't have to make his bed, rake leaves, or clear the table. He interrupted. He had his shows. He ate more cookies than anybody else. It wasn't right and we had done nothing—just sat there and watched—while first Mommy, then Daddy, then Mommy again, made exceptions for David.

"Fairness is important," I said. "Michael, here's this huge unfairness, right in the middle of everything. Every day."

Paul turned his attention away from the engine for a moment. "It has to be fair," he said.

Michael shook his head. "Judy, it is not a big deal. You make such a big deal out of stuff. Look, Paul, see the band connecting the pistons start to move when they move? That goes to the wheel. But here," Michael added, "first you have to push down the lever so the steam collects in the tank—you want to close it? That's okay, the handle's wood, it doesn't get hot. Yeah, move the lever and shut off the wheel."

"Somebody needs to ask them why."

"So go ask them, that's okay," Michael replied, increasingly annoyed. "I'm busy."

"Doing what?" I asked.

Michael just looked at me.

"Come on, Michael, I moved the lever," Paul urged.

Michael crouched down and reached his fingers delicately into the underside of the rubber belt running from the engine to the pistons. "So you take the band off and that disconnects the pistons," he explained to Paul. "And then when the steam builds up, we'll get the whistle!"

"Yeah, do the whistle!" said Paul.

The steam built up in its little copper tank.

"It takes a while," Michael explained to Paul.

"You're the oldest," I said, returning us to the topic at hand.

"You're the guuurrrl," he replied, stretching out the word as though being a girl was a synonym for being a well-pampered idiot.

I was the best arguer, anyway. I always stuck to it and I always had something to say.

Paul smiled with satisfaction. "Yeah, Judy," he said, "you go do it." He was waiting for the whistle. He knew he wouldn't have to ask; he was the baby.

I knew it had to be done. I knew I could do it.

"I'll do it but I'm not going to ask Daddy," I said. "I'll ask Mommy."

"And report back," said Michael. "I don't think there's an answer so I'd like to hear it."

"Yeah," grinned Paul, showing his dimples. I left them staring at the engine like it was the TV, or a miracle about to happen.

I went downstairs, past David doing a show in the living room, *Superman* as I recall, and found my mother out on the porch. We were living in the house on Lenox Street, with its great porches. Joan had turned the porch table upside down and was starting to drill into a small block of wood. She had an idea in her head that she could make the table the right height for having drinks on (something we did every night at six-thirty), so that when the weather was warm, we could drink out on the porch.

When I asked her why there were two sets of rules, she put down the drill.

But maybe at this point I should explain about the shows.

David performs television shows. He has been doing this for decades. My oldest brother is now more than fifty years old, and I don't remember a time when his shows weren't part of a normal day with him.

Throughout our childhoods, David would walk from room to room in our house, being different people, talking in different voices, a squeaky one for Doberman of *Sergeant Bilko* or Jimmy Olsen of *The Adventures of Superman*, a self-assured, slippery voice for Bilko or for Bud Abbott when he did an Abbott and Costello movie, holding his body in different ways to represent the different characters, breaking for advertisements and announcing different products.

He does dialogue, music, and gestures.

These are not word-for-word re-creations, but condensed versions, featuring the pivotal moments of each scene, drawing on the language that drives the plot, like a storyboard of a show, or a series of friezes telling the familiar story of a holy figure moving through his destiny.

David also does interview shows. He does *Meet the Press.*

My brother David is a tall man with dark hair, nicely cut in the traditional style. For the interview shows he sits at the dining room table. He keeps a tumbler of water, at room temperature, to his left, and he often wears sunglasses, which he puts on and takes off as he talks, depending on who is speaking.

He does everybody: it used to be Lawrence E. Spivak was moderator in David's world, but then Martin Agronsky got the job, and David also does various members of the *Meet the Press* panel: Marianne Means of the Associated Press, Allen Otten of *U.S. News & World Report.*

David does the guests, who cover the political spectrum. Sometimes David, who knows the middle name of every member of the House and Senate who has served during his lifetime, will give the guests new jobs. He sent Elliot Richardson to France as ambassador for a while there. Sometimes he'll keep people alive; he interviewed Patrice Lumumba into the 1970s.

After Bill Clinton was elected president, David interviewed the former governor of Alabama, George Wallace. The music of political discourse filled the interview.

"Well, Governor Wallace, what is your choice in the political party caucus?"

"Well, we expect we have the party choices and party gimmicks that are needed."

"Governor Wallace, don't you think the Clinton administration might outlaw a presidential veto?"

"Well, Mister Otten, the Clinton administration might assure us that many democracies are strong, favorable, and more powerful."

David does commercials, too, often one in a squeaky voice: Don Adams for Allstate Insurance. "Our alternate sponsor," says David.

Around the time he turned forty-five, David started to frame the interview shows with five-minute renditions of stories featuring Twinkles, the Magic

Elephant. The Twinkles cartoons, originally a segment within a cartoon half hour, were brief and tightly told. He performed these in entirety: the title, the narration, and all the dialogue, apparently word for word. These segments all feature strong punch lines, which David socked home.

David's performances were almost always without audience. Sometimes I'd tune in for a few minutes, but for the most part they were background sound, something we paid as little attention to as we paid to Mommy making dinner in the kitchen or Michael mixing gunpowder for a miniature homemade bomb or Paul and I playing with our tiny wooden animals in the Mouse House.

Even now, when David comes to my mother's house, he has all his shows on a careful schedule, his own schedule, which has nothing to do with what is on the television at that particular moment but everything to do with a system that we don't understand but which David does and feels strongly should be respected. He can get very angry if the schedule has to change. He drums on his head with his long fingers, his face becomes red, he repeats phrases and names over and over. If you give David some time, though, he can work it out. He makes adjustments.

The shows have gone on for years, never one exactly like the other. I don't know where David first got the idea.

Before answering my question, Joan looked over her tools—the drill, the four short Phillips head screws, the second small wooden block, the two sets of hooks and eyes, the screwdriver, and the pliers—as if to make sure they were all in place so that she would be able to pick up where she had left off, after the conversation. Or maybe she was taking a minute to think about what to say and how exactly to say it, although it is certain that she had been waiting for some time for this question, or one like it, to be asked.

She turned her attention to me and said, in a matter-of-fact way, "Well, Judy, David gets some things easier because a lot of ordinary things are harder for him. Getting through the day is harder for David than it is for the rest of us."

"Hard?" I replied. His life didn't look so hard to me. "Mommy!"

My mother paused.

"You know the way you look at something, Judy, and it's just there? Or the way you hear something, and it's just a sound?

"What David sees or hears breaks into a lot of little pieces before it gets to him. So he needs to put it all back together. This goes on all the time, and it's a lot of work. The parts of his brain are the same—it's the way they're connected that's different."

I stopped arguing. There were times when I could almost see the gears in David's head spinning, as he said the same things quickly over and over, his hands dancing in the air, sometimes drumming on his head. No wonder.

"Things arrive splintered," said my mother.

She was about to continue but I interrupted.

"Okay, Mom, I *get* it."

I stood there for a minute. Just as I had taken the dirty clothes from my floor and put them into the hamper, I moved David from one classification to another. He went from being an incomprehensible pain in the neck to someone who, although an incomprehensible pain in the neck, had a tough situation and needed protection. Poor David. And all that was wrong was the wiring. Otherwise his brain could have been mine. And vice versa.

"Okay, Judy?" asked my mother. "You sure?"

"Yeah I guess," I said, somewhat begrudgingly.

"Okay, then," she replied, whereupon she returned to fixing the table. I went back upstairs, past David doing his show, to report.

I found my brothers in the upstairs back bathroom. Michael was making sure that Paul, who had touched the fuel cube, got his hands clean.

I explained what I had been told.

"That's great, Judy," said Michael. "That's what I said. David is David."

Paul turned to Michael. "Blow on my fingers," he said. They had been singed by the hot cube.

Michael blew, gently.

"Does that feel better?"

Paul nodded.

"We got the whistle to go," Paul told me. "You want to see?"

The three of us went back down the hall to the bedroom.

Reluctantly, I sat down next to Paul and Michael and the tiny combustion system that only did one thing, over and over, but which fascinated my brothers. There was probably an explanation for the two of them, just like there was an explanation for David.

Michael slid in another cube of fuel. He lit it and we waited as the steam built up. The whistle was louder than I had expected. It hit a high, long note.

4 A Quiet Evening at Home with the Karasiks

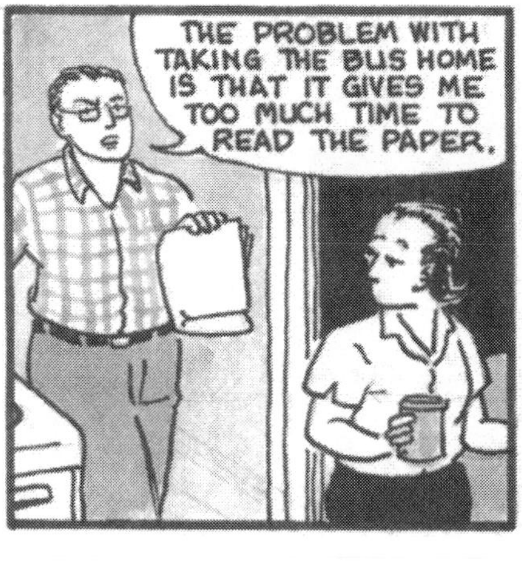
THE PROBLEM WITH TAKING THE BUS HOME IS THAT IT GIVES ME TOO MUCH TIME TO READ THE PAPER.

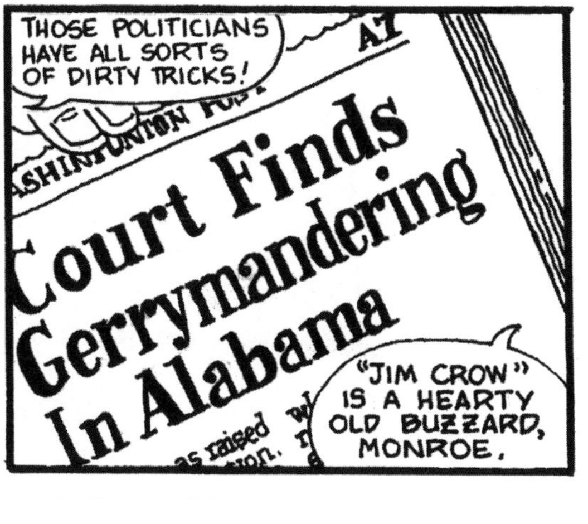
THOSE POLITICIANS HAVE ALL SORTS OF DIRTY TRICKS!
Court Finds Gerrymandering In Alabama
"JIM CROW" IS A HEARTY OLD BUZZARD, MONROE.

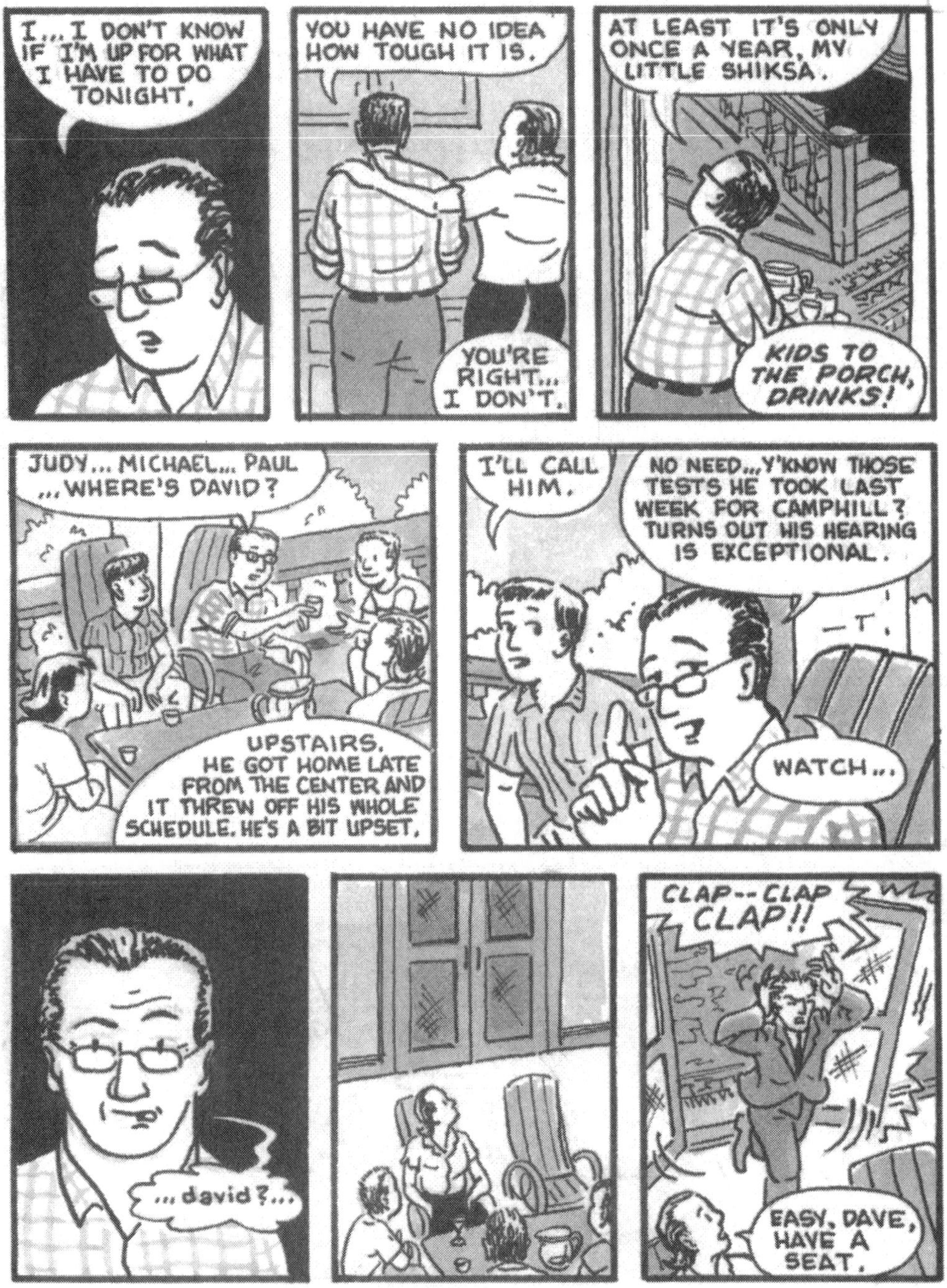
I... I DON'T KNOW IF I'M UP FOR WHAT I HAVE TO DO TONIGHT.
YOU HAVE NO IDEA HOW TOUGH IT IS.
YOU'RE RIGHT... I DON'T.
AT LEAST IT'S ONLY ONCE A YEAR, MY LITTLE SHIKSA.
KIDS TO THE PORCH, DRINKS!
JUDY... MICHAEL... PAUL ...WHERE'S DAVID?
UPSTAIRS. HE GOT HOME LATE FROM THE CENTER AND IT THREW OFF HIS WHOLE SCHEDULE. HE'S A BIT UPSET.
I'LL CALL HIM.
NO NEED...Y'KNOW THOSE TESTS HE TOOK LAST WEEK FOR CAMPHILL? TURNS OUT HIS HEARING IS EXCEPTIONAL.
WATCH...
...david?...
CLAP--CLAP CLAP!!
EASY, DAVE, HAVE A SEAT.

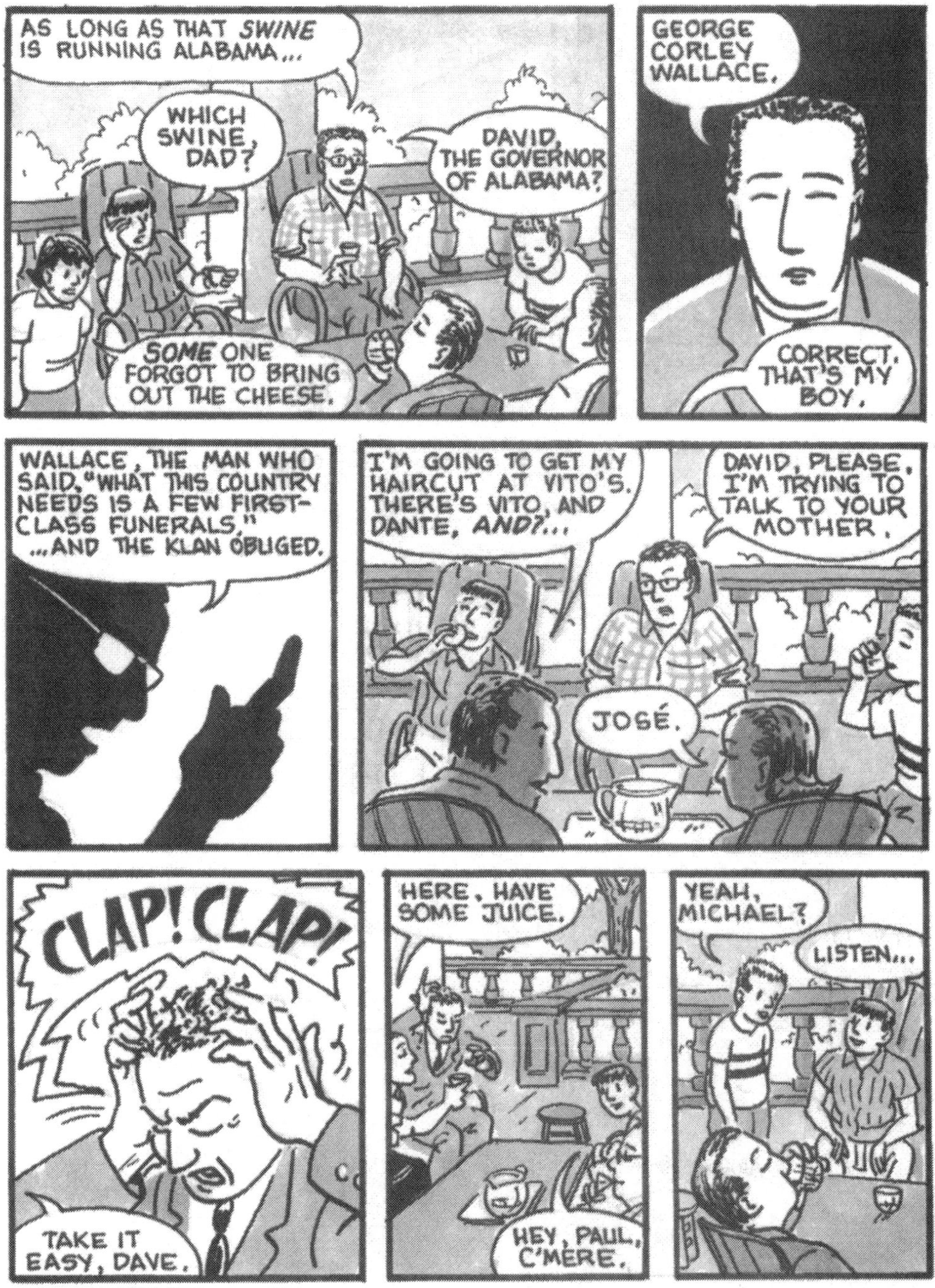
AS LONG AS THAT SWINE IS RUNNING ALABAMA...
WHICH SWINE, DAD?
DAVID, THE GOVERNOR OF ALABAMA?
SOME ONE FORGOT TO BRING OUT THE CHEESE.
GEORGE CORLEY WALLACE.
CORRECT. THAT'S MY BOY.
WALLACE, THE MAN WHO SAID, "WHAT THIS COUNTRY NEEDS IS A FEW FIRST-CLASS FUNERALS," ...AND THE KLAN OBLIGED.
I'M GOING TO GET MY HAIRCUT AT VITO'S. THERE'S VITO, AND DANTE, AND?...
DAVID, PLEASE, I'M TRYING TO TALK TO YOUR MOTHER.
JOSÉ.
CLAP! CLAP!
TAKE IT EASY, DAVE.
HERE, HAVE SOME JUICE.
HEY, PAUL, C'MERE.
YEAH, MICHAEL?
LISTEN...

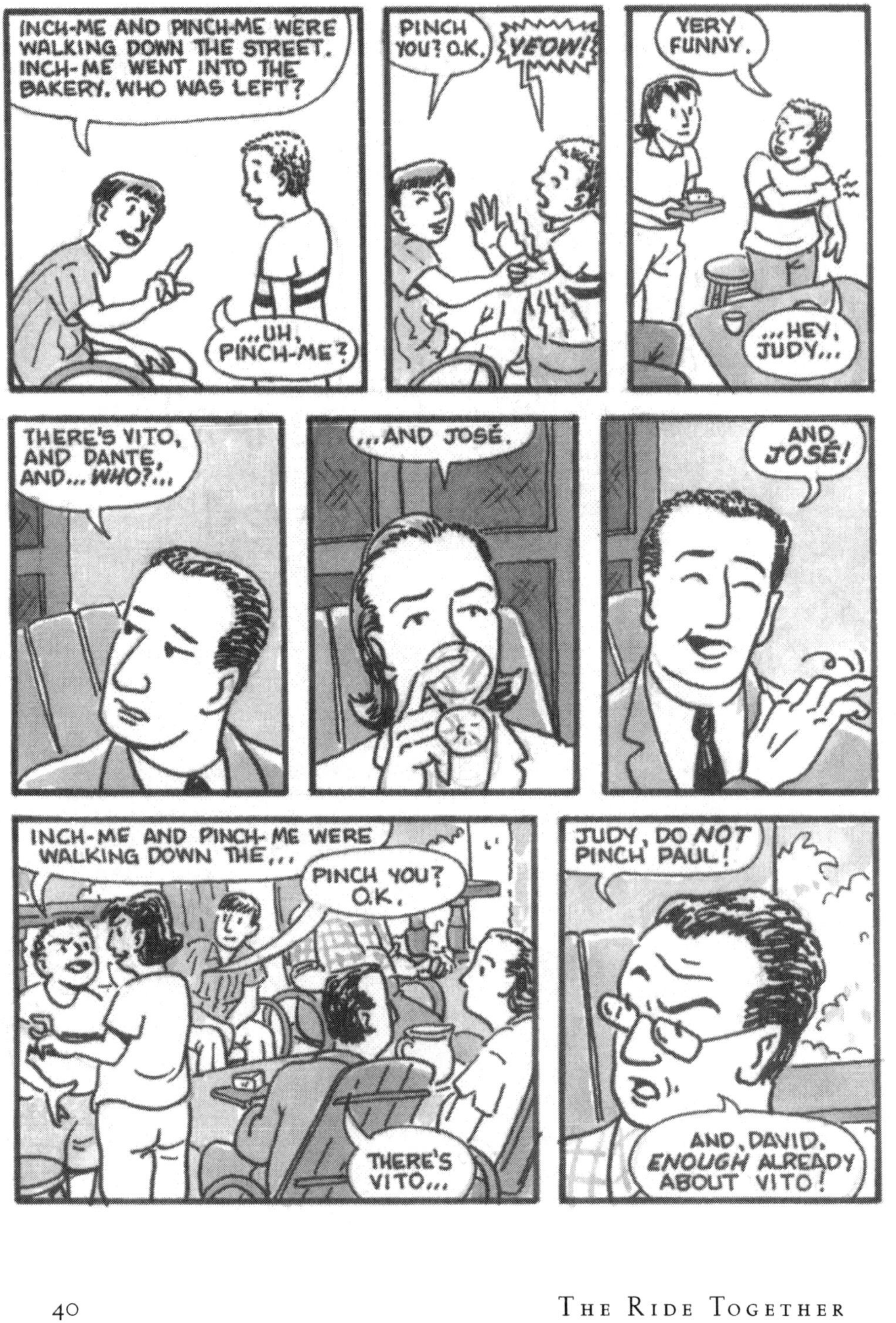
INCH-ME AND PINCH-ME WERE WALKING DOWN THE STREET. INCH-ME WENT INTO THE BAKERY. WHO WAS LEFT?
...UH, PINCH-ME?
PINCH YOU? O.K.
YEOW!
VERY FUNNY.
...HEY, JUDY...
THERE'S VITO, AND DANTE, AND... WHO?...
...AND JOSÉ.
AND JOSÉ!
INCH-ME AND PINCH-ME WERE WALKING DOWN THE...
PINCH YOU? O.K.
THERE'S VITO...
JUDY, DO NOT PINCH PAUL!
AND, DAVID, ENOUGH ALREADY ABOUT VITO!

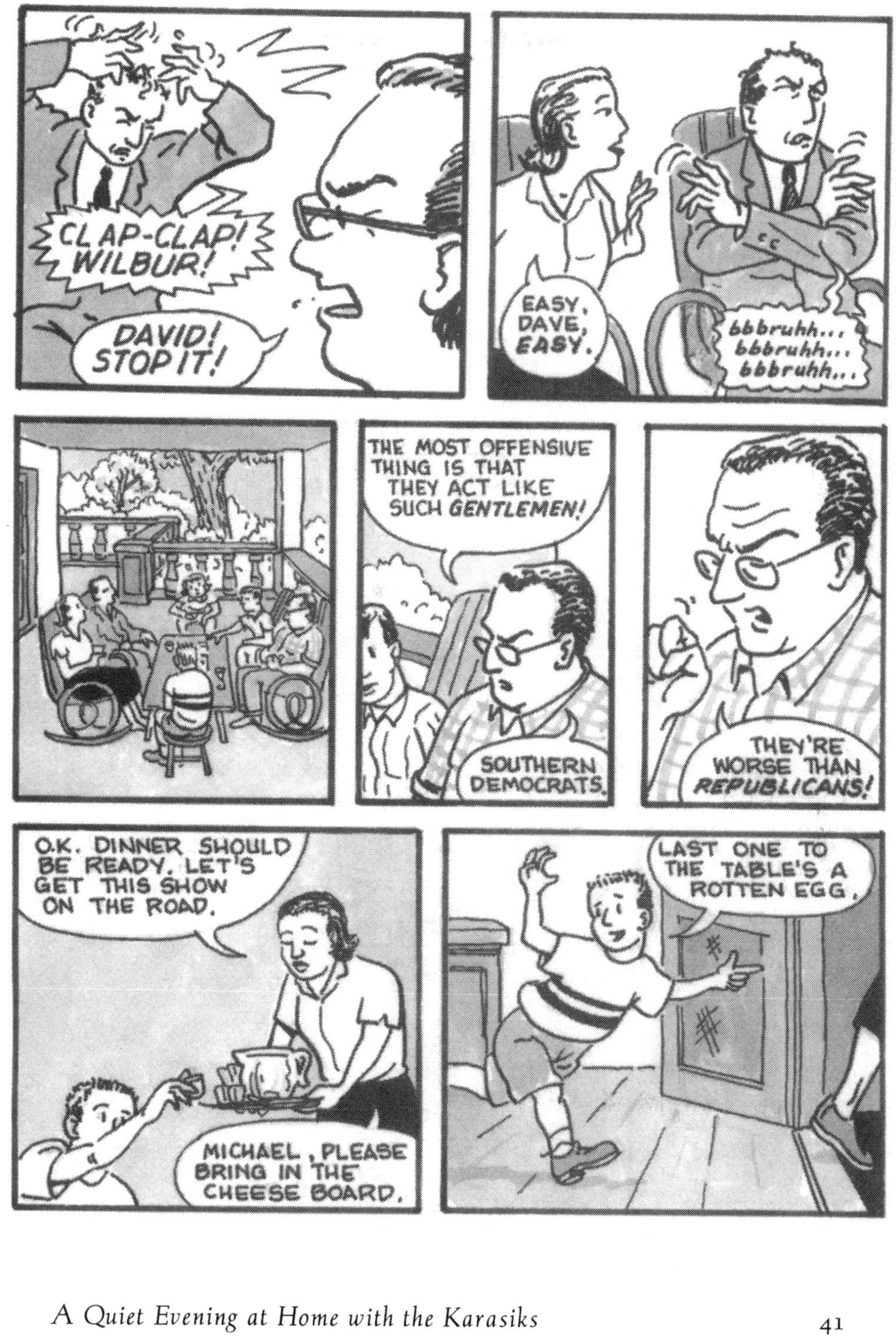
CLAP-CLAP! WILBUR!
DAVID! STOP IT!
EASY, DAVE, EASY.
bbbruhh... bbbruhh... bbbruhh...
THE MOST OFFENSIVE THING IS THAT THEY ACT LIKE SUCH GENTLEMEN!
SOUTHERN DEMOCRATS.
THEY'RE WORSE THAN REPUBLICANS!
O.K. DINNER SHOULD BE READY. LET'S GET THIS SHOW ON THE ROAD.
MICHAEL, PLEASE BRING IN THE CHEESE BOARD.
LAST ONE TO THE TABLE'S A ROTTEN EGG.

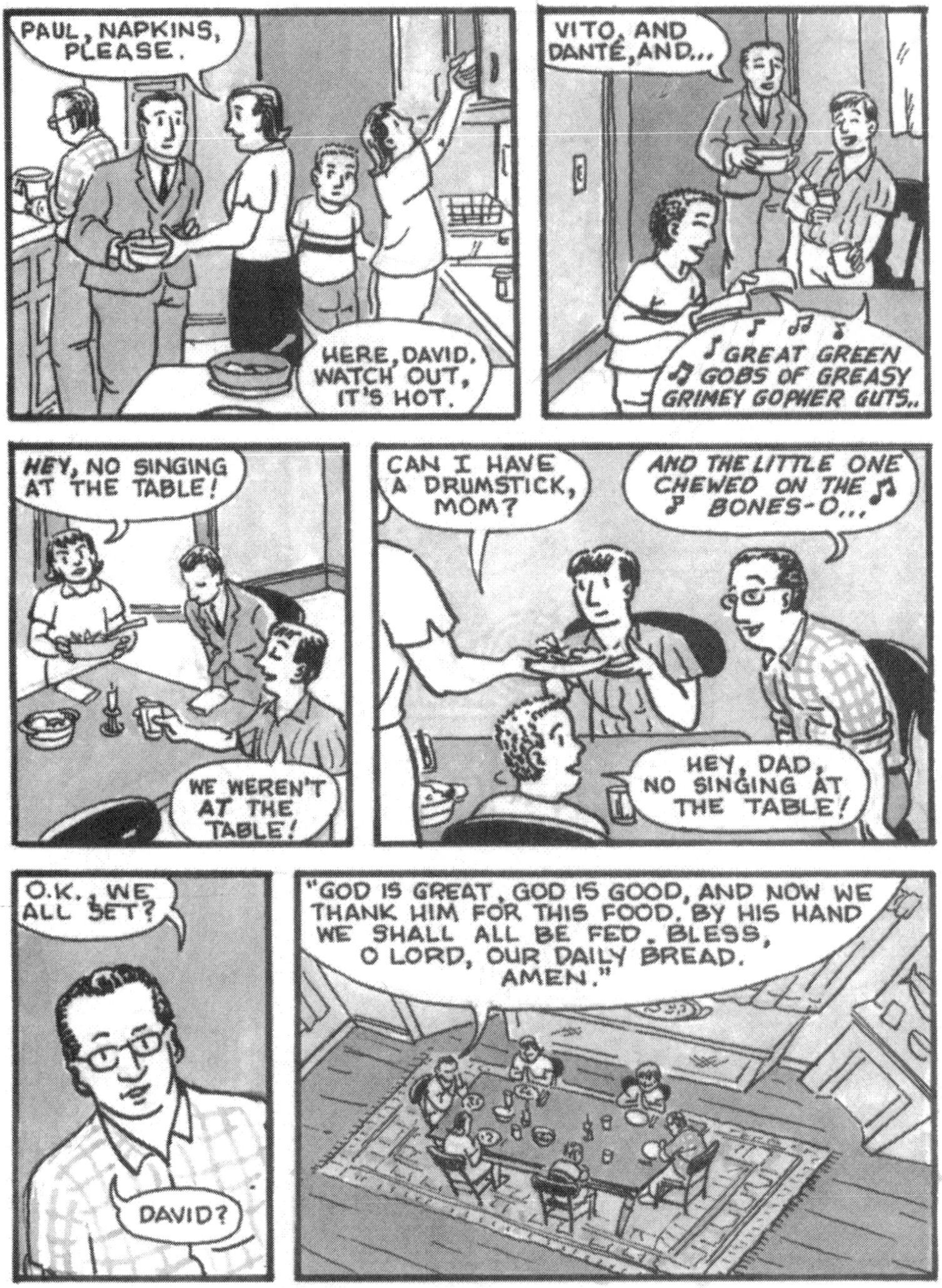
PAUL, NAPKINS, PLEASE.
HERE, DAVID. WATCH OUT, IT'S HOT.
VITO, AND DANTÉ, AND...
GREAT GREEN GOBS OF GREASY GRIMEY GOPHER GUTS..
HEY, NO SINGING AT THE TABLE!
WE WEREN'T AT THE TABLE!
CAN I HAVE A DRUMSTICK, MOM?
AND THE LITTLE ONE CHEWED ON THE BONES-O...
HEY, DAD, NO SINGING AT THE TABLE!
O.K., WE ALL SET?
DAVID?
"GOD IS GREAT, GOD IS GOOD, AND NOW WE THANK HIM FOR THIS FOOD. BY HIS HAND WE SHALL ALL BE FED. BLESS, O LORD, OUR DAILY BREAD. AMEN."

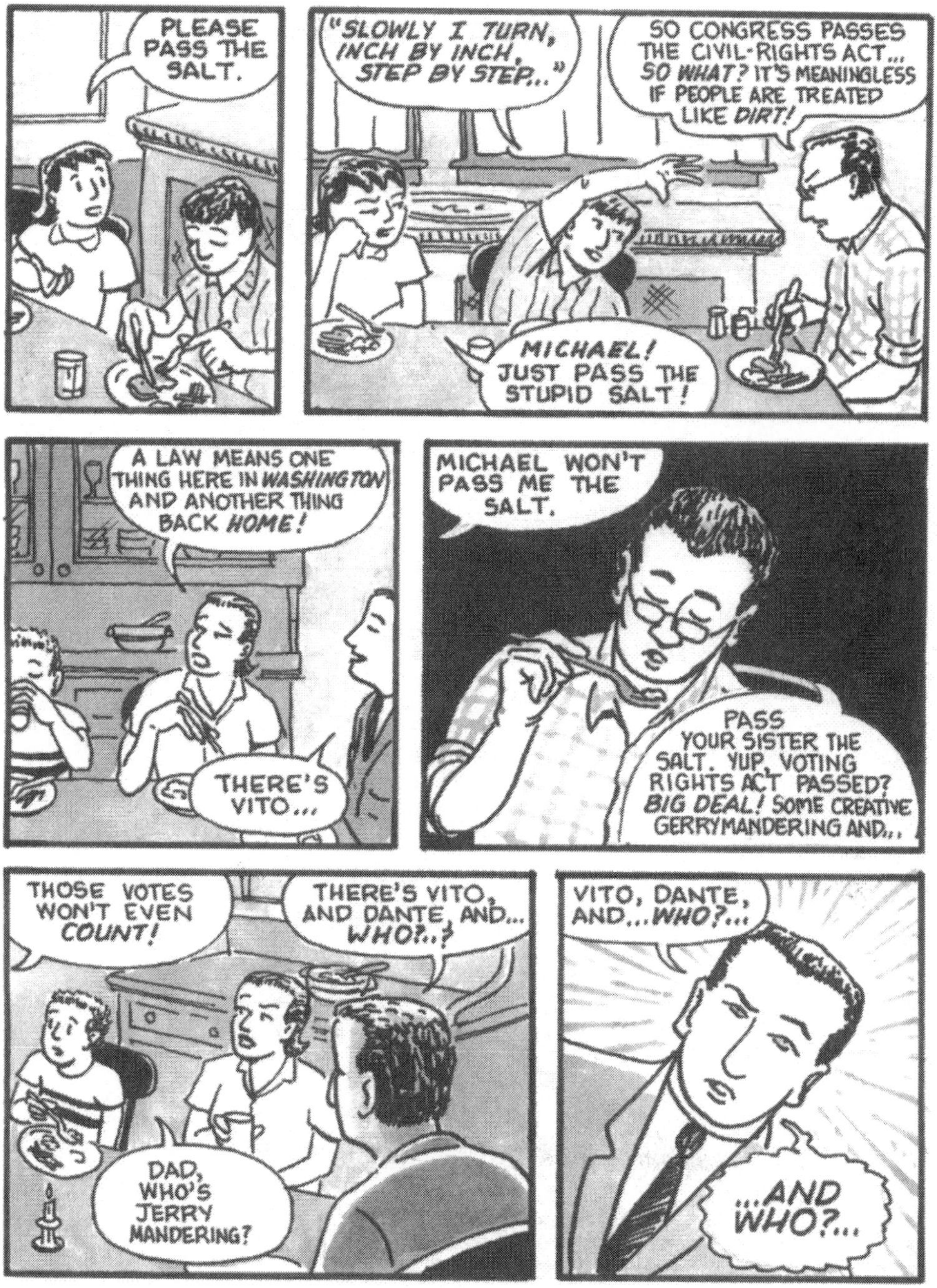
PLEASE PASS THE SALT.
"SLOWLY I TURN, INCH BY INCH, STEP BY STEP..."
SO CONGRESS PASSES THE CIVIL-RIGHTS ACT... SO WHAT? IT'S MEANINGLESS IF PEOPLE ARE TREATED LIKE DIRT!
MICHAEL! JUST PASS THE STUPID SALT!
A LAW MEANS ONE THING HERE IN WASHINGTON AND ANOTHER THING BACK HOME!
THERE'S VITO...
MICHAEL WON'T PASS ME THE SALT.
PASS YOUR SISTER THE SALT. YUP, VOTING RIGHTS ACT PASSED? BIG DEAL! SOME CREATIVE GERRYMANDERING AND...
THOSE VOTES WON'T EVEN COUNT!
THERE'S VITO, AND DANTE, AND... WHO?..?
DAD, WHO'S JERRY MANDERING?
VITO, DANTE, AND...WHO?...
...AND WHO?...

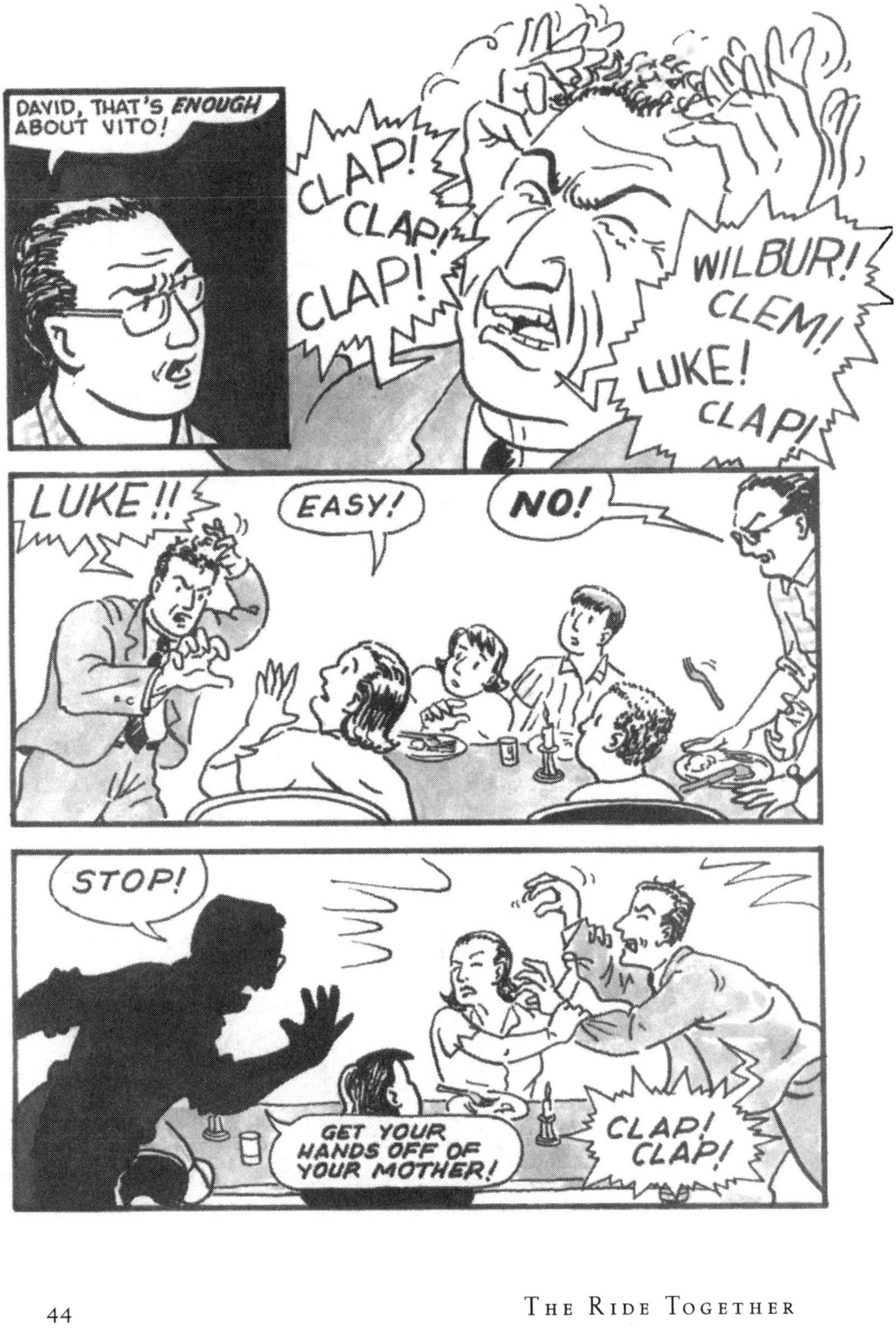
DAVID, THAT'S ENOUGH ABOUT VITO!
CLAP! CLAP! CLAP!
WILBUR! CLEM! LUKE! CLAP!
LUKE!!
EASY!
NO!
STOP!
GET YOUR HANDS OFF OF YOUR MOTHER!
CLAP! CLAP!

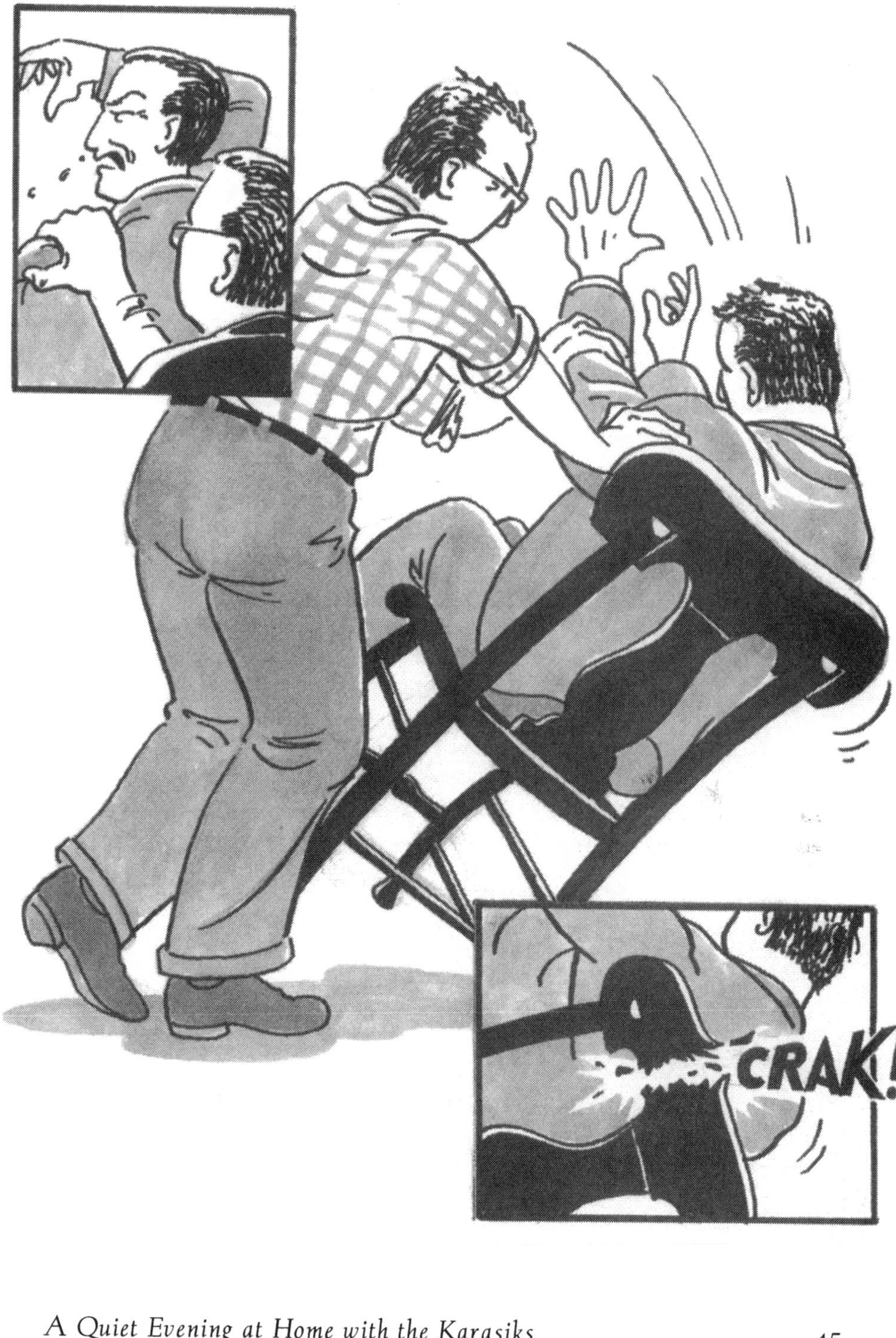
CRAK!

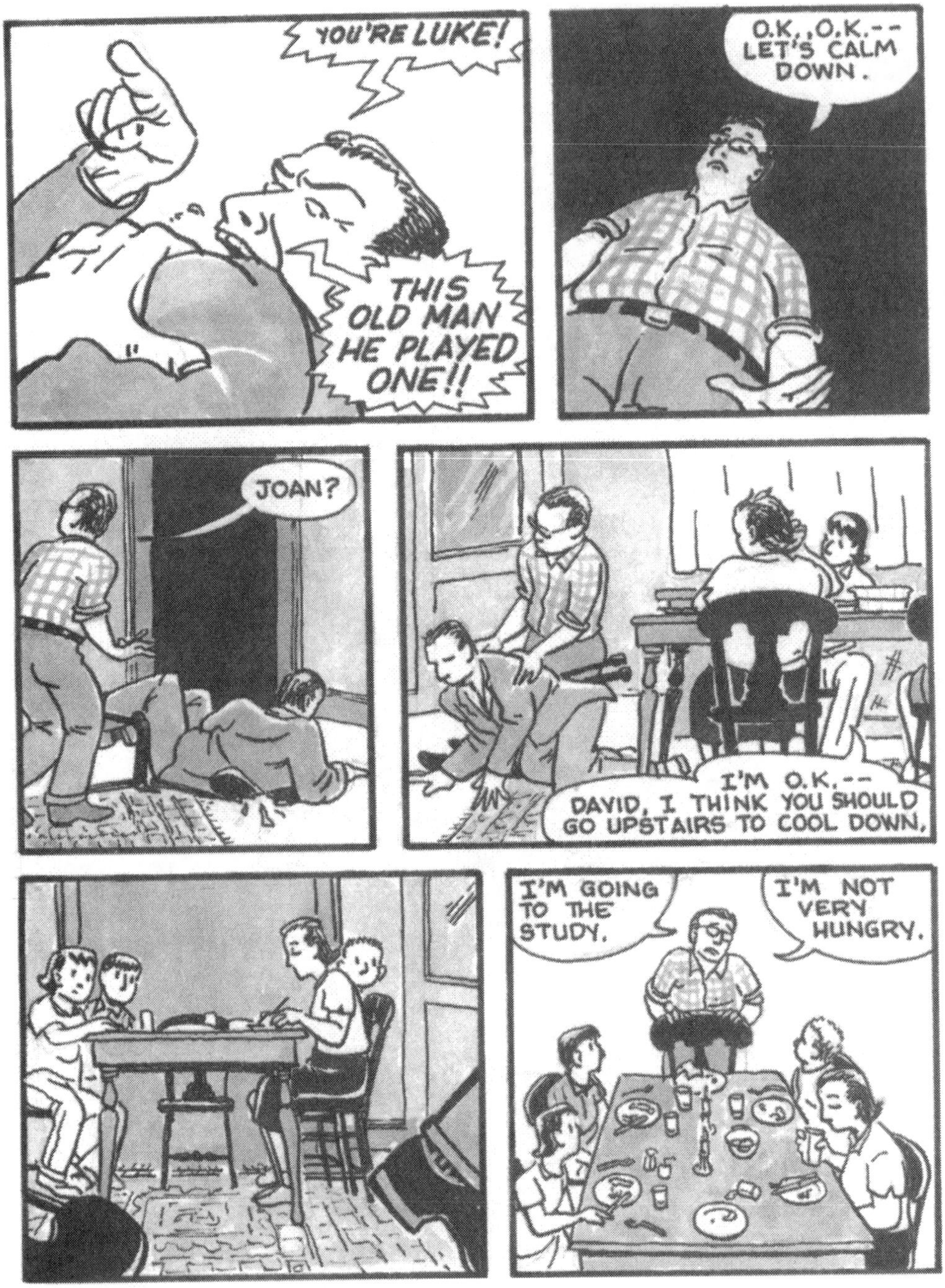
YOU'RE LUKE!
THIS OLD MAN HE PLAYED ONE!!
O.K., O.K.-- LET'S CALM DOWN.
JOAN?
I'M O.K.-- DAVID, I THINK YOU SHOULD GO UPSTAIRS TO COOL DOWN.
I'M GOING TO THE STUDY.
I'M NOT VERY HUNGRY.

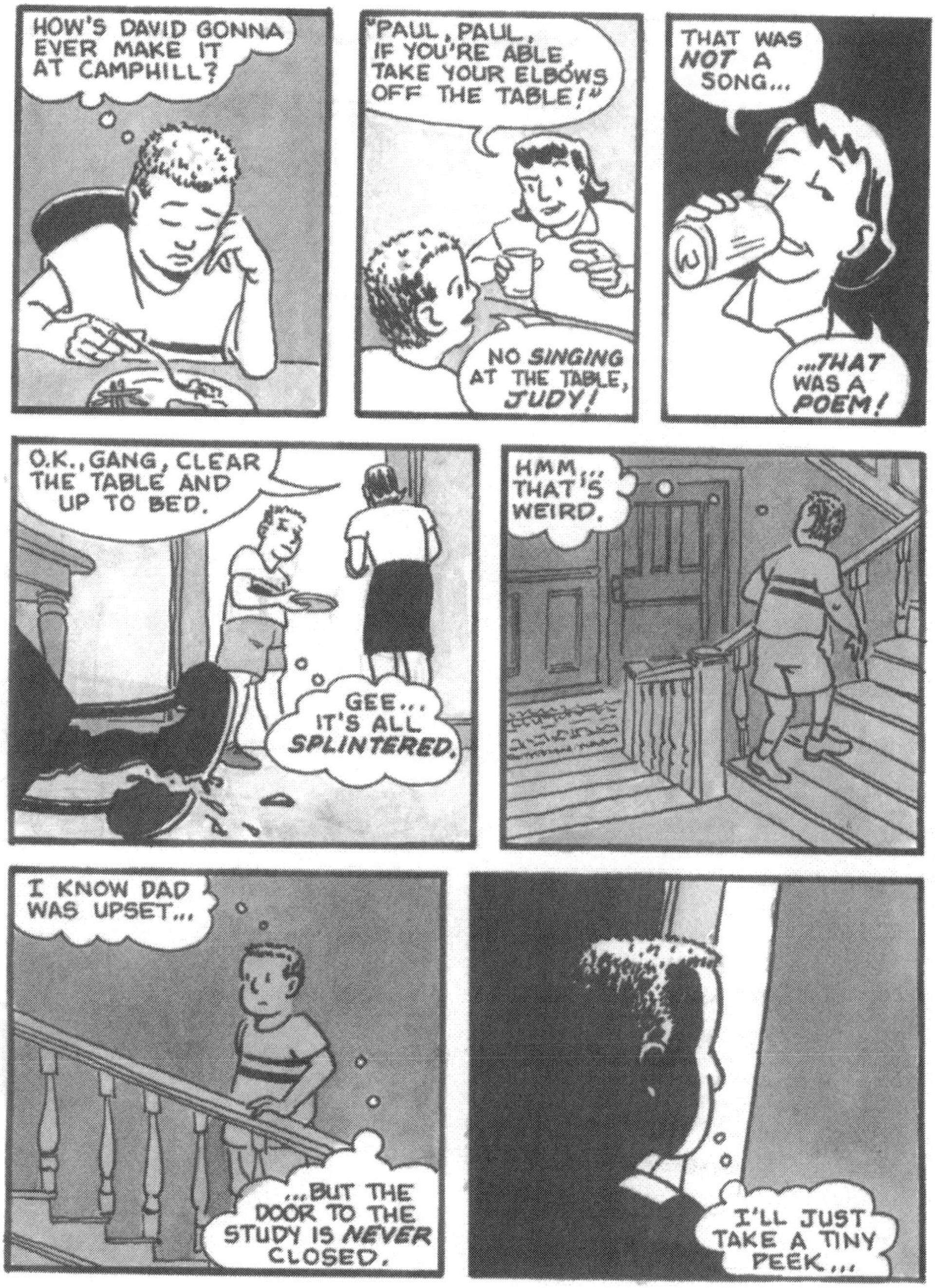
HOW'S DAVID GONNA EVER MAKE IT AT CAMPHILL?
"PAUL, PAUL, IF YOU'RE ABLE, TAKE YOUR ELBOWS OFF THE TABLE!"
NO SINGING AT THE TABLE, JUDY!
THAT WAS NOT A SONG...
...THAT WAS A POEM!
O.K., GANG, CLEAR THE TABLE AND UP TO BED.
GEE... IT'S ALL SPLINTERED.
HMM... THAT'S WEIRD.
I KNOW DAD WAS UPSET...
...BUT THE DOOR TO THE STUDY IS NEVER CLOSED.
I'LL JUST TAKE A TINY PEEK...

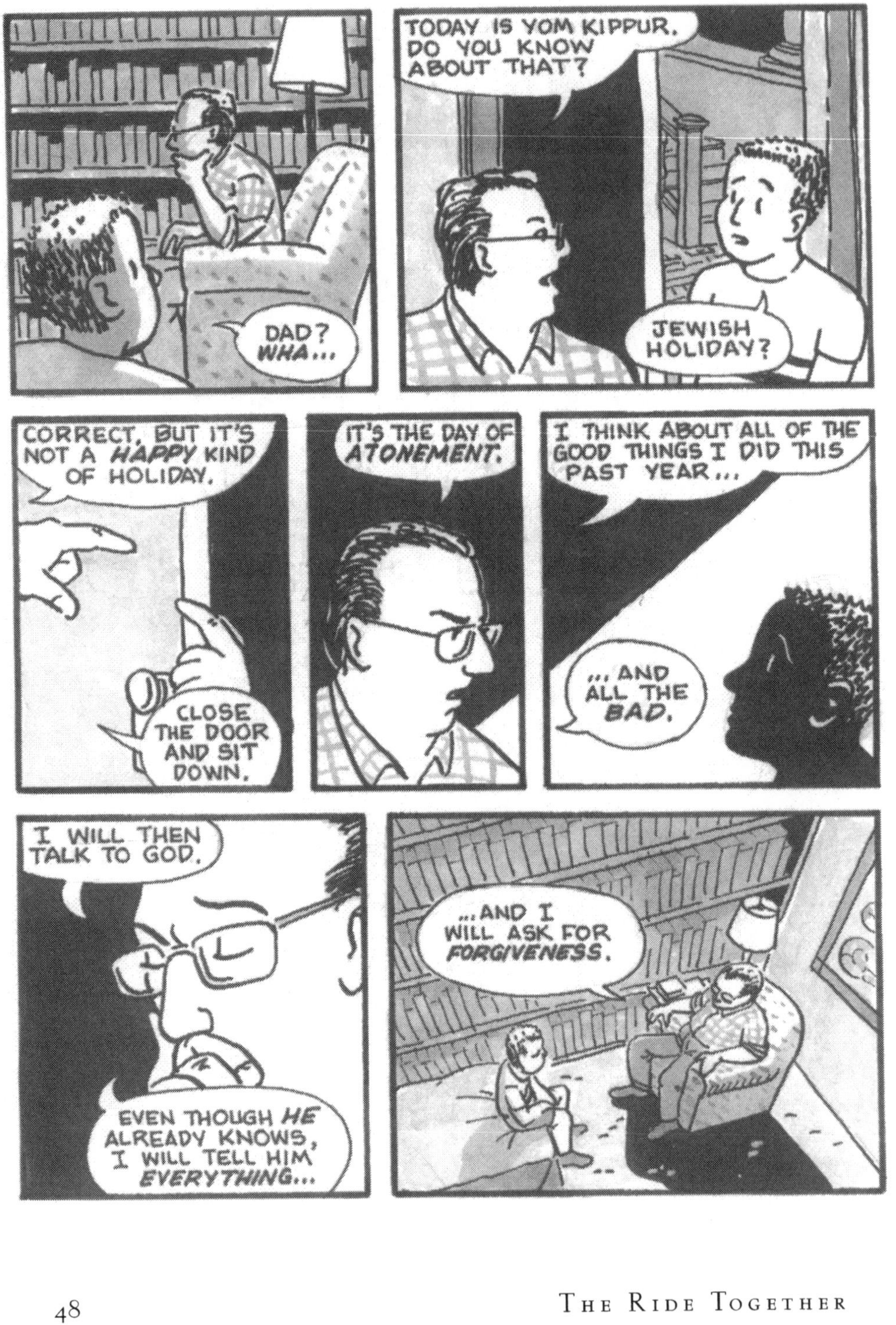

DAD? WHA...
TODAY IS YOM KIPPUR. DO YOU KNOW ABOUT THAT?
JEWISH HOLIDAY?
CORRECT, BUT IT'S NOT A HAPPY KIND OF HOLIDAY.
CLOSE THE DOOR AND SIT DOWN.
IT'S THE DAY OF ATONEMENT.
I THINK ABOUT ALL OF THE GOOD THINGS I DID THIS PAST YEAR...
...AND ALL THE BAD.
I WILL THEN TALK TO GOD.
EVEN THOUGH HE ALREADY KNOWS, I WILL TELL HIM EVERYTHING...
...AND I WILL ASK FOR FORGIVENESS.

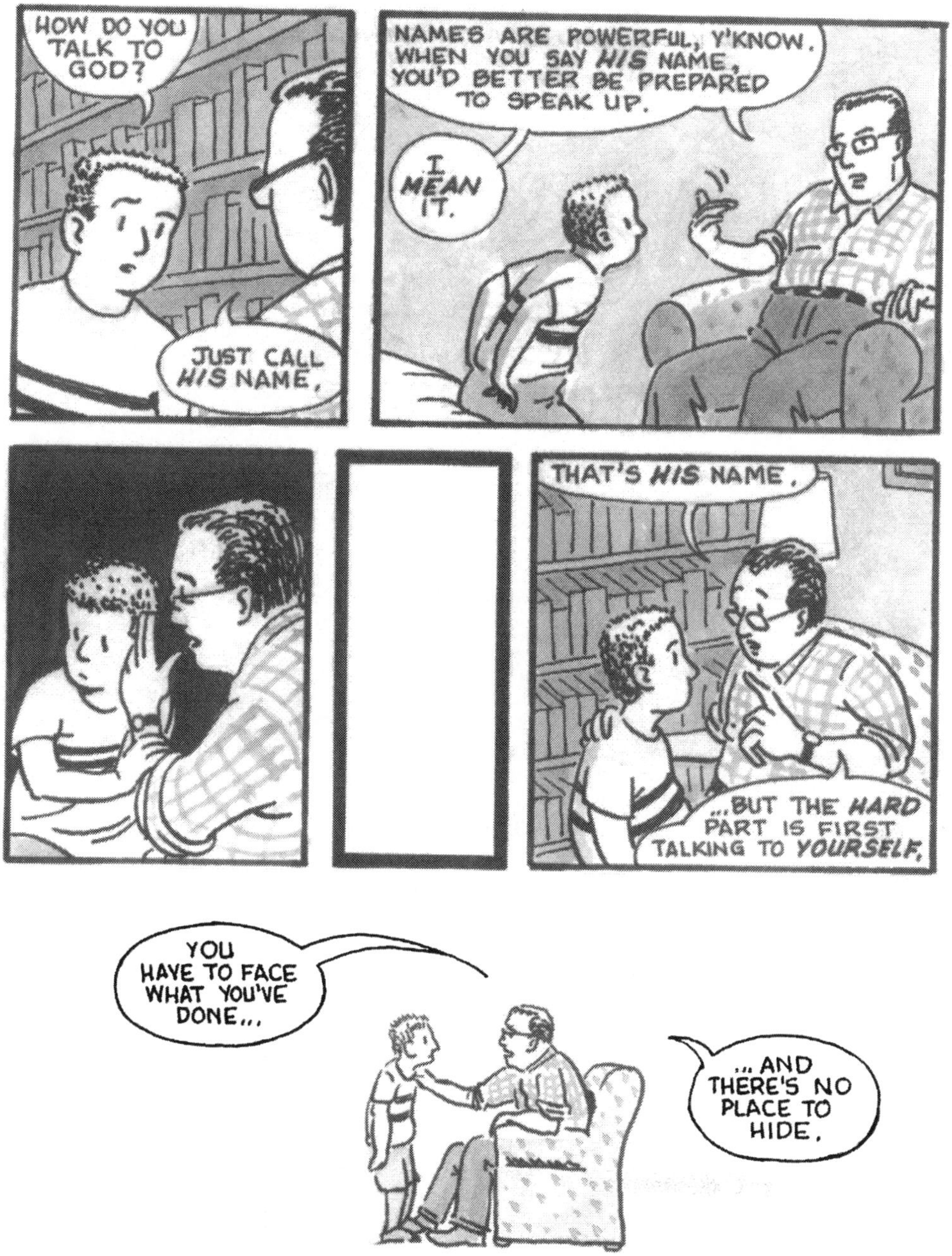
HOW DO YOU TALK TO GOD?
JUST CALL HIS NAME.
NAMES ARE POWERFUL, Y'KNOW. WHEN YOU SAY HIS NAME, YOU'D BETTER BE PREPARED TO SPEAK UP.
I MEAN IT.
THAT'S HIS NAME.
...BUT THE HARD PART IS FIRST TALKING TO YOURSELF.
YOU HAVE TO FACE WHAT YOU'VE DONE...
...AND THERE'S NO PLACE TO HIDE.

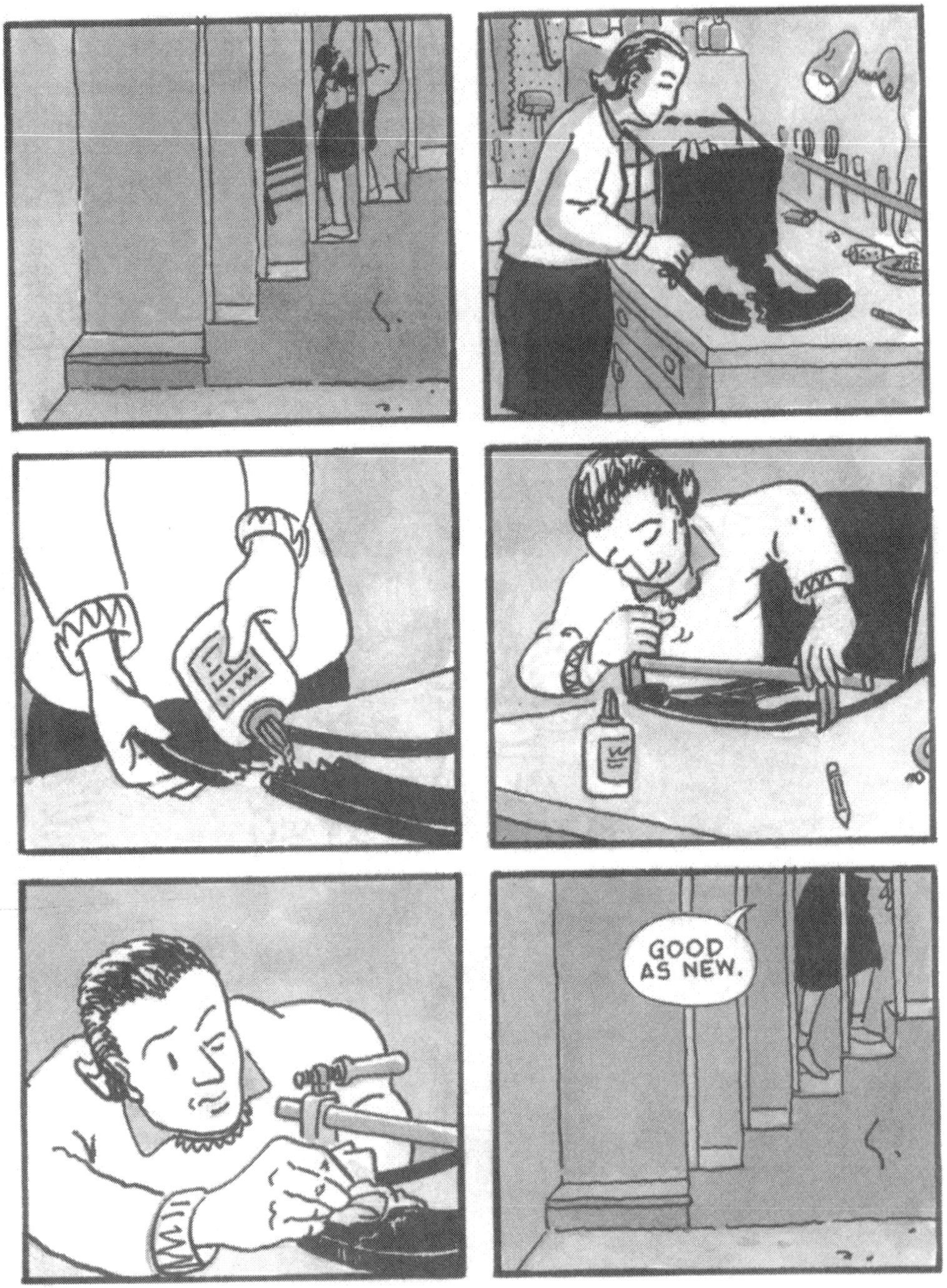
GOOD AS NEW.

5 *Playing Poker with Miss Murphy*

Every August, we rented a big old house on an island off the coast of Massachusetts for the whole month. Sadie Attaquin's house on Martha's Vineyard. We didn't see other people much—it was just us together as a family, swimming and doing jigsaw puzzles and picking blueberries and climbing the beach cliffs, living in the hot salty air—but sometimes visitors came to stay.

One summer Miss Murphy came, with her best friend, Miss McKenna.

We knew Miss Murphy from Washington, but she was originally from Maine. "Down East," she said. "Helen Murphy from Down East." She was a knobby, short woman with short, slicked-back hair the color of old white piano keys and strong but stubby arms. Miss McKenna's first name was Florence. She looked like a Florence—curly reddish bangs and pink skin that made her look always astonished and thick pale blue glasses that hung on a golden chain around her neck. If Miss McKenna had been a dog she would have been a poodle.

Miss McKenna was nice enough, in a fluttery way. But it was Miss Murphy who was dear to our hearts, because Miss Murphy loved my brother David.

Miss Murphy had been David's teacher before he went away to Burgoyne School in Delaware. Burgoyne hadn't worked out in the end. Joan and Monroe liked the place and the people, but David was miserable there. Finally, one time they were saying good-bye to Dave, dropping him off after a visit home, and he lay down on his bed and cried. He came home soon after. Maybe he was just too young to go away to school.

The only thing I remembered about Burgoyne was once when I was standing with Paul and Michael on a wide green lawn waiting for our parents outside. We heard a voice roaring upstairs, a voice without words, and we looked up from the green lawn and saw bars on the windows. When I told Mom the place scared me, she assured me that it wasn't a bad place, that David would never have to be in a bad place.

Now, Dave was in a local day program run by a non-profit, since kids like David couldn't go to public school. Through all these changes, Miss Murphy had remained a family friend.

"Hey, Dave!" said Miss Murphy when she saw him as the women first got out of their car at the Attaquin house. "Hey, Dave!" she said. "Give me a hug." And she grabbed him, a little less roughly than she grabbed anything else.

"You're a good boy, Dave," growled Miss Murphy cheerfully.

He dashed away after the hug, but he was smiling. Because it was hard to tell what David was thinking, not many people knew how to be friendly with him, how to be genuine, and so it was nice to have somebody around who did.

During the day, Miss Murphy and Miss McKenna wore hats and drove around the island. One morning they took me with them, over to watch my father and my brother Michael fish off the Menemsha jetty. Those were the days when you could still catch something off the Menemsha jetty.

By breakfast time Dad and Michael were just finishing off a good day's fishing. They had gotten up in the dark of night to fish.

That morning, I followed the two women out to the tip of the jetty, jumping from one big rock to another. By the time I got out there, Michael was pulling in a flounder, the fish with two eyes on one side of its head, like the face on a card from a deck of playing cards, and my father was cursing the seagulls for stealing his bait.

Dad used the words we weren't allowed to use, the words we heard every August, at the beginning of the month and at the end, when we crept through the traffic in steaming downtown Providence, Rhode Island.

Michael and I looked at each other and smiled. Someday we would be able to use those words, too.

"Why, Monroe!" cried Miss McKenna to my father, hearing the words. "Heavens!" she cried, in delighted shock.

My father begged her pardon, a gentleman at least on the outside, but Michael and I knew what he was thinking. He was savoring the day when he would have his revenge on the seagulls.

My father had a plan. When he died, I was going to put his ashes in a bottle and break the bottle on the rocks of the Menemsha jetty. The seagulls would cut their feet on the broken glass and that would be Pop's revenge.

It was my job because I was the only girl and so, special to my father in a way.

Miss Murphy was examining Michael's fish.

"It's a flounder," I said. "See the two eyes on the same side of its head? Like on a deck of playing cards."

Miss Murphy squinted in the sun. "You kids play cards?" she asked.

"Sure," said Michael, taking the fish away from Miss Murphy and pulling the hook out of its mouth, getting his fingers all bloody. "Poker," he said. "You like poker?"

Miss Murphy grinned. "Michael, my boy," she told him, "You're only a kid. Take some advice. Don't play poker with an Irishwoman."

Michael grinned right back. He was fourteen years old.

"You scared to play with me?" Michael asked Miss Murphy.

Like Dad had his idea of revenge against the seagulls, Michael loved the idea of spectacularly beating somebody who thought he was only a kid, who thought he didn't know anything about cards.

And so that evening's entertainment was set. Michael was part Irish, too. We all were, in addition to being part Jewish. What happened that night, though, had nothing to do with how Irish or how Jewish or how anything else we were— just about how the night air and the night fog can bring out the unusual, the part that's not normal in young boys.

After dinner that evening, Dad went into the living room to read, having been a good father all day. Miss McKenna sat with him, also with a book. The rest of us cleared the round dining room table, with the white glass globe lit above, and set up the table to play.

David was set to head upstairs. He had his little transistor radio and earplug in his hand. Then Miss Murphy said, "Here, Dave, sit next to me."

David had endured our conversation at dinner, which probably made very little sense to him, but he had sat through it politely, and like Dad he was looking for a little peace and quiet. He was susceptible to Miss Murphy, however, so he plugged his transistor radio into his ear, sat down between her and Michael, and watched.

Paul and I wanted in, too, so Mom made us each little cheat sheets, listing what the different hands meant and which was better: from one pair, to two pairs, to three of a kind, through a straight, a flush, a full house, four of a kind, a straight flush, right up to a royal flush.

Mom counted out the chips, a set made of Bakelite we had found in the house, and the game began.

Michael took one look at his cards and slapped them onto the table, like he'd remember them forever. Then the next instant he picked them up again and rearranged them all.

Miss Murphy used both hands to hold her cards. She moved to sip her whiskey, or to tilt her glance toward David.

Mom had a glass of red wine by her ashtray. Paul, between her and Michael, glowered at his cards. "Sit closer," my mother said to him. Even though he'd just turned nine years old Paul was still her baby.

"Don't look at my cards," replied Paul, snuggling up tight.

"I wouldn't dream of it," said Mom, palming her own cards so he couldn't see her hand, either.

The cards grew sticky in our hands, sticky with the smell of the sea. Fog circled outside, tossed in the cool, soft, black air.

Michael kept bidding like a rocket wooshing into the wild blue.

Miss Murphy watched Michael. She countered him and sipped and kept on steadily. From time to time, she peered at David, tipping her hand in his direction, tying him to the game, although David also listened at the same time to things the rest of us couldn't hear, sounds that came in through the transistors from the airwaves in the wind and the night. The chips piled up between them.

Mom sipped absentmindedly, and absentmindedly played. Her game wasn't poker. Her game was Scrabble. She was just waiting for us to get old enough to play *that* every night after dinner.

Occasionally Mom asked Paul if he needed help with his cards. Paul kept saying no. He stared at his hand like it was a book he was reading, reading hard. That was the way he read everything, because he still read very slowly. He made his bids, his little boy bids, while I wondered what the odds were for my hand to somehow become a full house. I held three of a kind and two unmatched cards. What were the odds to get dealt a pair, one right after the other, if I let go of both cards? Not likely. And if I only let go of one? Out of all those cards, I'd get back what I wanted? That didn't seem any more likely.

With thoughts like these, I could never be a serious player.

Above, moths bumped up against the white glass ceiling globe. Below, cards shuffled and slapped on the wooden table. And Michael grew less and less normal.

Mom and Paul folded after a spectacular leap in bidding by Michael. Paul was more interested in making piles of chips in different patterns—two red, one white, two red, one white; three blues, one red, two whites—than in playing. Mom shoved a bunch of her chips over to him when he ran out of blues.

I stayed in, even though I knew I was cutting my own throat. I wanted to see what would happen.

"You are doomed, Judy," Michael told me. "You are doomed." Satisfied, he turned his smile to Miss Murphy, the same grin he'd stretched across his face on the jetty, half schoolboy, half maniac. "How about it?"

Miss Murphy didn't give Michael so much as a glance. She turned to my mother, politely. "A touch more bourbon, Joan, if you would," she said.

My mother poured her the whiskey. "No ice?" she asked. Miss Murphy nodded no in agreement. She watched the whiskey rise in the glass but did not drink immediately. First, she leaned back like a well-paid lawyer after a good meal and curved the tight fan of her cards toward David.

"Have we got it, Dave?" she asked. "What do you say?"

David looked at Miss Murphy. He made no answer but took the plug out of his ear and laid the radio on the table next to the chips. He massaged his scalp with his long fingers, humming to himself and smiling fiercely.

Miss Murphy raised Michael.

Michael raised her right back and he had the cards, all right. A lineup of jacks.

"These two in particular," said Michael, "are my pals. See the eyes both on the same side of the face? These are my little flounder-prince pals," said Michael, raking in the chips.

That hand killed me. Michael was ecstatic when he forced me to fold for the night. He swore that this moment, this win, meant that his life had changed. Not just his luck, but his whole life.

Miss Murphy watched him the next round. She watched him hard. I watched him, too. We all watched. Even David, silent but watching like the rest of us.

After all of the deal was laid down, Miss Murphy watched as he picked up each card. She watched Michael's face. He tried to hide it but he couldn't.

She was Irish and she could tell. Like the rest of us could tell. He had a great hand. Card after card, you could just tell: the whole thing was falling into place.

Maybe he was right. Maybe his whole life *had* changed.

Miss Murphy remained calm. She turned to David. "Worth fishing, Dave?" she asked, the cards held hard, their curve like the knee pad for a suit of armor. "With this," she said, pushing up one card slightly, the one second from the left end, "have we got it?"

David, shaking a little with the excitement of the evening, wiggled the radio into the breast pocket of his shirt and drummed both hands on the table.

"Clem Kadiddlehopper!" he cried happily. This was the name of a favorite character on the Red Skelton show on TV. "Oh Clem!"

That was enough to satisfy Miss Murphy. She matched Michael. She didn't raise him, but she saw him.

At this point Mom folded. Paul stayed in, mostly to have the puzzle of rearranging his stacks. He let go of chips in patterns, five whites and a blue instead of two blues or a single red—that was *his* game.

Meanwhile Michael raised Miss Murphy again and again. She saw him and saw him and saw him but still she had more chips. Paul was able to keep up, bankrolled by Mom until she had nothing left; he stayed in the game.

Paul, however, was not on the table as far as Michael was concerned. All he saw was Miss Murphy. He wanted to clean her out. He wanted it so bad he started lifting scallop shells off the windowsill and betting them in an effort to get all Miss Murphy's chips on the table.

She was a good sport. She said she was glad to have the opportunity to clean out his shells.

"Kid," said Miss Murphy, "I admire your style." She showed him the chips she had left, even after she'd matched all the scallop shells. "And if you beat me, I'll throw in these for free."

Either she was bluffing or she had a great hand.

Michael put two baby scallop shells in the places where his eyeballs fit, like they were monocles in each eye. "I am King!" said Michael. "I am King!"

Miss Murphy sipped her whiskey. "Okay, kid," she said, and put down what she had.

"Clem!" cried David, his fingers twisting the cord of the radio.

A pair of twos. Nothing lower in the world.

Playing Poker with Miss Murphy

"Clem indeed," said Mom.

Michael grinned. "Well," he said, laying down his cards, "You beat me."

Miss Murphy beat my brother Michael with a pair of twos.

Michael had nothing but his raw nerve. The only way he could have won was if Miss Murphy had folded in the sight of his mighty confidence. If she had folded, he would have been able to win without revealing his empty hand.

Michael was a real poker player all right.

But then, just as Miss Murphy had stretched out her strong short forearm to rake in the chips, the chips that now were hers, Paul spoke.

"Wait," said the little boy.

And he put down his cards in a beautiful fan. And there were the faces of the king and queen of diamonds and three jacks: hearts, clubs, spades.

My mother lit a cigarette and smiled and didn't say a thing.

" 'This old man he played one!' " said David. " 'He played knickknack!' "

And then it was Paul against Miss Murphy.

Paul looked across the table at his opponent. "No asking David," he said.

Michael and David faded into the fog. It was no longer their game.

Paul didn't speak another word and it took him five hands to clean her out. He played very, very slowly, but he completely cleaned her out and she was playing as hard as she could.

"I'll be darned," said my mother when it was over. "Now brush your teeth, my little riverboat gamblers. It's time for bed. Time for bed on the riverboat."

She picked up the deck and shuffled it. We each came with clean teeth to kiss her good night.

All night, as the wind squeezed through the shingles of the Attaquin house, which was old even back then, in 1965, I dreamed of shuffling cards. I dreamed of letting go of one card and getting dealt another, one I'd never seen. I dreamed of the riverboat and the riverboat gamblers and the river and the wind and the cards, and my three brothers, three of a kind, and Miss Murphy and Miss McKenna, a pair, and my parents, another pair, all of them wild cards scattered in the wind.

6 *Bizarro World*

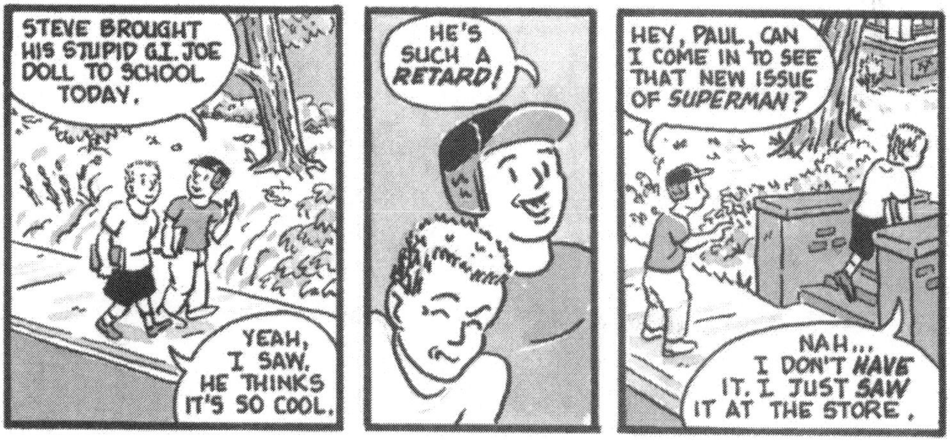
STEVE BROUGHT HIS STUPID G.I. JOE DOLL TO SCHOOL TODAY.
YEAH, I SAW. HE THINKS IT'S SO COOL.
HE'S SUCH A RETARD!
HEY, PAUL, CAN I COME IN TO SEE THAT NEW ISSUE OF SUPERMAN?
NAH... I DON'T HAVE IT. I JUST SAW IT AT THE STORE.

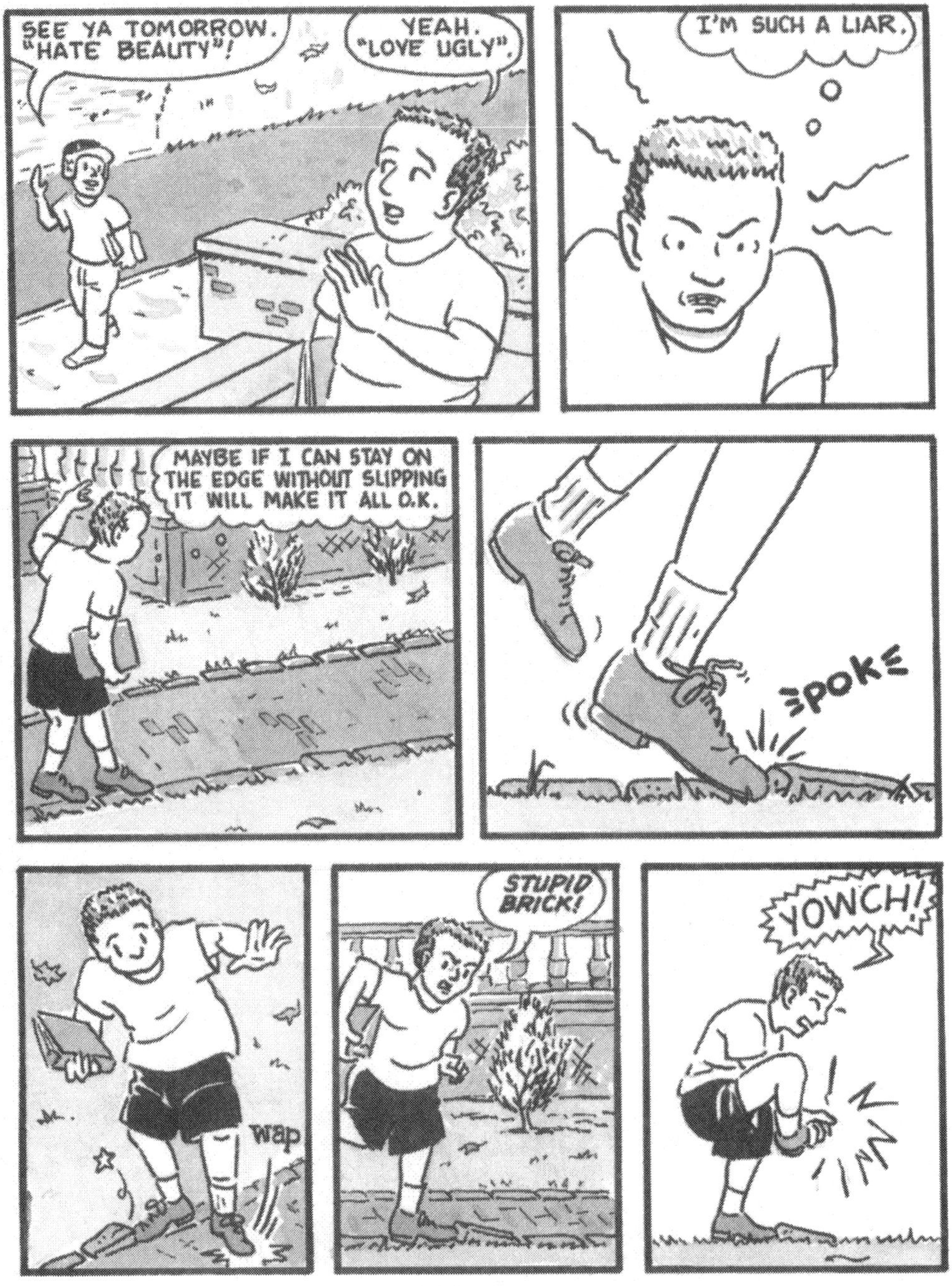
SEE YA TOMORROW. "HATE BEAUTY"!
YEAH. "LOVE UGLY".
I'M SUCH A LIAR.
MAYBE IF I CAN STAY ON THE EDGE WITHOUT SLIPPING IT WILL MAKE IT ALL O.K.
POKE
WAP
STUPID BRICK!
YOWCH!

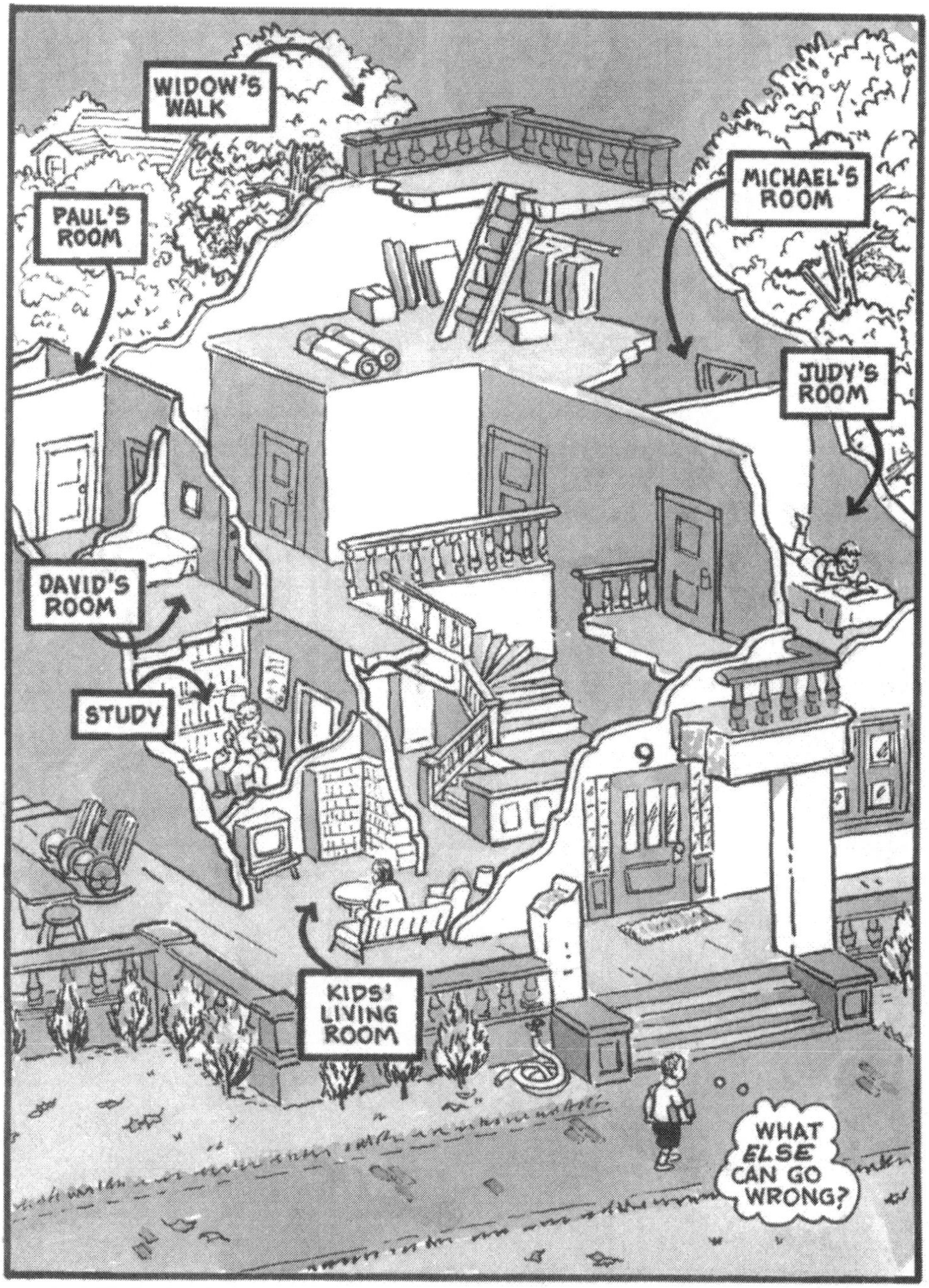
WIDOW'S WALK
PAUL'S ROOM
MICHAEL'S ROOM
JUDY'S ROOM
DAVID'S ROOM
STUDY
KIDS' LIVING ROOM
WHAT ELSE CAN GO WRONG?

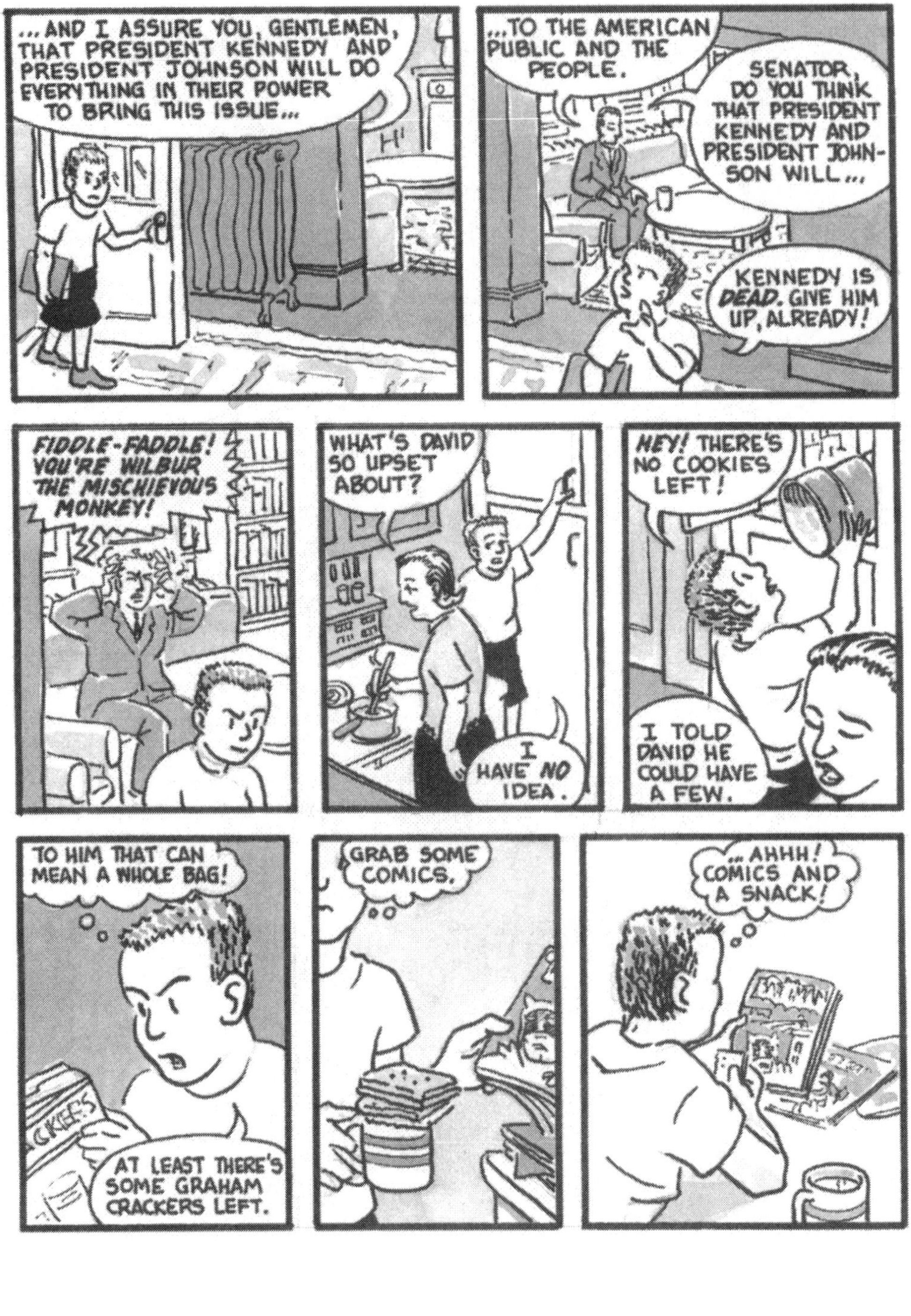
...AND I ASSURE YOU, GENTLEMEN, THAT PRESIDENT KENNEDY AND PRESIDENT JOHNSON WILL DO EVERYTHING IN THEIR POWER TO BRING THIS ISSUE...
HI
...TO THE AMERICAN PUBLIC AND THE PEOPLE.
SENATOR, DO YOU THINK THAT PRESIDENT KENNEDY AND PRESIDENT JOHNSON WILL...
KENNEDY IS DEAD. GIVE HIM UP, ALREADY!
FIDDLE-FADDLE! YOU'RE WILBUR THE MISCHIEVOUS MONKEY!
WHAT'S DAVID SO UPSET ABOUT?
I HAVE NO IDEA.
HEY! THERE'S NO COOKIES LEFT!
I TOLD DAVID HE COULD HAVE A FEW.
TO HIM THAT CAN MEAN A WHOLE BAG!
AT LEAST THERE'S SOME GRAHAM CRACKERS LEFT.
GRAB SOME COMICS.
...AHHH! COMICS AND A SNACK!

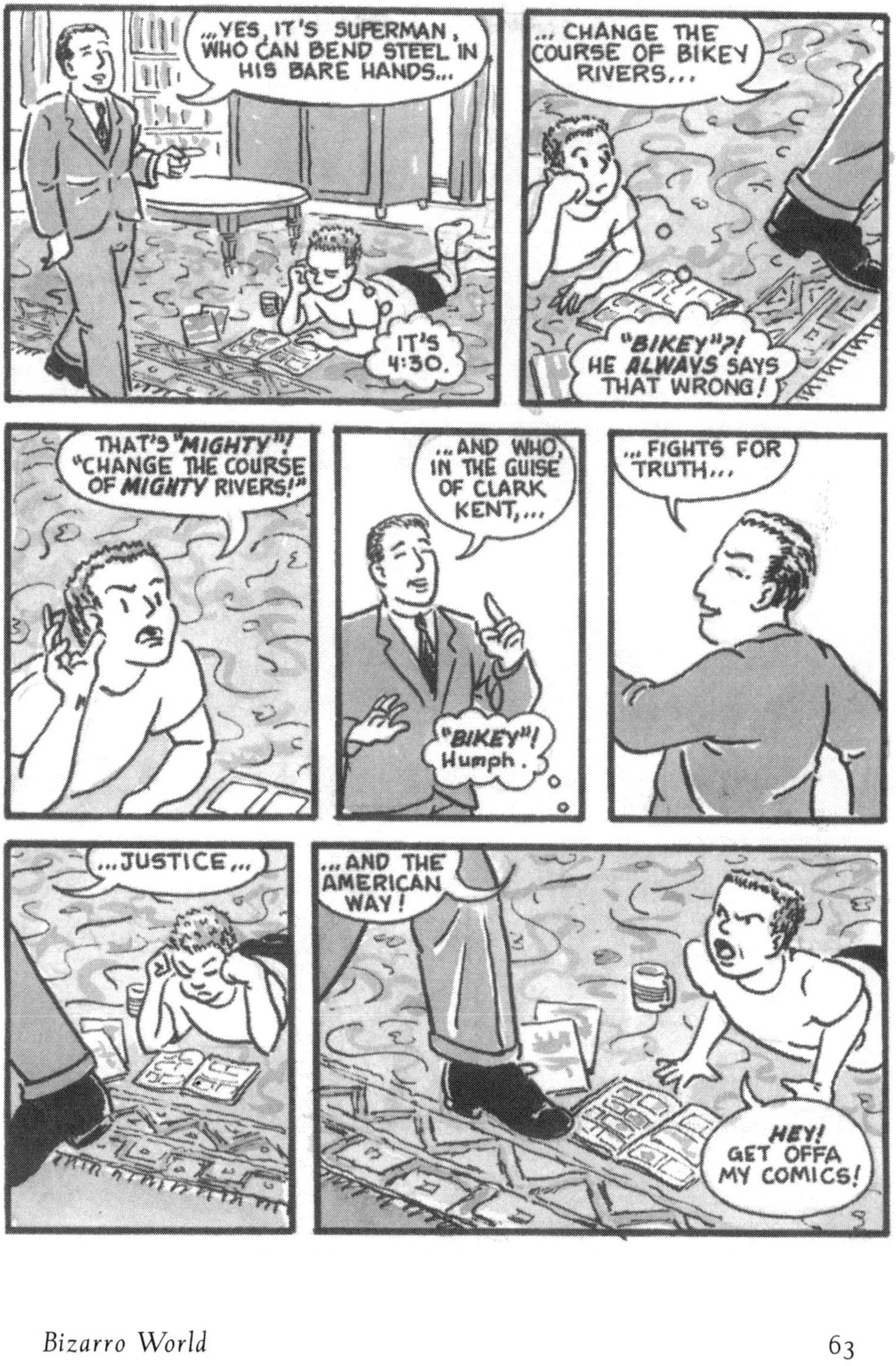

...YES, IT'S SUPERMAN, WHO CAN BEND STEEL IN HIS BARE HANDS...
IT'S 4:30.
... CHANGE THE COURSE OF BIKEY RIVERS...
"BIKEY"?! HE ALWAYS SAYS THAT WRONG!
THAT'S "MIGHTY"! "CHANGE THE COURSE OF MIGHTY RIVERS!"
...AND WHO, IN THE GUISE OF CLARK KENT,...
"BIKEY"! Humph.
...FIGHTS FOR TRUTH...
...JUSTICE,...
...AND THE AMERICAN WAY!
HEY! GET OFFA MY COMICS!

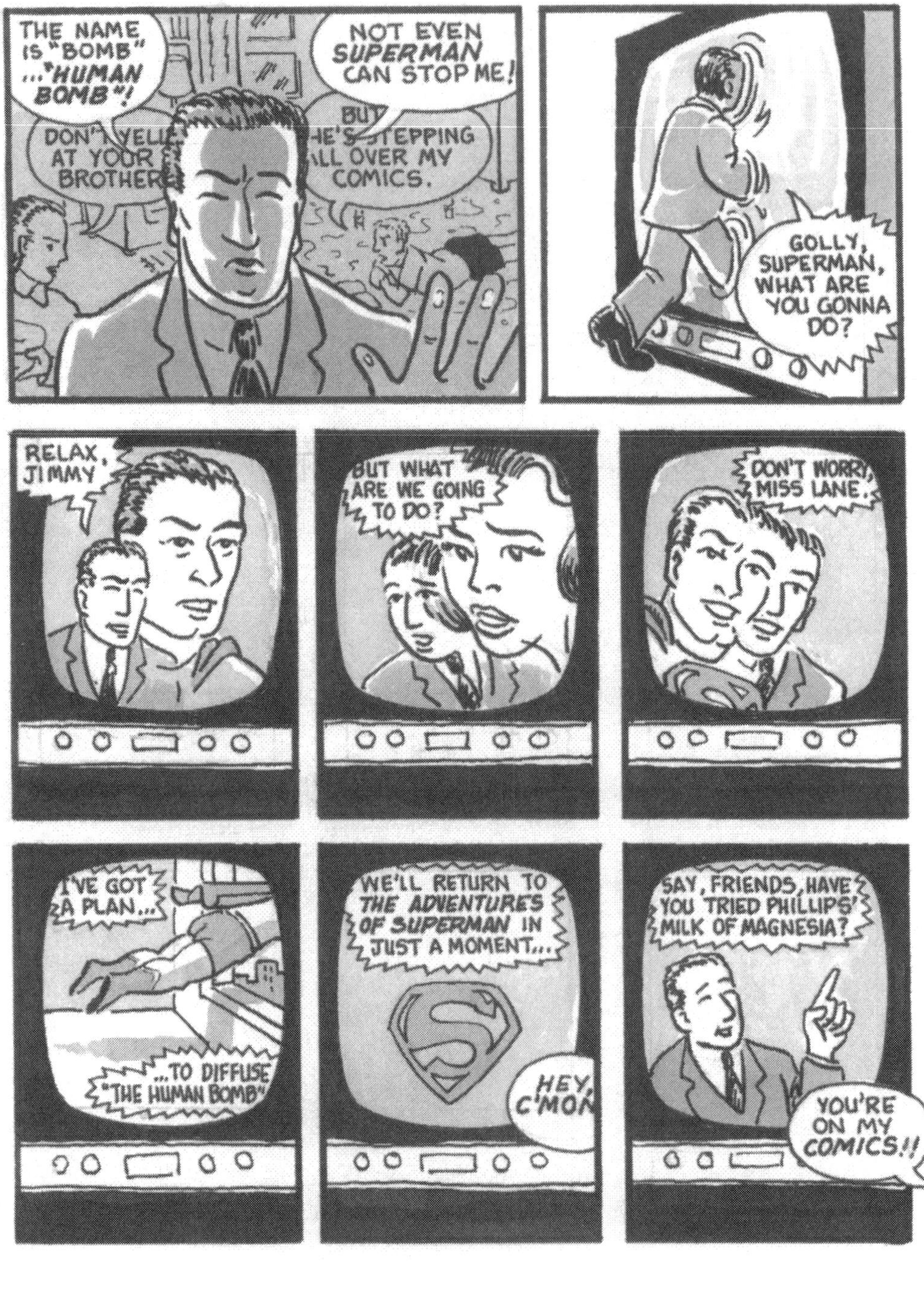
THE NAME IS "BOMB" ..."HUMAN BOMB"!
NOT EVEN SUPERMAN CAN STOP ME!
DON'T YELL AT YOUR BROTHER.
BUT HE'S STEPPING ALL OVER MY COMICS.
GOLLY, SUPERMAN, WHAT ARE YOU GONNA DO?
RELAX, JIMMY
BUT WHAT ARE WE GOING TO DO?
DON'T WORRY, MISS LANE.
I'VE GOT A PLAN...
...TO DIFFUSE "THE HUMAN BOMB"
WE'LL RETURN TO THE ADVENTURES OF SUPERMAN IN JUST A MOMENT...
HEY, C'MON
SAY, FRIENDS, HAVE YOU TRIED PHILLIPS' MILK OF MAGNESIA?
YOU'RE ON MY COMICS!!

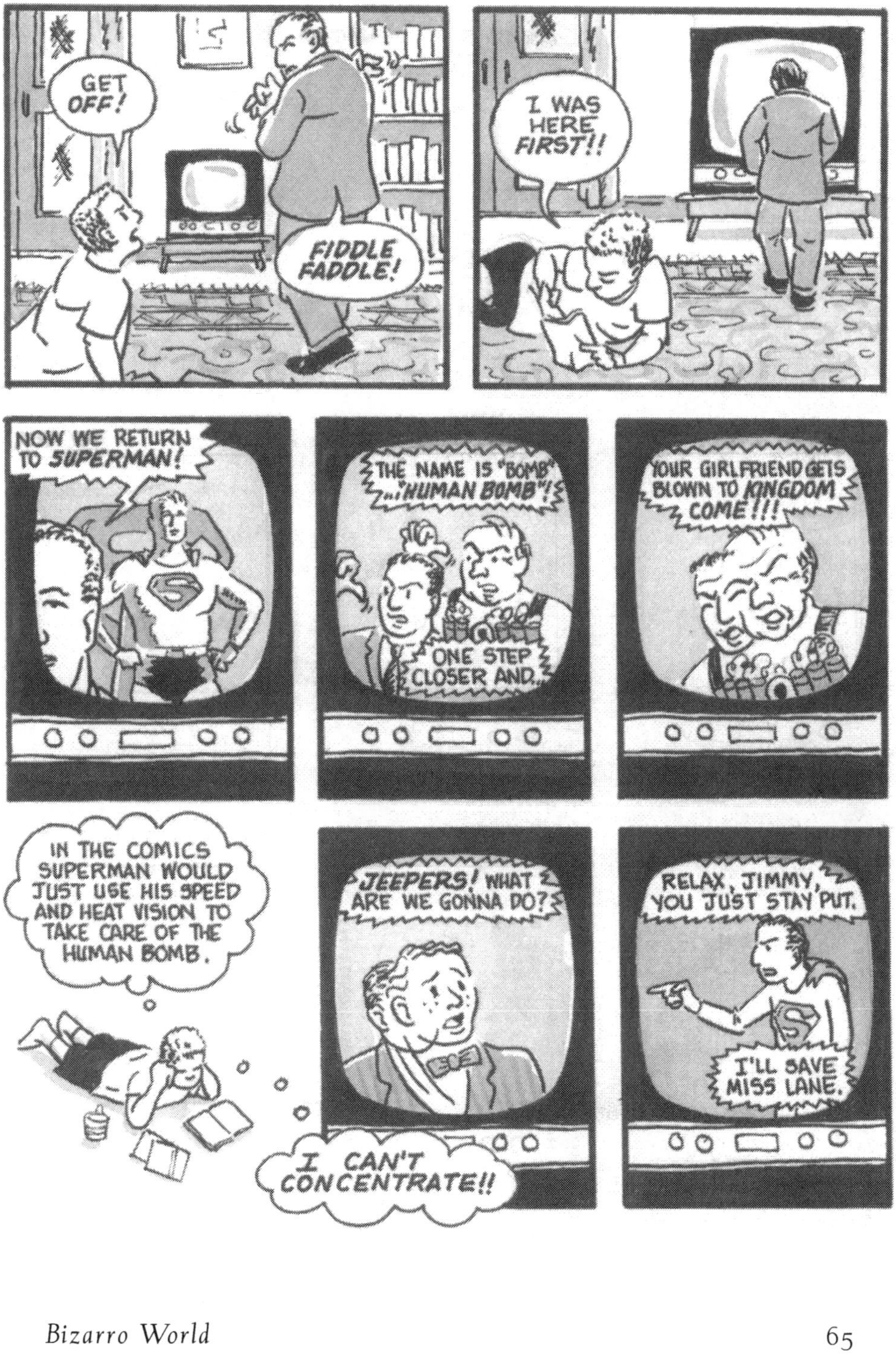
GET OFF!
FIDDLE FADDLE!
I WAS HERE FIRST!!
NOW WE RETURN TO SUPERMAN!
THE NAME IS "BOMB" ..."HUMAN BOMB"!
ONE STEP CLOSER AND..
YOUR GIRLFRIEND GETS BLOWN TO KINGDOM COME!!!
IN THE COMICS SUPERMAN WOULD JUST USE HIS SPEED AND HEAT VISION TO TAKE CARE OF THE HUMAN BOMB.
JEEPERS! WHAT ARE WE GONNA DO?
I CAN'T CONCENTRATE!!
RELAX, JIMMY, YOU JUST STAY PUT.
I'LL SAVE MISS LANE.

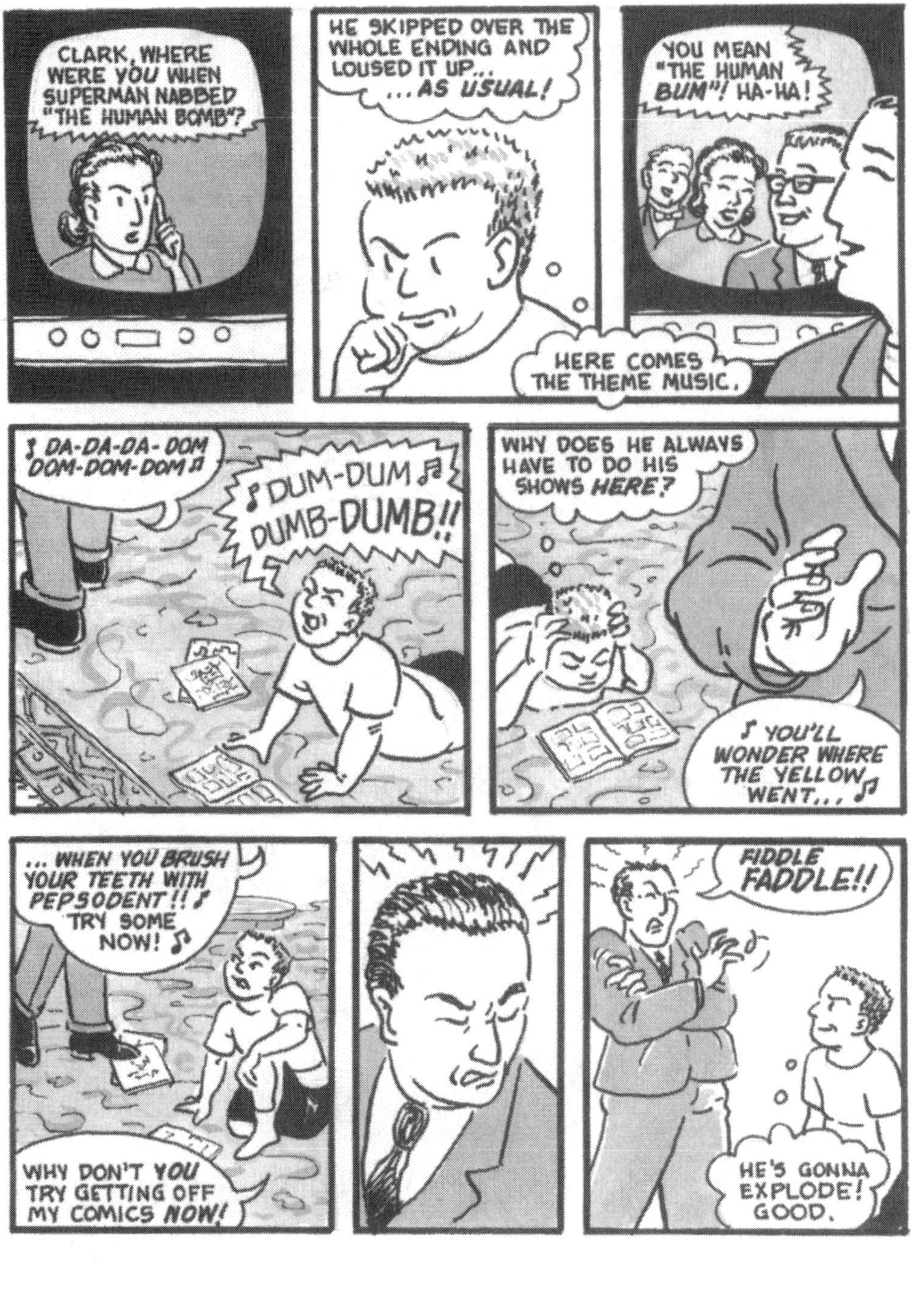
CLARK, WHERE WERE YOU WHEN SUPERMAN NABBED "THE HUMAN BOMB"?
HE SKIPPED OVER THE WHOLE ENDING AND LOUSED IT UP... ...AS USUAL!
YOU MEAN "THE HUMAN BUM"! HA-HA!
HERE COMES THE THEME MUSIC.
DA-DA-DA-DOM DOM-DOM-DOM
DUM-DUM DUMB-DUMB!!
WHY DOES HE ALWAYS HAVE TO DO HIS SHOWS HERE?
YOU'LL WONDER WHERE THE YELLOW WENT...
... WHEN YOU BRUSH YOUR TEETH WITH PEPSODENT!!! TRY SOME NOW!
WHY DON'T YOU TRY GETTING OFF MY COMICS NOW!
FIDDLE FADDLE!!
HE'S GONNA EXPLODE! GOOD.

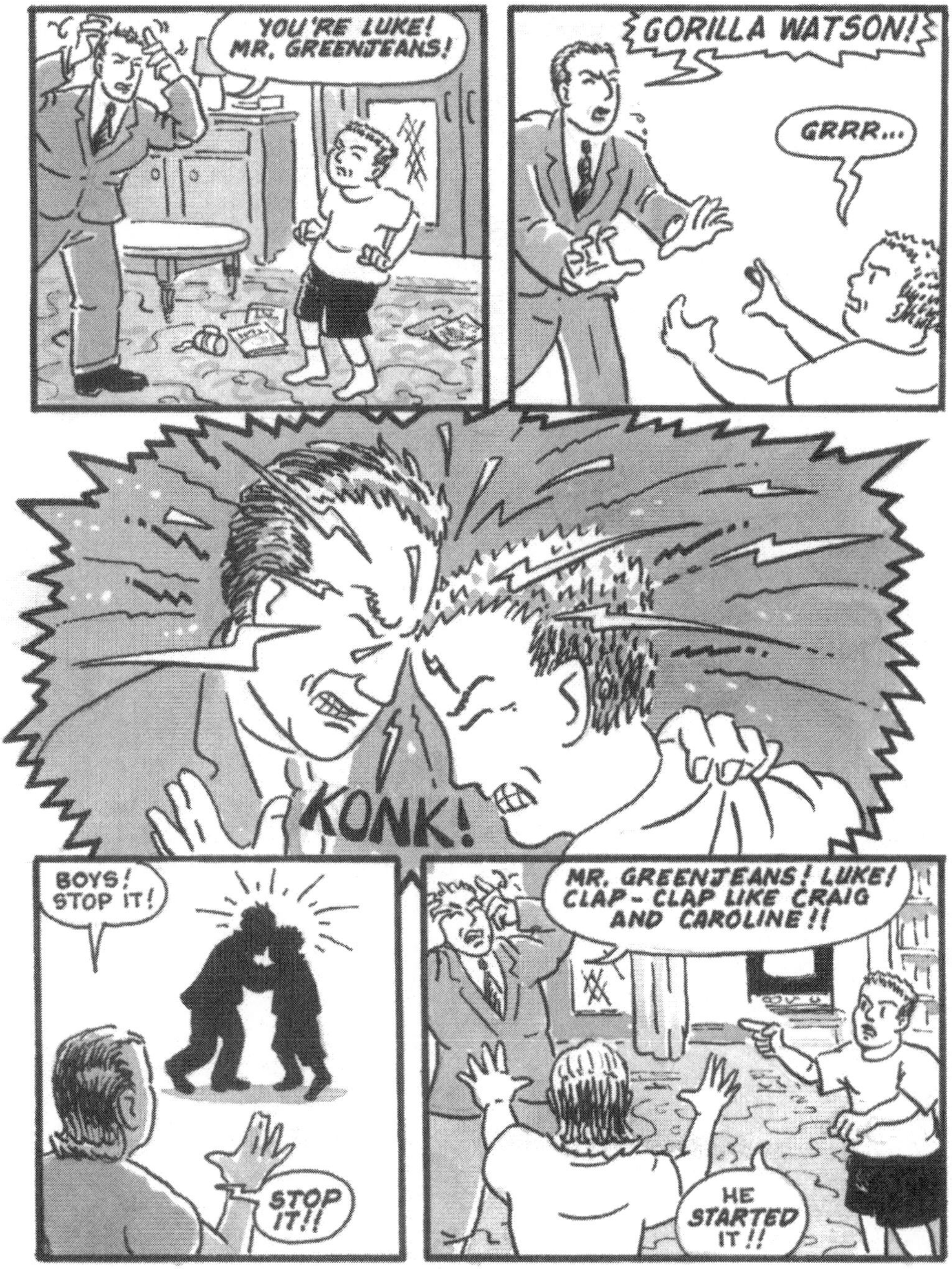
YOU'RE LUKE! MR. GREENJEANS!
GORILLA WATSON!
GRRR...
KONK!
BOYS! STOP IT!
STOP IT!!
MR. GREENJEANS! LUKE! CLAP-CLAP LIKE CRAIG AND CAROLINE!!
HE STARTED IT!!

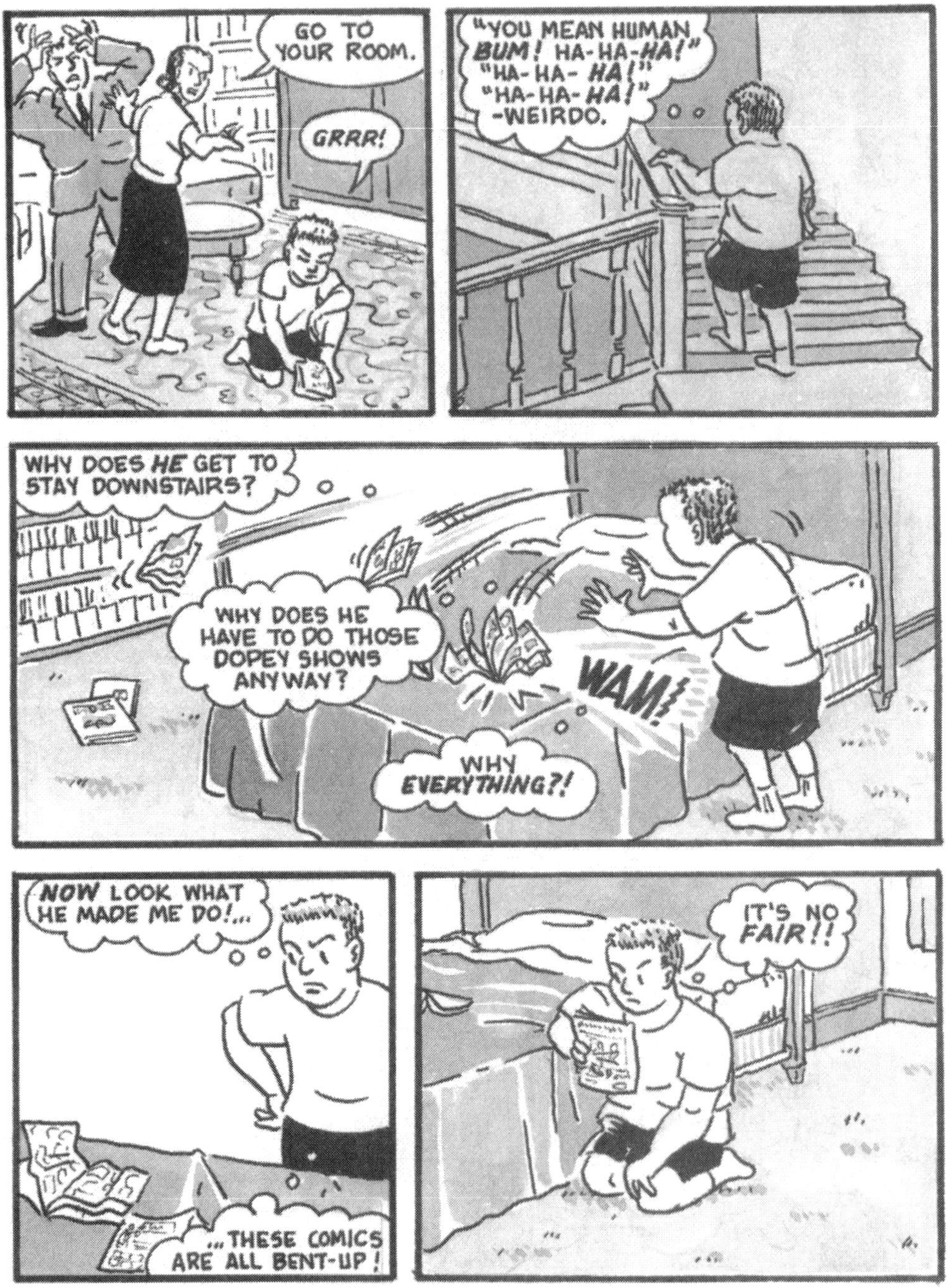
GO TO YOUR ROOM.
GRRR!
"YOU MEAN HUMAN BUM! HA-HA-HA!" "HA-HA-HA!" "HA-HA-HA!" -WEIRDO.
WHY DOES HE GET TO STAY DOWNSTAIRS?
WHY DOES HE HAVE TO DO THOSE DOPEY SHOWS ANYWAY?
WAM!
WHY EVERYTHING?!
NOW LOOK WHAT HE MADE ME DO!...
...THESE COMICS ARE ALL BENT-UP!
IT'S NO FAIR!!

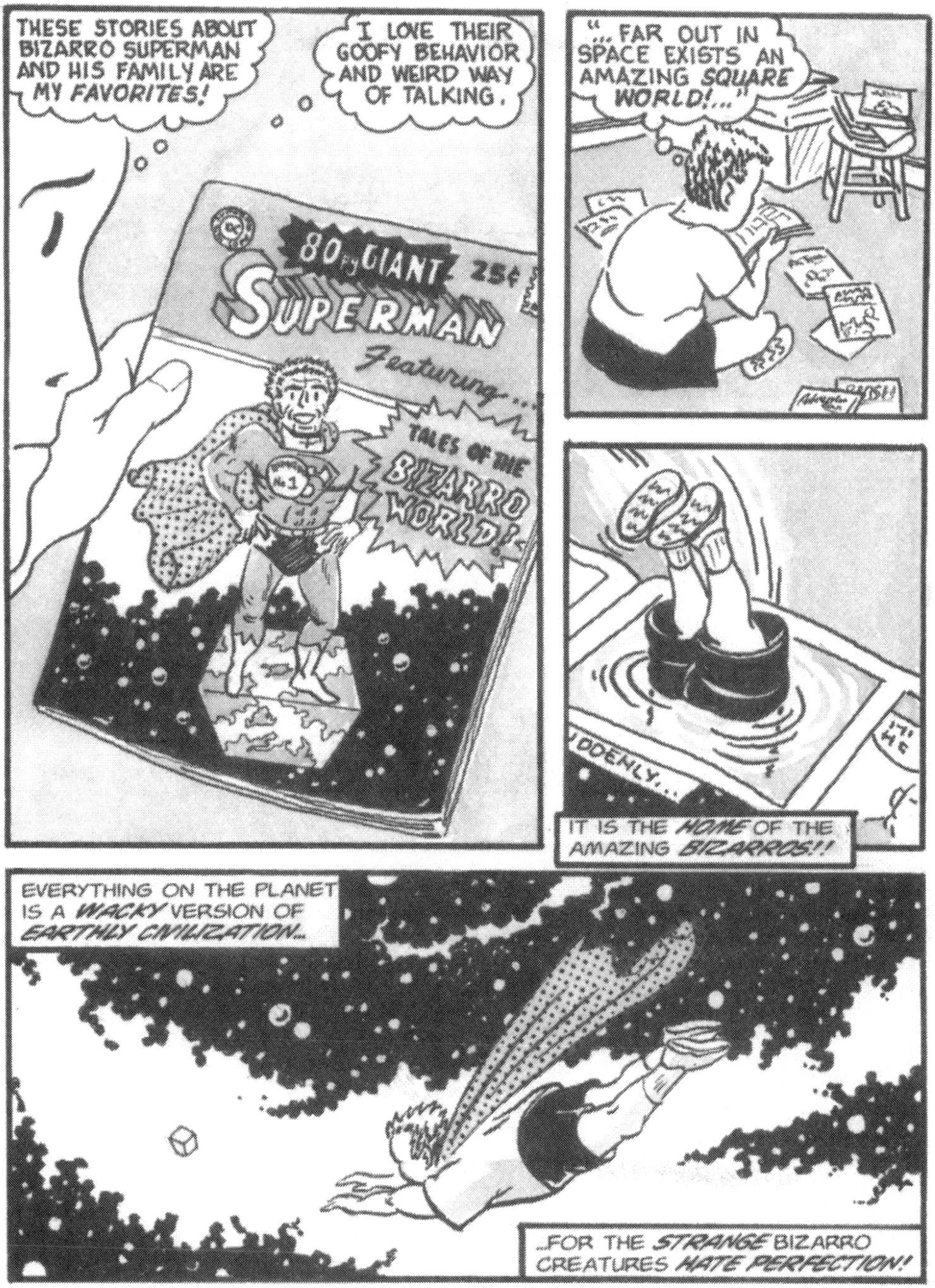
THESE STORIES ABOUT BIZARRO SUPERMAN AND HIS FAMILY ARE MY FAVORITES!
I LOVE THEIR GOOFY BEHAVIOR AND WEIRD WAY OF TALKING.
80 PG GIANT
25¢
SUPERMAN
Featuring...
TALES OF THE BIZARRO WORLD!
"...FAR OUT IN SPACE EXISTS AN AMAZING SQUARE WORLD!..."
SUDDENLY...
IT IS THE HOME OF THE AMAZING BIZARROS!!
EVERYTHING ON THE PLANET IS A WACKY VERSION OF EARTHLY CIVILIZATION...
...FOR THE STRANGE BIZARRO CREATURES HATE PERFECTION!

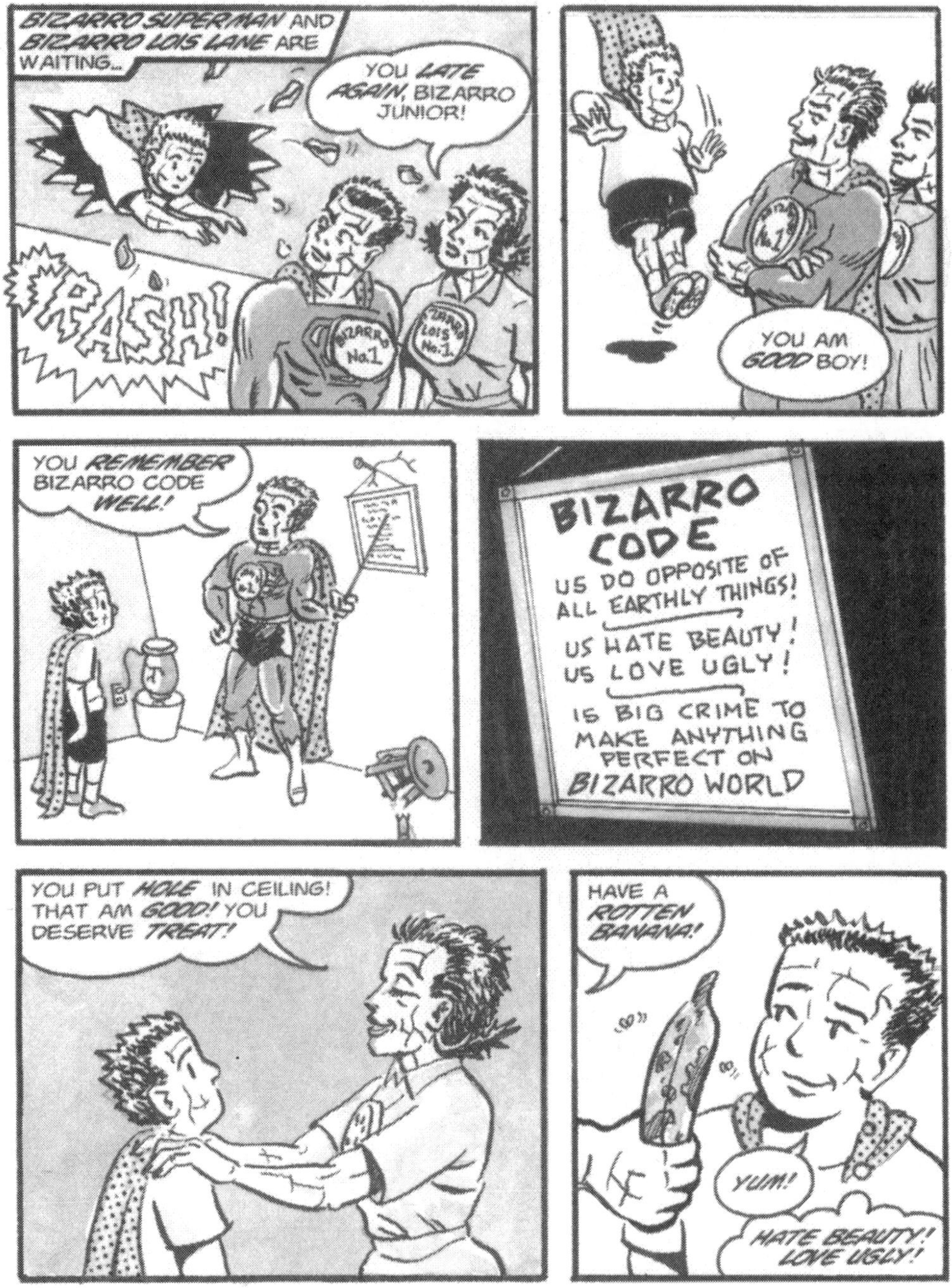
BIZARRO SUPERMAN AND BIZARRO LOIS LANE ARE WAITING...
YOU LATE AGAIN, BIZARRO JUNIOR!
RASH!
BIZARRO No.1
BIZARRO LOIS No.1
YOU AM GOOD BOY!
YOU REMEMBER BIZARRO CODE WELL!
BIZARRO CODE
US DO OPPOSITE OF ALL EARTHLY THINGS!
US HATE BEAUTY! US LOVE UGLY!
IS BIG CRIME TO MAKE ANYTHING PERFECT ON BIZARRO WORLD
YOU PUT HOLE IN CEILING! THAT AM GOOD! YOU DESERVE TREAT!
HAVE A ROTTEN BANANA!
YUM!
HATE BEAUTY! LOVE UGLY!

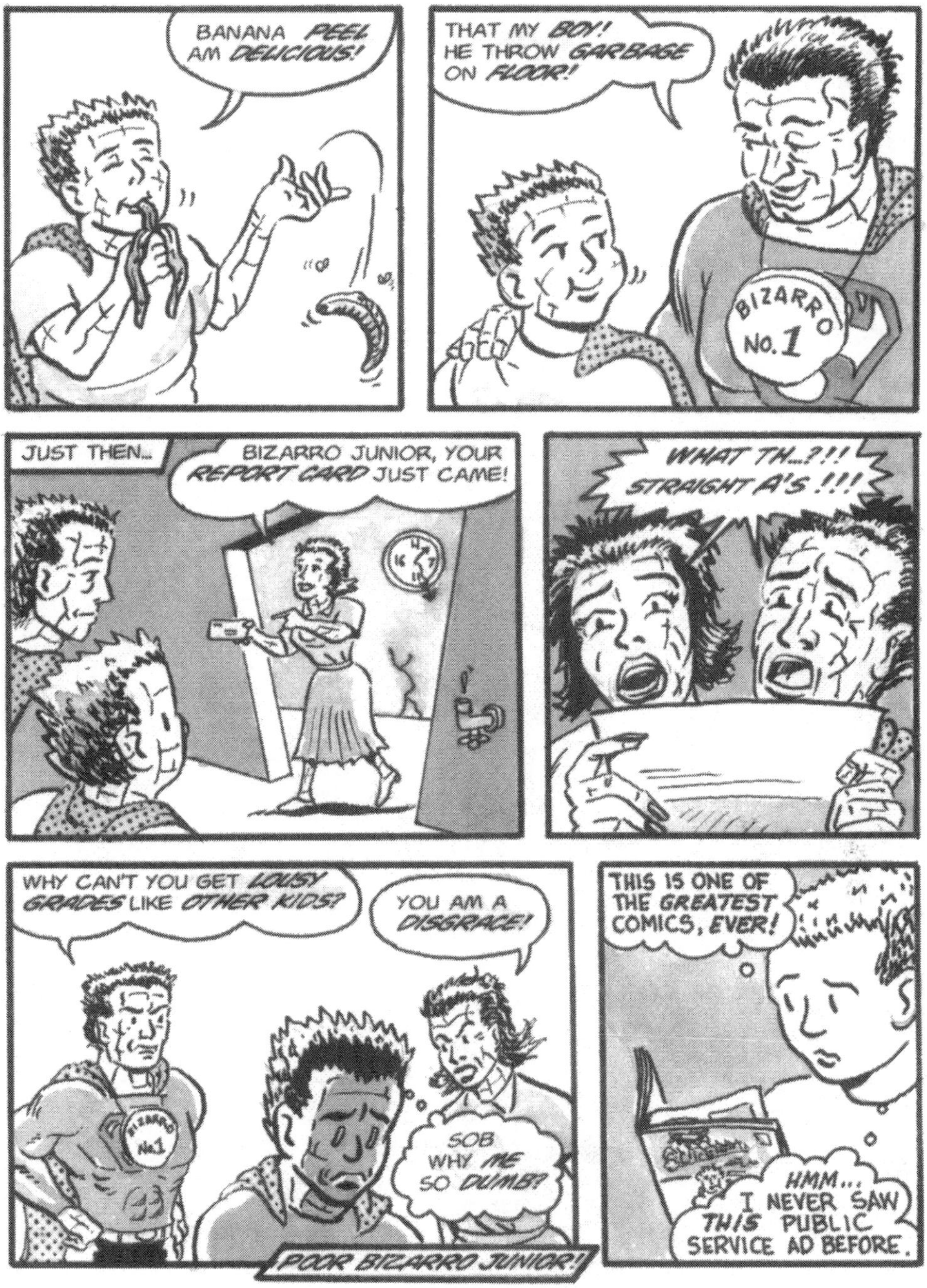
BANANA PEEL AM DELICIOUS!
THAT MY BOY! HE THROW GARBAGE ON FLOOR!
BIZARRO No.1
JUST THEN...
BIZARRO JUNIOR, YOUR REPORT CARD JUST CAME!
WHAT TH...?!! STRAIGHT A'S !!!
WHY CAN'T YOU GET LOUSY GRADES LIKE OTHER KIDS?
YOU AM A DISGRACE!
SOB WHY ME SO DUMB?
POOR BIZARRO JUNIOR!
THIS IS ONE OF THE GREATEST COMICS, EVER!
HMM... I NEVER SAW THIS PUBLIC SERVICE AD BEFORE.

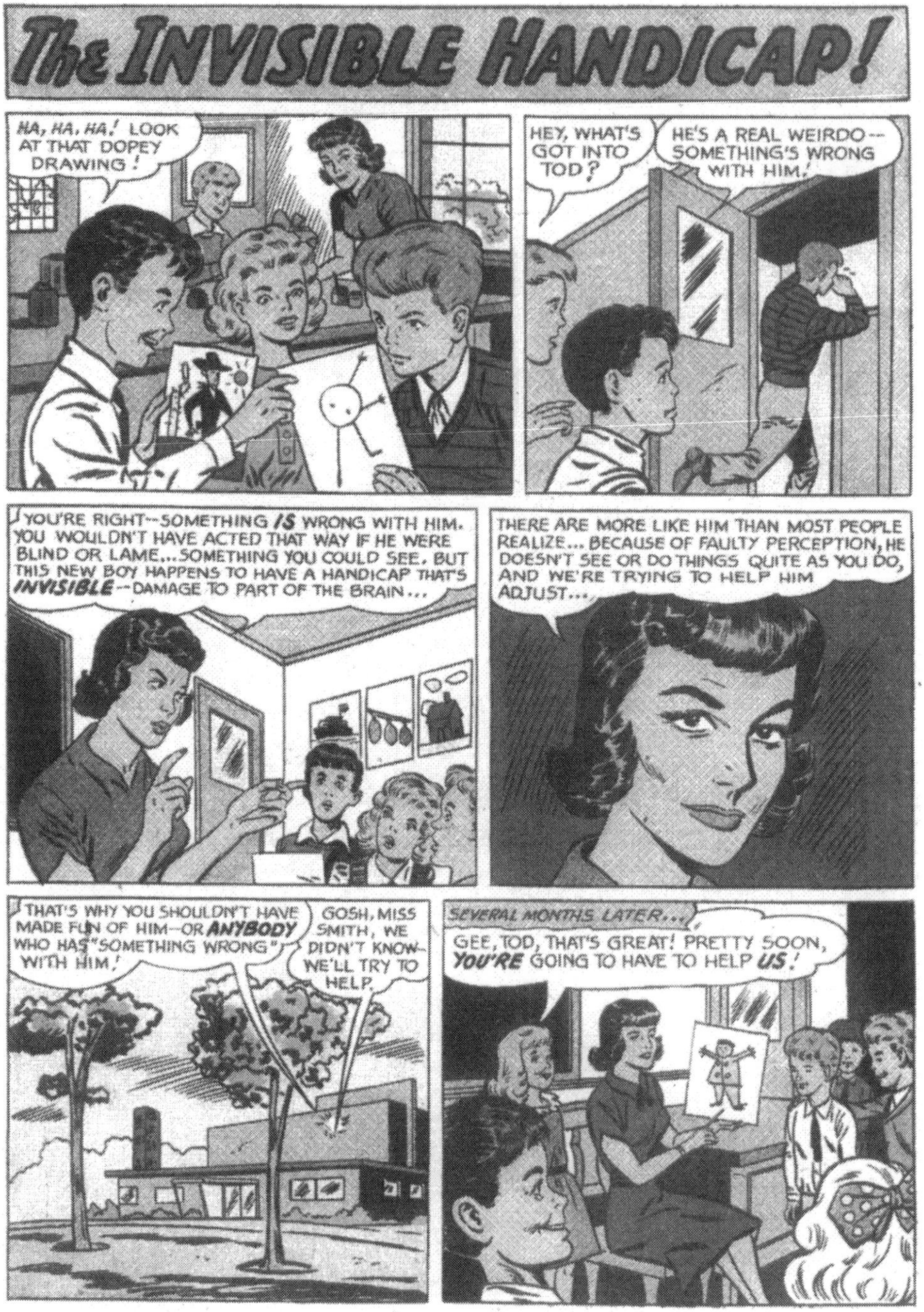

The INVISIBLE HANDICAP!
HA, HA, HA! LOOK AT THAT DOPEY DRAWING!
HEY, WHAT'S GOT INTO TOD?
HE'S A REAL WEIRDO--SOMETHING'S WRONG WITH HIM!
YOU'RE RIGHT--SOMETHING IS WRONG WITH HIM. YOU WOULDN'T HAVE ACTED THAT WAY IF HE WERE BLIND OR LAME...SOMETHING YOU COULD SEE. BUT THIS NEW BOY HAPPENS TO HAVE A HANDICAP THAT'S INVISIBLE--DAMAGE TO PART OF THE BRAIN...
THERE ARE MORE LIKE HIM THAN MOST PEOPLE REALIZE... BECAUSE OF FAULTY PERCEPTION, HE DOESN'T SEE OR DO THINGS QUITE AS YOU DO, AND WE'RE TRYING TO HELP HIM ADJUST...
THAT'S WHY YOU SHOULDN'T HAVE MADE FUN OF HIM--OR ANYBODY WHO HAS "SOMETHING WRONG" WITH HIM!
GOSH, MISS SMITH, WE DIDN'T KNOW-WE'LL TRY TO HELP.
SEVERAL MONTHS LATER...
GEE, TOD, THAT'S GREAT! PRETTY SOON, YOU'RE GOING TO HAVE TO HELP US!

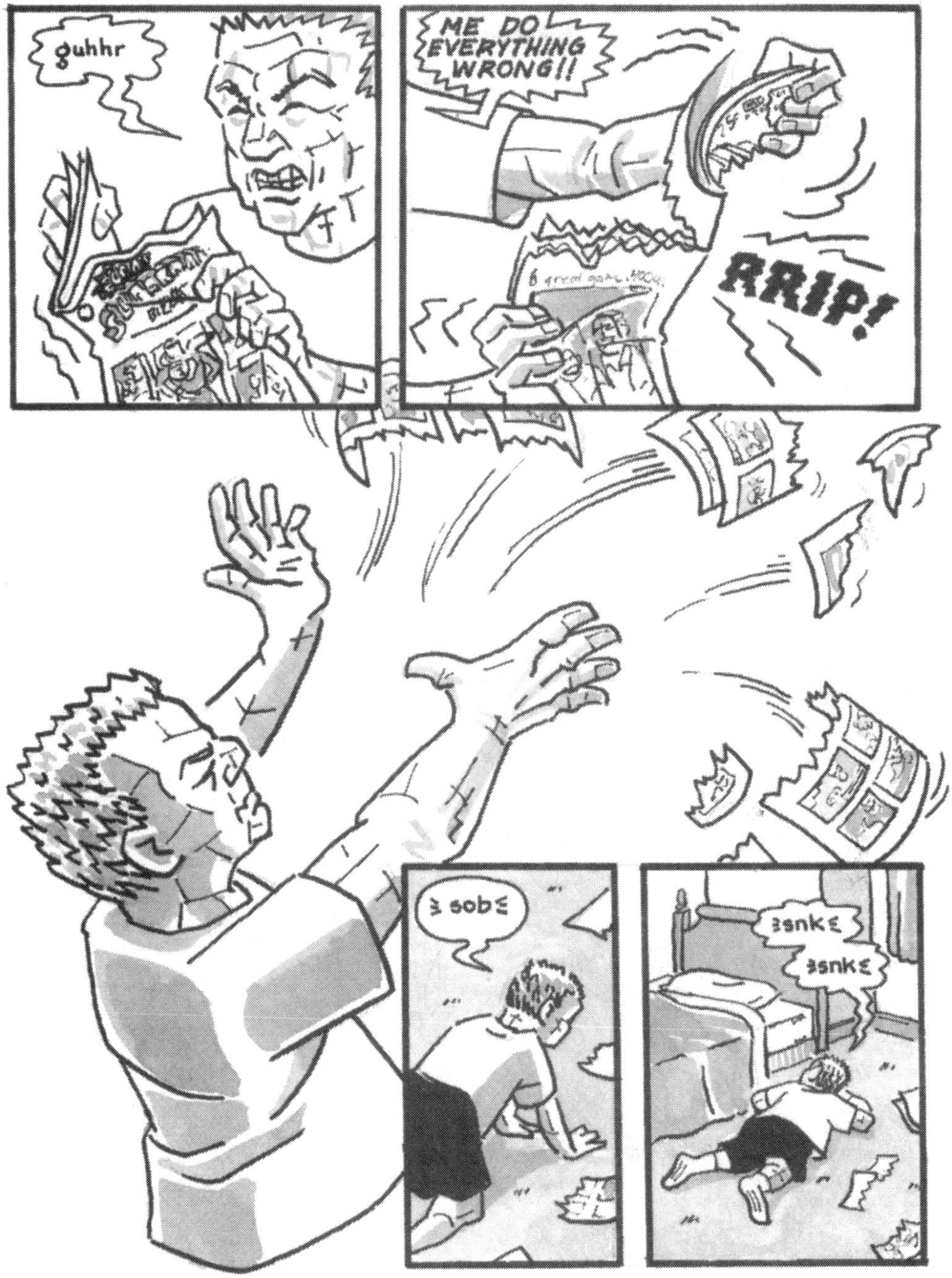
guhhr
ME DO EVERYTHING WRONG!!
RRIP!
sob
snk
snk

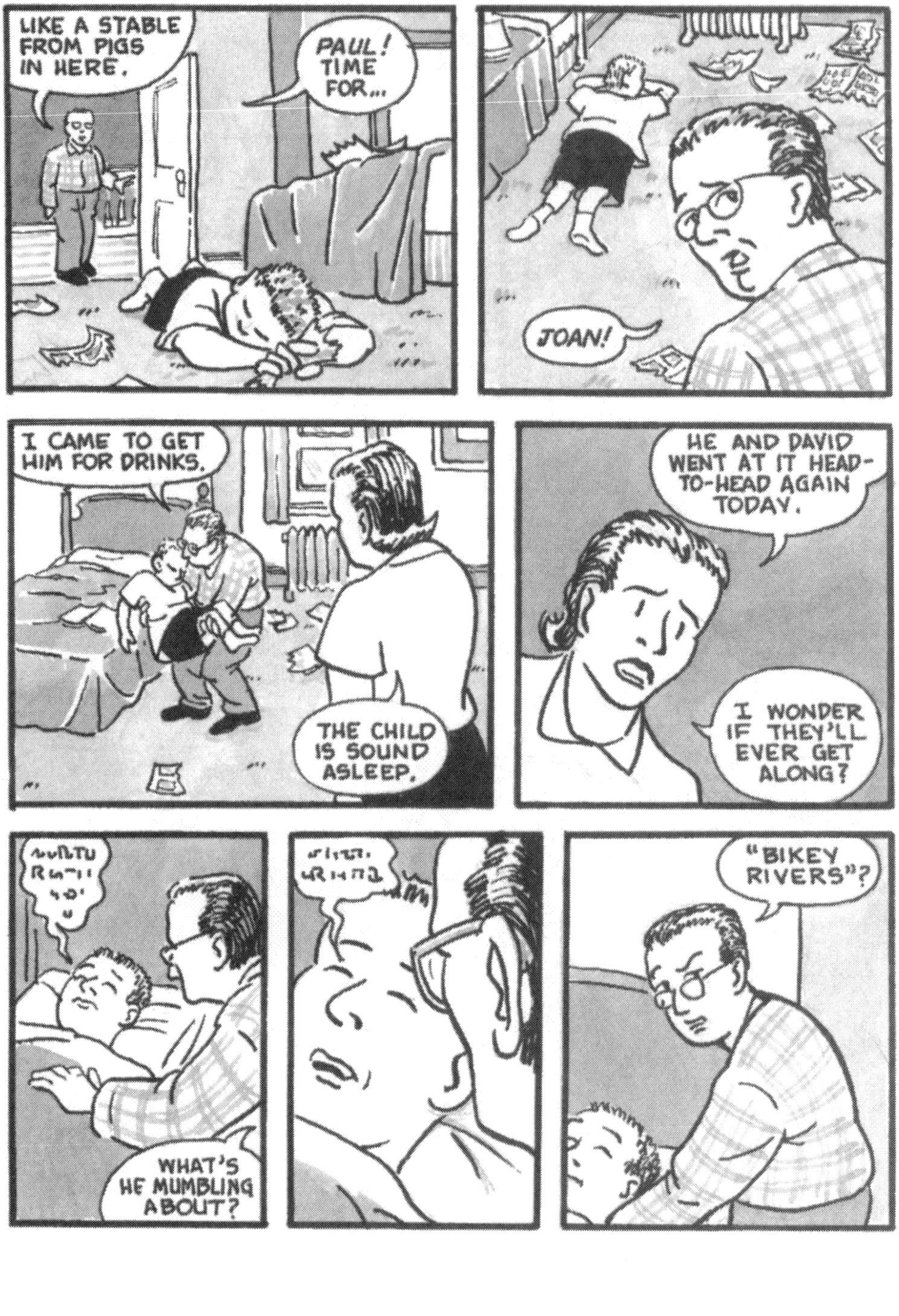
LIKE A STABLE FROM PIGS IN HERE.
PAUL! TIME FOR...
JOAN!
I CAME TO GET HIM FOR DRINKS.
THE CHILD IS SOUND ASLEEP.
HE AND DAVID WENT AT IT HEAD-TO-HEAD AGAIN TODAY.
I WONDER IF THEY'LL EVER GET ALONG?
WHAT'S HE MUMBLING ABOUT?
"BIKEY RIVERS"?

7 Kurt Mo Has Done It Again

Anyone who walked past Paul's bedroom door that Saturday afternoon could hear the two of us talking in the different voices of the small wooden animals. We did the motorcycle-driving greaser mouse, the poet mouse, the scientist dog with his British accent, the scientist's puppy dog assistant, the southern belle mouse with her southern accent, the housekeeper mouse who sounded as though she hailed from north central Illinois, the artist mouse, the sloppy pig, the miserly rich frog. Paul and I had made them a home in an old set of shelves we named the Mouse House.

The animals got into all kinds of difficulties with one another, in stories and adventures that would go on for days, usually by one character ruining life for every-one else by a single willful action. The greaser mouse drove his motorcycle forty-eight hours straight on the masking-taped speedway on the top of the bookshelf and all the paintings fell off the walls and nobody got any sleep. The mousewife insisted that everyone take cooking lessons. This resulted in competition, scorn, ridicule, and much spilled peanut butter. When a china spaniel puppy joined the household, he chanted religious prayers until he drove everyone crazy. The poet mouse defended the spaniel on the grounds of free speech, the pig stuffed toilet paper into the chapel until the puppy could barely breathe, and the southern belle mouse saved the day by inventing very chic little earplugs that could be customized to fit a wide range of ears.

Paul and I had made them beds and tables and shelves and either found or made tiny accessories. The scientist had a microscope, the greaser mouse had a record album Paul had made, one side containing "VROOM I" and the other side "VROOM II," which we pretended contained the sounds of motorcycle engines being revved. The two sides of Marvin's album had different names but it was understood that the motorcycle noises were exactly the same on both. I'd manufac-tured two sets of periodicals, fashion magazines for the southern belle and a kind of mousy *Family Circle* for the housekeeper mouse with recipes and perky, idiotic tips on managing difficult domestic behavior. I also wrote a few poems for the poet mouse; I tried to make them so they were funny to us but serious to her, with lots of short lines and words like "silence" and "forever."

Paul and I were behaving very well that afternoon, but we knew we didn't have to make it last. David was away, in a permanent placement this time we hoped, and as a consequence Paul and Michael and I felt freer to get on one another's nerves.

Dave, who would soon turn eighteen, was at a place called Camphill Village. He'd been there since the fall, coming home for holidays. Camphill Village really *was* a village, where everybody helped and had their part in supporting daily life, in the kind of fairy tale way that all the adult elephants under King Babar had their jobs in Celesteville—one elephant was the farmer, another the sculptor, another the street cleaner. Dave lived in the house where the bakery was located, as a member of the family with the husband and wife bakers and their four blond-haired pigtailed little girls. Because he could read, David was responsible for delivering the bread and roll orders to the other houses. I didn't understand it, but Camphill was a really wholesome place, a really sane place, in its own wacky European way. David liked it.

With our brother gone, Michael and Paul and I got into more fights, especially physical ones. It was as though the household had its required level of surface tension and we got to fill it in when David was away. We could be very petty when the pressure was off, but at the same time it was interesting to live the life that other kids presumably lived all the time, to live as though David didn't exist.

That afternoon, however, even though Paul and I were playing with something we'd gotten a little too old for, we felt no need to be nasty. We were making up something new.

I folded white paper into tiny pages, cut out a set of curled shapes from some wallpaper samples my best friend had given me, and then showed Paul how we'd make a book.

"These are waves, okay?" I explained, holding the curls flat on the palm of my hand. "Three different waves, three different sizes. If I glue them in, page by page—smaller, bigger, and really big—they make a novel." I shoved in the curls, one by one. "The story of a disaster—a giant tidal wave that first gets one person, then a whole city, and finally the whole world."

"Great," said Paul. "I'll draw a cover."

"Let's just call it *The Wave*," I said. "Something short and menacing."

"Yeah," said Paul, bent over the tiny book. "It's by Kurt Mouse." (Kurt Vonnegut was one of the few novelists' names he knew.) Paul, however, still had fairly wiggly writing at the age of nine and couldn't get all of the name on the cover, so the author became Kurt Mo.

"Let me have it," I said, grabbing the tiny little thing. "I want to put quotes on the back. Books always have quotes where people say stupid things." I thought for a minute. "How about this? 'Kurt Mo has done it again.' We don't say *what* he's done, just that he's done it again. And we can make other disaster books and then he'll have a series. And use the same quote on the back."

"'Kurt Mo has done it again,'" said Paul. "That's really good, Judy. It's really stupid."

"Thanks," I replied modestly.

About half an hour after the birth of Kurt Mo, Mom and Dad called all three of us kids downstairs. Our parents stood in the front hall. From the top of the stairs we could see Dad's hands making tight, impatient wheels in the air.

"I *looked* there, Joan," he said. "I do wish that occasionally you would listen to me."

Mom nodded evenly. Our parents had a rule, which was that when one of them got angry, the other was not allowed to get angry. It was almost always Mom who was not allowed to get angry, but she was allowed to think. As Paul and I came clomping down the staircase, followed closely by Michael, I could see that Mom was thinking; I just couldn't see *what* she was thinking.

"Now where the hell is Michael?" asked Dad.

"Right here," Michael replied. "What's the problem?"

Dad looked at him, eyes in cold black focus. "I'll tell you what the problem is," he said, as if Michael were the problem. Although Michael got none of the advantages of being the oldest son, he had all the responsibility that goes with the job. "The problem is that my reading glasses have disappeared, goddammit. How am I supposed to get anything *accomplished*? Not that this seems to *matter* to anyone in this house."

Our father truly loved the world inside his head. There were times in there, places in there, where a kind of fun happened that didn't happen anywhere else.

"Goddammit," he muttered. "Goddammit to hell." The four of us silently waited around a fuming Monroe.

"We've looked everywhere," said Mom to us kids.

"We'll try upstairs," I replied.

Upstairs, away from Dad, the three of us looked at one another. "If you were a pair of glasses," I said, "where would you hide?"

"Under all the stuff on my floor," said Michael.

Michael was currently employing the pile method of personal organization. One pile was the limp spongy skin of his wet suit and his scuba diving mouthpiece, another was scripts from plays he ran lights for, or manuals on how to run and repair film projectors. (When other students were enduring the study of Longfellow's *Evangeline* or distinguishing belts of global winds by drawing fleets of arrows in opposing directions or trying to remember the name of those little doors that let in oxygen on the underside of plant leaves, Michael was gliding along the halls of his junior high moving audio visual equipment from one classroom to another.) There were piles of boy clothing, piles of underground magazines and comic books, and piles that were mysterious combinations, usually including broken colored pencils, based on reasoning known only to Michael. He could always find what he was looking for in one pile or another.

"Dad can be such a jerk," he added.

"Let's get this over with," I replied.

We looked under beds and chairs and behind rows of books and inside shoes and in the backs of dresser drawers. Paul checked the pockets of all of Dad's Viyella shirts. I looked inside the bucket where Mom kept bathroom cleaning supplies.

It was Michael who hit the jackpot, in the bottom of the laundry hamper in the front bathroom. We all tromped down to the study with the trophy, Paul and I following the genius who was our big brother, and Mom came in to witness.

"You are my good son," said Dad. "You may live another day."

Michael grinned a half grin.

"Okay, Mon?" asked our mother.

"Very much okay," said Monroe, which is the closest he came to admitting he'd behaved badly.

Mom sighed and finally said what had been on her mind the whole time.

"You know, if David was here, we wouldn't have to wonder if something got lost. We'd just blame it on him."

Suddenly I wondered what it would be like to come home to a place where anything that went wrong could always be your fault.

After a silence, Dad said quietly, "I'm afraid that's something for all of us to think about."

He looked at our mother and something passed between them.

"And perhaps," Monroe added, a little too pleasantly, "this would be a good time to sit down with you kids and talk about something. Something on a somewhat different topic. We need to let you in on something that's happening."

"Now?" asked Paul.

"No time like the present," said Mom.

We sat down in the grown-ups' living room and our parents explained to us that David was coming back home.

The nine-month trial had failed.

"He just couldn't make it at Camphill," said Mom.

"So it's like he flunked out," Michael commented.

"I guess you could say so," replied Dad. "It's a good place—"

"Really one of the best, we think," Mom added.

"But there wasn't enough structure at Camphill Village," continued Dad.

David had flunked out, I thought, just like Michael said. He couldn't make the cut. He wasn't a cooperative and attractive retarded person like the people who lived in the fairy tale of Camphill, he was just our brother.

"You kids know how David needs things to happen in an ordered way. The program is ordered at Camphill, but it isn't ordered like David," said Dad.

"And the program expects the villagers to participate in cultural and other activities, to get involved with the philosophy behind the place," Mom explained. "And you know, David already has a lot going on in his head. He needs time to himself and he's not so flexible about that. So there's been frustration on both sides—and one of the results has been that, about every month, David has gone out of control, violently. They don't have the people there, the levels of supervision, that would be needed to keep things safe for everyone, David included."

Michael and Paul and I all knew what David was like when he was out of control. He started by rapping and fiddling his fingers on his skull, as though he were revving an engine. If whatever was going on inside of him got worse, he attacked people—it didn't always make sense who. He could pull your head to his and grind his forehead against yours, repeating the names of people who didn't exist outside of television. It hurt.

The three of us nodded, listening to our parents, thoughtful, so good on the outside, and so disappointed and discouraged and disgusted on the inside.

My adventure in normal life was ending. I would need to be able to predict with some certainty that the friends I invited over the house could handle David, that they would be cool enough to act as though he was like everyone else if he was having a good day, that they would be smart and fast enough to get out of the way if he was upset. I would have to know if people liked me before I invited them over to the house, because kids who didn't could say things about David behind my back after they left, things I didn't like to imagine but which made me murderously angry when I did. I had to protect him. We all did. We could have only friends who were very, very loyal. Only insiders.

I would have to be nice about the little things, which can be the hardest things to be nice about: not getting the extra piece of pie, but letting it go to him; not minding the noise of the shows, the shows that happened whenever David wanted them to; not getting a ride to the bus, but walking down there and back.

Even worse, it was completely clear that we were doing the right thing. David couldn't endanger other people at Camphill—that wasn't okay. David couldn't get sent back to Burgoyne, which wasn't a good place for him—that, too, was clear. We were lucky to be flexible enough to keep David at home if that was what was needed; most families with people like David had to send their Davids away, and send them to bad places. Finally, David deserved to have a family, just like the rest of us. I knew that, in an unpleasant way, this was going to make me a better person, that I deserved to have David as he deserved to have me. It was just that right then and there I didn't want to be a better person. I wanted that ride to the bus.

"So he's coming home," said Mom. "There's a program we have in Montgomery County, a day program, the one he was in before, and David has been accepted back into that."

We understood. David was coming home and life would change again. We would all need to operate around him.

"Your mother and I, it's our responsibility to find a place for David," said Dad, "and so we shall. A permanent place, somewhere he can make a contribution. Everyone needs to be able to make a contribution."

"But we're sure there are other options out there," Mom added.

"You kids should not worry," said Dad.

"It's only temporary," said Mom.

I knew we couldn't count on that to be true, and so did Paul and Michael.

Mom went off to do a laundry—she thought that if Dad's glasses could be found in a hamper that maybe she should be paying better attention in that area. She told us to go play outside. Maybe she thought we needed the fresh air (if so, she was right); maybe she just didn't want to have us around (also understandable).

"Get lost," she added, trying to make it into a joke. "Go practice crossing the street."

Michael pulled on his jacket. "Don't follow me, you guys," he added. "I'm going over to Thom's."

In addition to running lights in school plays, Michael was running lights on a show for an older kid over on Melrose Street. Thom had created an entire working theater in his basement, adapted books into plays, and had kids put on the shows. I had wanted to be part of it all, but Michael had gotten there first, and by no accident. There were plenty of girls who wanted to act, but very few kids could rig lighting boards and manufacture working lights with gels out of tin cans and scrounged colored cellophane and God knows what kinds of wires.

"What's wrong with him?" asked Paul.

"Who knows?" I shrugged. Figuring out Michael was a task I had no time for. Certainly not today.

Monroe picked up his book, a history of the English language, and lifted his precious reading glasses out of his pocket.

I wondered how my parents felt. But anything would have been a guess. Our parents didn't want us to have their feelings as one more thing to consider. They worked out those feelings for themselves, or they tried to, and we followed that example—or tried to. If they could be grown-ups about the complications of life in this family, there was no reason why the rest of us couldn't be, too.

"How about you and me, we go down the street and crawl up the culvert?" I proposed to my little brother. This, like the Mouse House, was something we used to do much more often when we were younger.

Paul and I walked to the end of Lenox Street and through a muddy abandoned garden to the creek, then walked upstream to where the creek bank was high. Here, embedded in the bank, was the circular mouth of a tunnel—the end of a long concrete culvert that drained water from the curb gutter down to the creek. We entered from the creek end and began to crawl uphill, up a passage that grew narrower and narrower the closer it got to the street.

The fresh air smelled of shallow running water bumping itself across the muddy irregular edges of rocks and damp red Maryland clay, warmed for the first time since winter, and the early sprouts of onion grass and jack-in-the-pulpits and may apples.

"You know spring is when the flash floods come, Paul," I said to my little brother just as he wiggled into the narrow part ahead of me. "And if that ever happens while we're in the pipe, it's curtains for us." Suburban Maryland had never experienced flash floods in our lifetime, but all the kids in the neighborhood were waiting for them anyway.

"Shut up, Judy," Paul replied calmly.

"You've got a really big rear end, Paul," I said. "If it gets stuck in this pipe it could be all over for you when the flash floods come."

"You're the one with the really big rear end," he answered, "in addition to having a really big mouth."

"You stink," I said, because it was a familiar insult and I wanted this to be a vintage experience. I was getting too old for the culvert.

And Paul, who went first, had the wonderful adventure of seeing the tiny circle of light get larger and larger and finally coming out into the small rectangular concrete cell where the street drain poured into the pipe and then the moment of waiting to jump on the next person, who was me, when that person came out of the hole. We compared our muddy knees and tried to scare each other into not crawling back down the drain since, lying through our teeth, from what we could see of the sky through the sliver in the street gutter, it really was cloudy, and the flash floods would come really fast when they came. Once we milked it for all it was worth, we crawled back down toward the creek.

About midway down the pipe, when I was on my knees, crawling, doing something no self-respecting twelve-year-old should be caught doing, sadness hit me.

Already in the family photo album there were a few shots of Camphill. David standing next to a roughly hewn wooden fence, touching the nose of a big gentle horse; in the background stood a smiling woman wearing a baker's apron.

When he first walked into Camphill Village, we thought David was walking into an alternative universe, where time slowed down and space expanded, where he could be happy, where he was in the company of people who, although also wrapped in the static from their own noisy heads, were basically kind, and more like him than they were like us.

Now he was walking out.

There was no alternative universe for any of us, only this life. This life we all shared.

"Hey, Judy," said Paul, "keep going. My knees are starting to hurt."

I hadn't realized I was sitting still. "Okay," I said, crawling on.

"Hey, Judy," he continued, "what about a disaster book about an earthquake? First it gets a doghouse—that'll be funny, I can do the dog running away—then on the next page a whole regular house, then on the next page a city or something, then the United States?"

"Yeah," I said, climbing out at the creek end of the culvert and dusting off the seat of my pants. "You're going to have to figure out how to draw the earthquake deeper each time," thinking there was no wallpaper sample to provide the visuals for this one.

"It doesn't have to be deeper, just wider," he replied, getting out after me. "Wider is all you have to see. Deeper isn't the joke. The joke is the stuff falling in, dummy."

David was coming home.

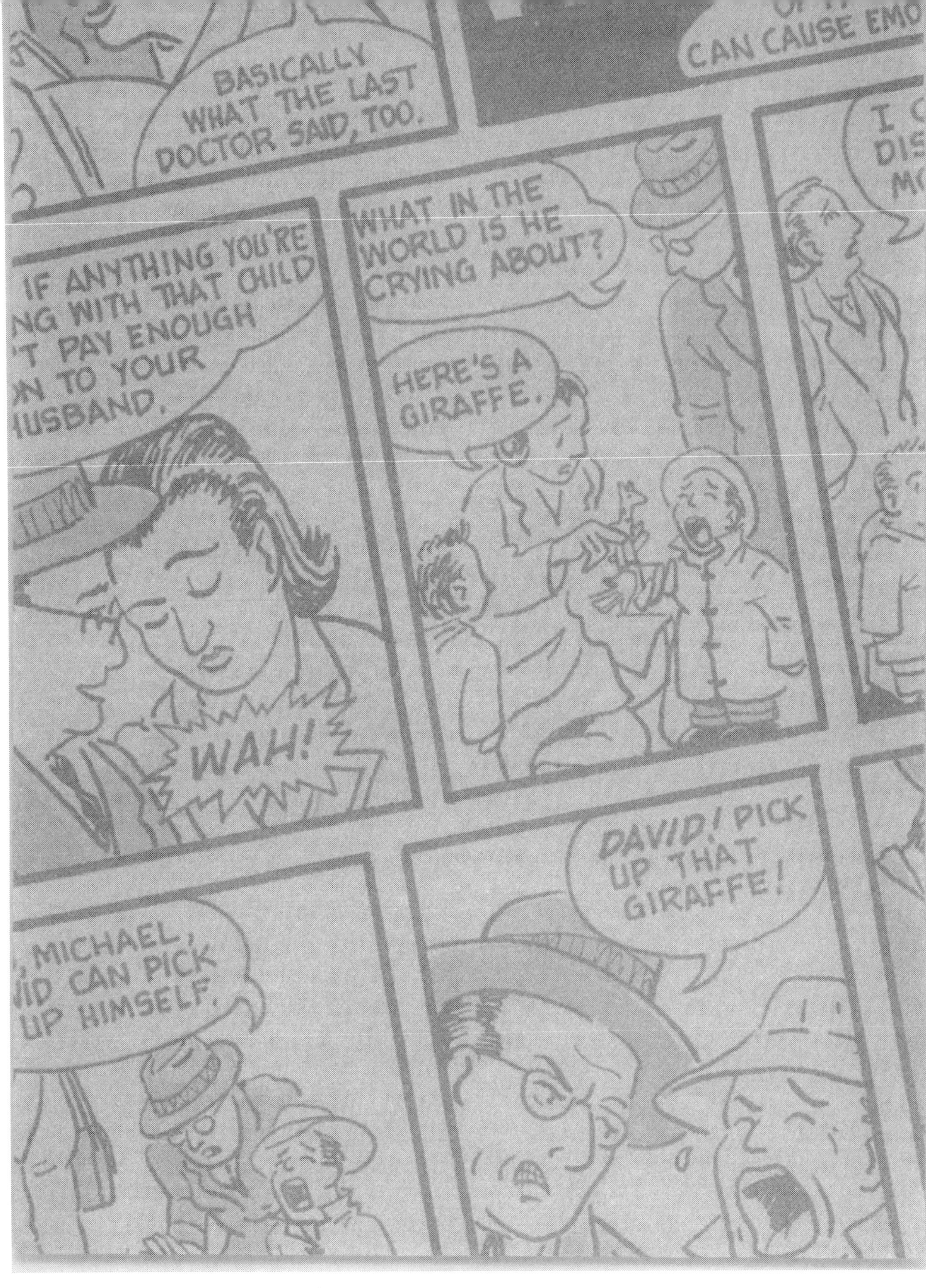

BASICALLY WHAT THE LAST DOCTOR SAID, TOO.
CAN CAUSE EMO
IF ANYTHING YOU'RE
WITH THAT CHILD
PAY ENOUGH
TO YOUR
HUSBAND.
WHAT IN THE WORLD IS HE CRYING ABOUT?
HERE'S A GIRAFFE.
WAH!
MICHAEL,
CAN PICK
UP HIMSELF.
DAVID! PICK UP THAT GIRAFFE!

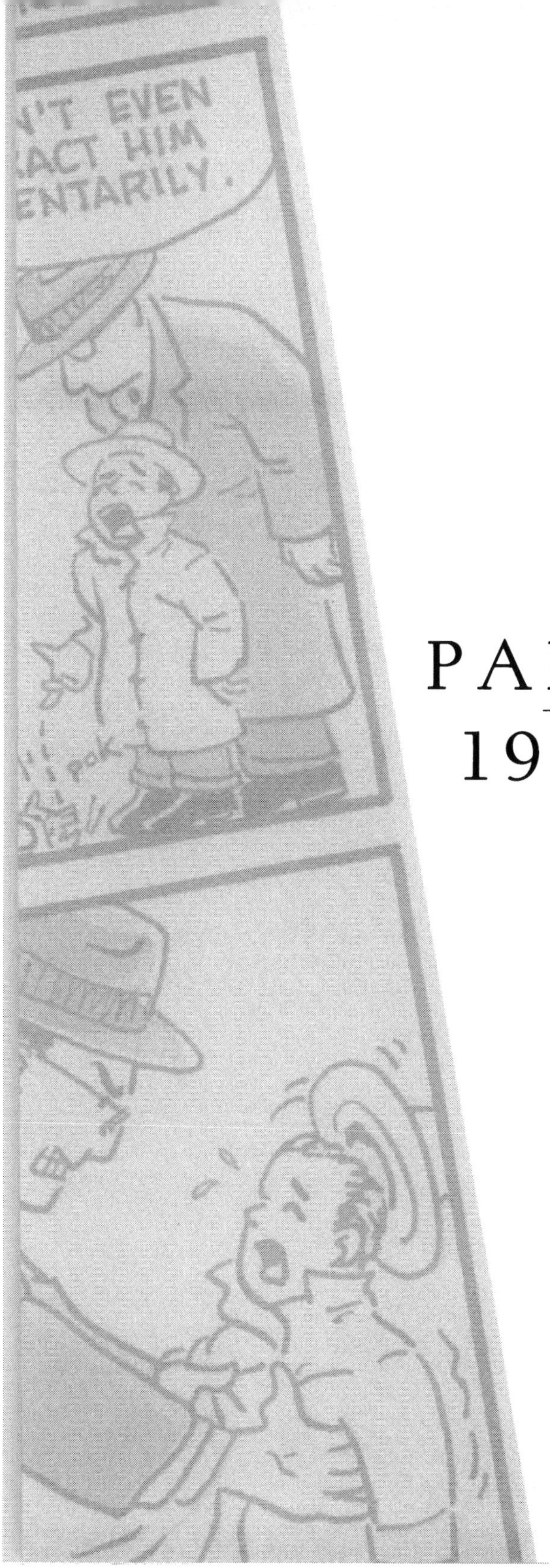
N'T EVEN
ACT HIM
ENTARILY.
POK

PART THREE

1967—1980

8 Independence

When Grandma Irene, Joan's mother, died from a stroke in 1967, my grandfather, Henry Pascal, and my aunt, who was called Sister, came to live with us. My parents, of one mind on what needed to be done, swiftly renovated the house so that the first floor could accommodate two people who couldn't manage stairs: adding a bedroom with a bath for Sister and enclosing the study as a bedroom for Grandpa.

The character of our house changed.

Shortly after they settled in, and things became as they would remain for the next several years, my life changed in a different way. I entered high school. More significantly, I left the public schools and so I was surrounded by a whole new set of people, in the thick of things. I wasn't required to help out at home; my parents were relieved that I had so much that kept me busy.

Occasionally I felt a brief, tiny, sharp sensation. I felt bloodthirsty to myself.

I was fifteen, running school-government committees, composing petitions and getting them signed, writing prizewinning sonnets, painting scenery, hanging lights, and waltzing around on stage pretending to be other people.

Then there was Grandpa and Sister—and Mom and Dorothy White taking care of them. And there was Dave. At the age of twenty, he was in the day program and likely to remain there.

Well, I told myself, somebody has to get out of the house. Somebody has to be strong and independent.

On top of Sister's chest of drawers was a double frame with a photo of Grandma Irene and one of Grandpa Henry, and a glass bottle of perfume with a lavender cap.

Sister loved the smell of that perfume. Every morning, after Joan had dressed Sister, she wiped a line of perfume against Sister's jawline and Sister groaned slightly and ground her teeth to show she was pleased.

Joan knew how to lift Sister and how to get her dressed. She knew what Sister liked to eat and what were the signs that meant her diet needed to be changed. She knew when Sister napped and how to wash Sister. She also knew that the perfume was important to Sister and she always remembered that line of scent.

Meanwhile, every morning, Monday through Friday, in Grandpa's room, Dorothy White got Doctor up.

That's what she always called my grandfather. "Doctor, here's your pills," she said each day.

He always counted them, even though she was always right, and she was fine with that.

Cornelia Pascal, my mother's only sibling, was born in late March 1920. The way it was explained to us, when she was born she suffered a massive cerebral hemorrhage that caused multiple, severe handicaps. Sister, as she was called, never walked; she was carried or she was wheeled. She had the ability to make groaning or snarling noises, but Sister never spoke. The gestures she made with her thin, wiry arms, the kicks of her legs, which were thin and wiry like her arms—she never developed leg muscles—even the way she would turn her head to examine something or tilt her head, gazing more generally, these movements usually came suddenly, in stages, in spurts, as though they were controlled partly by Sister and partly by some other force. We were told that her hearing was poor.

Once I had been afraid of Sister. I remembered Michael and I walking into Sister's room in my grandparents' house in Connecticut, a corner room with windows all around the exterior walls. It was stark—a hospital room with no rug, very little furniture—but full of light and the shadows of leaves, the shifting patterns of branch, light, and shade. When we came into the room, Sister turned her head, neck muscles tense, and gazed at us, like a captive lion. Michael was told to give her a kiss, and I was glad I wasn't supposed to.

She had scared me, this person who, it appeared, was only partly a human being.

By the time she came to live with us, I was not frightened. She was Sister. I wondered what was going on inside her head.

Dorothy White had come to work for my mother when David was a baby, and when it turned out that David would be complicated to raise and as more children came along to increase the complications, Dorothy continued to work for Joan. Dorothy was a large black woman who occupied space immediately, gracefully, and completely; there was no one in the world who could love as hard as Dorothy or scold as hard as Dorothy.

When the four of us kids got old enough to fend for ourselves, Dorothy was starting to think that her usefulness with us had come to an end. But then the house filled up with Grandpa and Sister and she was needed more than ever.

Dorothy's workday ended at six o'clock, dinnertime for Sister.

Dorothy put on her coat as Joan rolled the two wheelchairs next to each other. Every night, my grandfather leaned over and spooned in Sister's dinner, often bread sopped in a soft-boiled egg, then vegetables, and then a dessert.

"Night, Sissie," said Dorothy, ruffling Sister's short red hair. "Good evening, Doctor."

"Good evening to you, Dorothy," replied my grandfather, lifting his chin, smiling, and nodding in the direction of her voice. "And to your family."

Grandpa Henry was ninety-five years old and in a great deal of physical pain. He had busted both hips, falling first on one, then, a year later, on the other. He had shingles, a virus draped over his temples that left the nerve endings tattered and in pain, including the great nerve that encircled one eye. His pulse beat beneath a net of flaky skin. He could barely see. Henry Pascal was broken but he was too attached to life to die.

My grandfather had come over from Romania in 1888, at the age of fifteen, held a variety of jobs, mostly on the Lower East Side of Manhattan, learned English, avoided synagogues but continued to believe that as a Jew he had certain special responsibilities, entered New York University Medical College, and graduated first in his class in 1896. He became chief of surgery at Saint Elizabeth's in Washington Heights in upper Manhattan. The sisters of St. Francis loved and feared Doctor Pascal. He expected that everything he told people to do would be done immediately and well; he required that the staff treat patients efficiently, with dignity and respect.

My grandfather was a doctor for sixty-four years; as late as 1960 he drove into the city from his house in Connecticut to see patients and, occasionally, perform surgery. By that time they always sent a younger doctor into the operating room with him, but nobody could keep him out.

During the period when Grandpa and Sister lived on Lenox Street, caretaking was the main event in the house, while the rest of us, like performers with lesser business in a three-ring circus, slipped in and around my mother and Dorothy as they occupied themselves with one need or another.

They washed continuous loads of clothes and sheets, they brushed Sister's hair and talked to her and saw to it that her wheelchair found its way into a sunny spot in the living room, they prepared special meals, they kept an eye out for loose rugs when Grandpa was still using a walker and, later, popped his wheelchair over the bumps of the door frames, they dodged and kept an eye on David when he was home from the day program, as he dashed from one show to another, they managed Grandpa and Sister in and out of the shower stall, they handed out three separate sets of medication—painkiller for Grandpa's shingles, milk of magnesia for Sister's bowel movements, and phenobarbital for David's seizures.

Meanwhile, they raised the rest of us. Everyone was treated equally; the presiding spirit calmly asserted that this whole scene—wheelchairs, bedpans, and the constant static of unconnected language—was just another way people lived.

My mother said later that if it had not been for Dorothy White during that period she would have killed herself and probably the rest of us, too. Of course, given my mother's nature, she appeared to be completely at ease.

The two women, however different they were in background, religion, and, to a certain degree, temperament, were of one mind on the essential thing: housekeeping and nursing were, first of all, practical matters. To them, it was practical to treat people with respect, it was practical to keep a house clean and tidy and cheerfully lit, it was practical never to rush someone who was in your care (unless that person was a dawdling child), it was practical for food to be tasty and good-looking, it was practical to encourage as much activity as possible, no matter whose activity you were talking about. It was all practical because it enabled them to feel good about their work and so endure and even enjoy that work, and it enabled everyone else, from Sister to Michael to Monroe, to feel cheerful, most of the time, about life at 9 West Lenox Street.

In June of 1969, while Grandpa and Sister stayed in the house, the rest of us left for a vacation, which my parents needed and we kids expected. Dorothy took care of things during the day and a nurse came at night; in that period my parents were trying different arrangements, to see what would work best.

We took three weeks away, but I flew back early to take driver's education, so that I could complete my independence. I needed that car. For a week it would be just me and Grandpa and Sister and Dorothy in the house. And the nurse at night.

The nurse, a short, pale woman with a puffy Eastern European face, was watching the television. She crossed her arms over her bosom. Her forearms were mighty. She could lift people.

In the next room, my grandfather was calling for help.

It was night. It seemed like he had been calling since I had walked in the back door that afternoon, at the end of my journey home. The house seemed very empty.

The nurse wouldn't help him and I had never learned how to do any of this. The house was cluttered with the accessories of healing—wheelchairs, a walker, a tray for false teeth, bedpans, a potty chair, cotton wool, rubbing alcohol, a shower stall with a flexible stainless steel hose instead of a regular shower head—but still I was ignorant, the classic educated fool. I was afraid.

The nurse was unmovable as a tiny sumo wrestler cast in lead, washed blue, submerged in the television light.

My grandfather called again. He moaned.

"Please," called my grandfather. "Nurse," he called.

The nurse watched the screen.

"He needs something," I said.

She barely looked at me. "He'll quiet down," she said.

"Nurse," said Doctor Pascal. "Please. Nurse."

I went away.

My grandfather was still moaning. I came back.

The nurse looked at me. I stood there at the edge of the living room, staring at her to do something. I stared with the stare of a dog who wants to be let out but who has no hands to open the door.

"He'll quiet down," she said. "He gets like this."

I realized that this had been going on night after night.

"Nurse," my grandfather called. "Help," he said. I moved toward his voice.

"Don't you go in there," said the nurse. "Just stay away."

I stood at the entry to his room, unable to go in.

"Help," called my grandfather. "I'm in pain," he cried.

She stood up, walked down the short hall, looked at me. "Don't you go in there," the nurse said to me. "Don't you dare." She closed the door to the sickroom in my face. "You'll only get him riled up," she commented.

She walked back to the living room and sat down.

My grandfather started to moan.

From the television, the merry sound of a xylophone played. A woman's voice announced a prize. My grandfather moaned. And then he screamed.

He screamed for five minutes and he stopped.

I stood in front of the shut door to the sickroom. If I went in, I would only do the wrong thing, and everything would get worse. She wouldn't help if everything got worse. I would end up killing him.

It was like a terrible crack in life. This was why we never let people into our house who didn't understand us, I thought, people who didn't understand how you had to behave if you were going to be part of this family. These were the consequences when you let someone in who didn't understand.

The stairway formed a square well in the middle of the house. All of the house's sounds floated up the well. I walked upstairs, through the echoes, into my parents' empty bedroom. I picked up the phone. At least I knew the number to call. I knew she would see it the way I did, because she was one of the people who had raised me to see it that way.

Dorothy answered the phone.

"Hello?" she said, like she always did, like she'd been interrupted, like she already couldn't wait for you to get off and leave her alone. "Hello?"

"Dorothy?" I asked.

She knew my voice. She listened while I didn't say anything.

"What's wrong, baby?" she said.

"Dorothy," I said. And then I cried and cried.

"She's so mean," I managed to say. "Dorothy. Dorothy, she's so mean." And then I couldn't say anything more.

"You at home?" she asked.

"Yes," I said.

God knows what she thought was going on. Or maybe she knew right away.

"You stay put," she said.

I went and sat on the stairs, where the sounds drifted up, the television and the ceaseless moans.

When Dorothy arrived, she put her arms around me and she kissed me and called me her baby and a good girl and told me to go to bed. Everything would be all right. She would straighten things out.

I could hear her voice, first with the nurse, briefly, and then with my grandfather.

"Doctor," she said, bright and professional, walking into his room. "Now tell me what we can do here."

I heard my grandfather sigh. Then he spoke. He did not moan; he spoke.

It wouldn't be until years later that I would learn how to lift someone, how to change a bed underneath someone, how to feed a grown person who ate only soft food. But that night I learned that a person needs to know these things, to be independent.

I sat on the stairs for a few moments more and then I went to bed, just as Dorothy had told me to.

It wasn't even something hard or complicated, Dorothy told my mother later. It didn't take but a minute. He was just uncomfortable.

I was asleep by the time she got back to talking to the nurse. I slept through that conversation. I imagined it in my dreams, though. Dorothy on a chariot. Dorothy, whose righteousness was her own flaming sword.

When I came downstairs early the next morning, the nurse was gone. In her place was Dorothy, who had slept that night on the couch.

9 *Secret Agent Man*

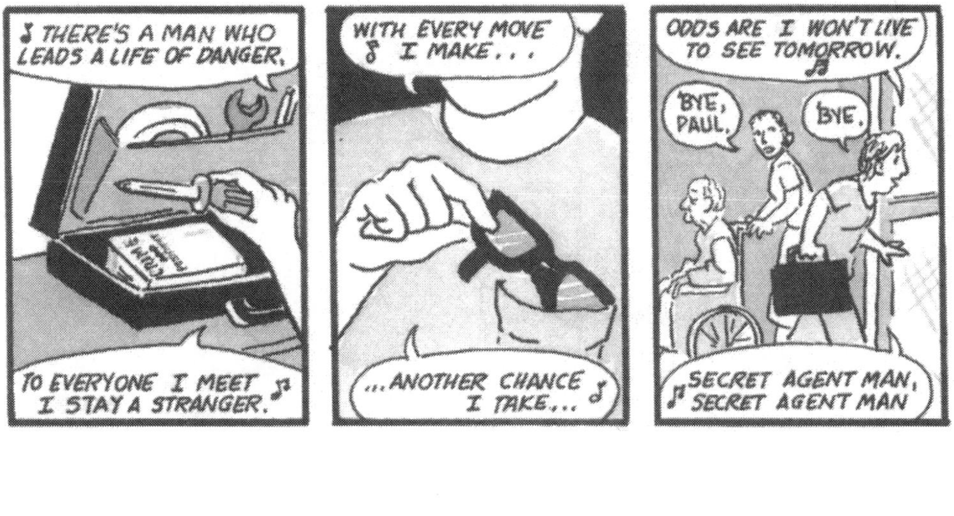

♪ THERE'S A MAN WHO LEADS A LIFE OF DANGER,
TO EVERYONE I MEET I STAY A STRANGER. ♫
WITH EVERY MOVE ♪ I MAKE...
...ANOTHER CHANCE I TAKE... ♪
ODDS ARE I WON'T LIVE TO SEE TOMORROW. ♫
'BYE, PAUL.
'BYE.
♫ SECRET AGENT MAN, SECRET AGENT MAN

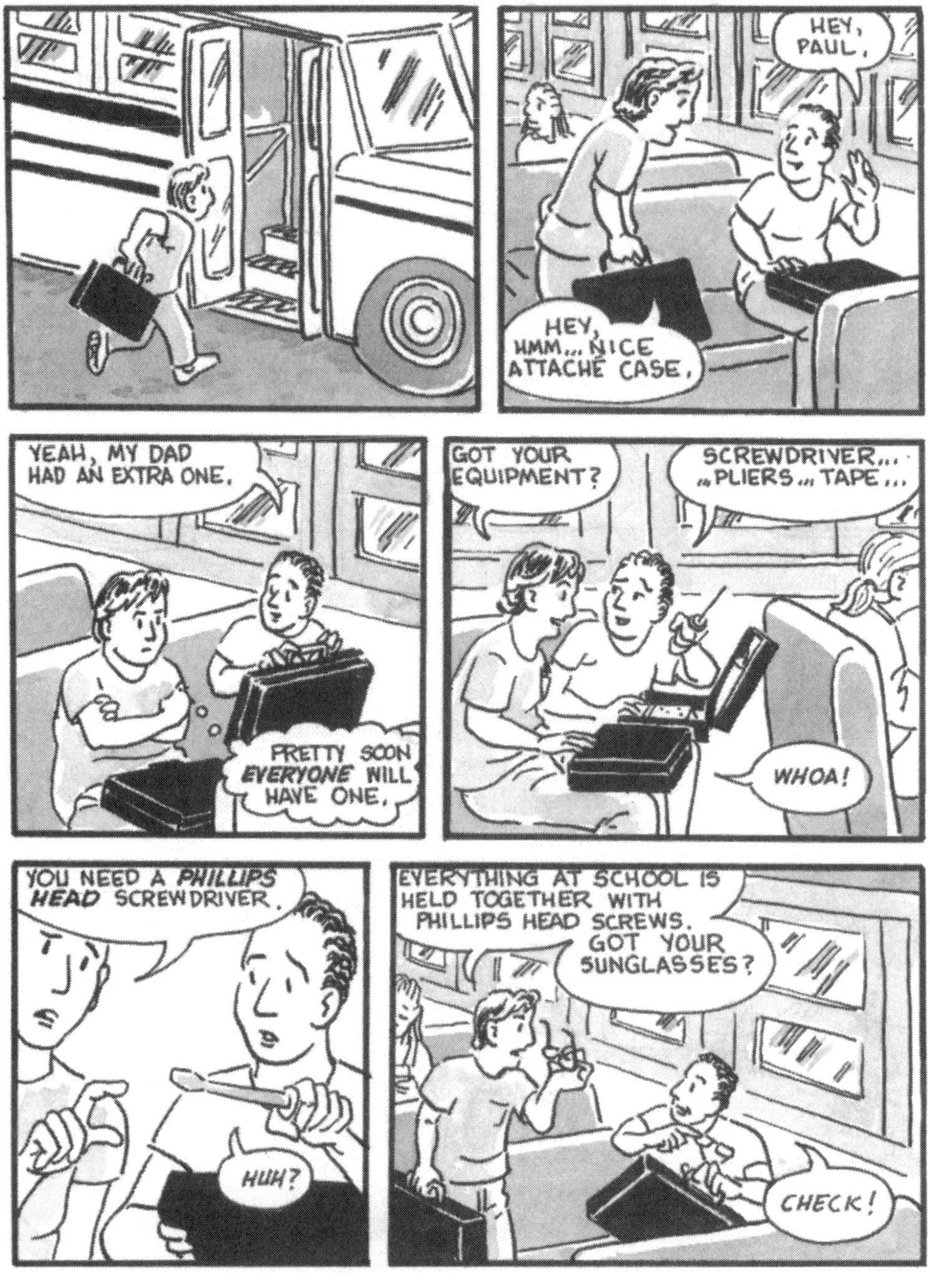
HEY, PAUL.
HEY, HMM... NICE ATTACHÉ CASE.
YEAH, MY DAD HAD AN EXTRA ONE.
PRETTY SOON *EVERYONE* WILL HAVE ONE.
GOT YOUR EQUIPMENT?
SCREWDRIVER... ...PLIERS... TAPE...
WHOA!
YOU NEED A ***PHILLIPS HEAD*** SCREWDRIVER.
HUH?
EVERYTHING AT SCHOOL IS HELD TOGETHER WITH PHILLIPS HEAD SCREWS.
GOT YOUR SUNGLASSES?
CHECK!

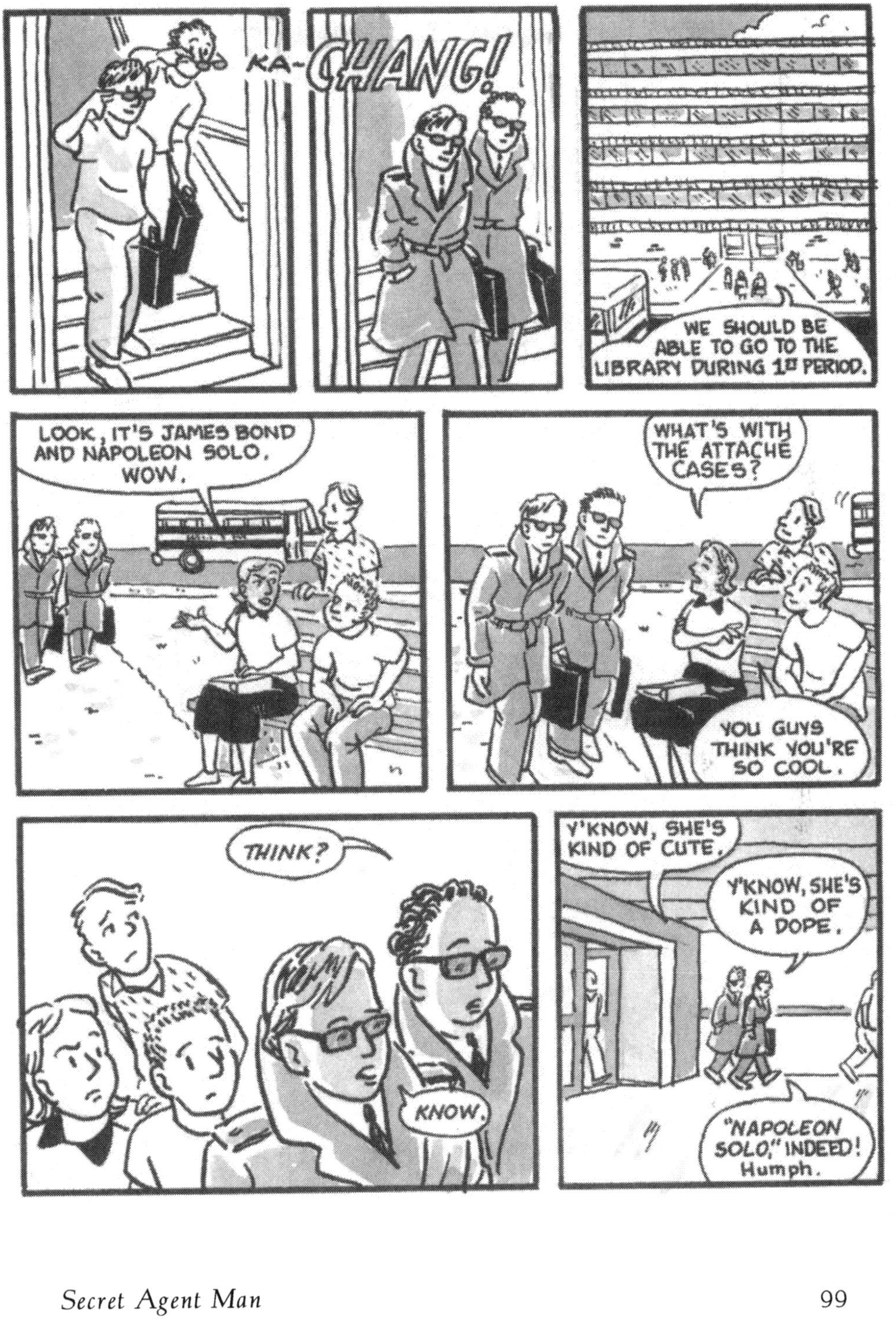
KA-CHANG!
WE SHOULD BE ABLE TO GO TO THE LIBRARY DURING 1ST PERIOD.
LOOK, IT'S JAMES BOND AND NAPOLEON SOLO. WOW.
WHAT'S WITH THE ATTACHÉ CASES?
YOU GUYS THINK YOU'RE SO COOL.
THINK?
KNOW.
Y'KNOW, SHE'S KIND OF CUTE.
Y'KNOW, SHE'S KIND OF A DOPE.
"NAPOLEON SOLO," INDEED! Humph.

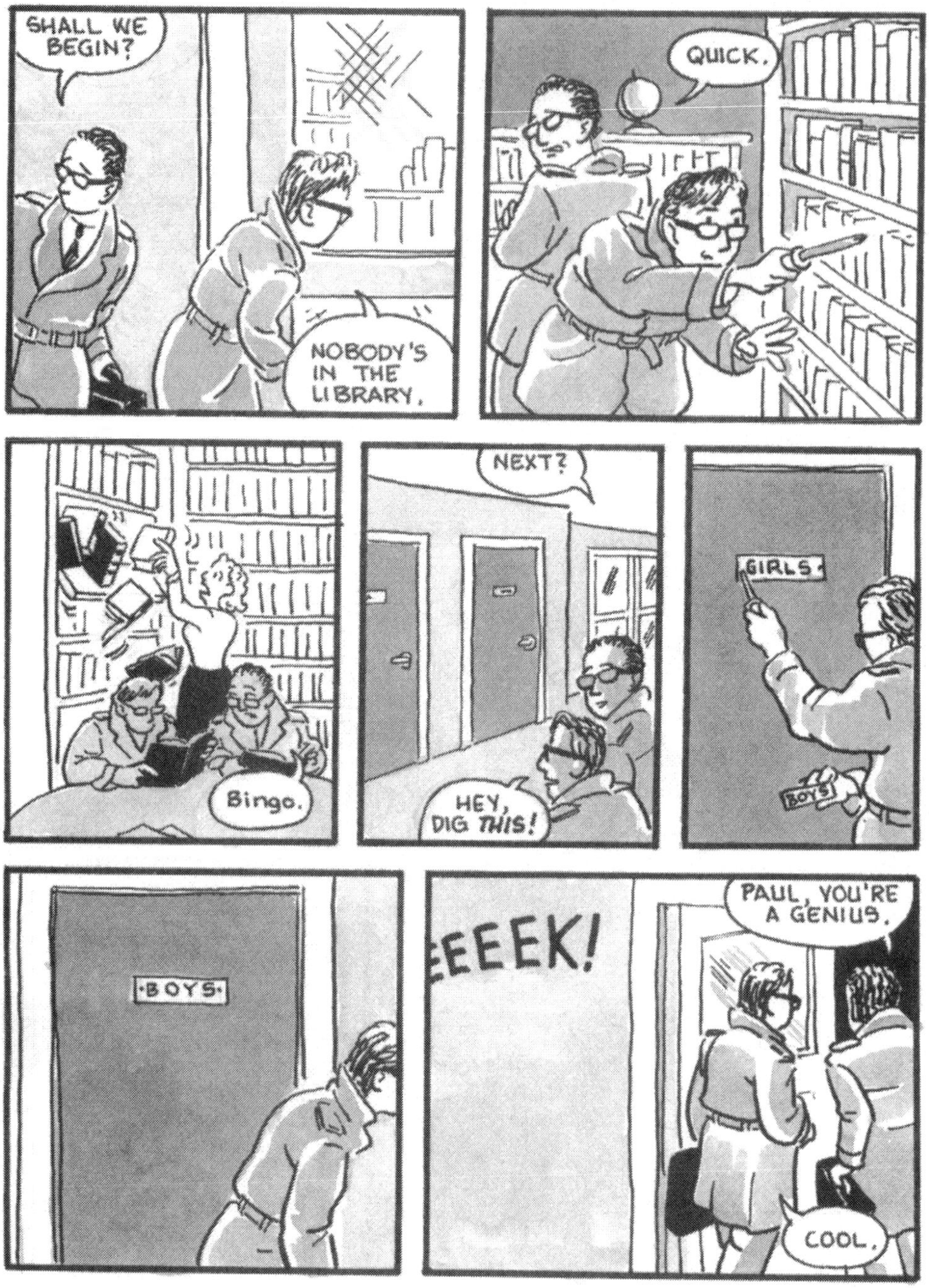
SHALL WE BEGIN?
NOBODY'S IN THE LIBRARY.
QUICK.
Bingo.
NEXT?
HEY, DIG THIS!
GIRLS
BOYS
BOYS
EEEEK!
PAUL, YOU'RE A GENIUS.
COOL.

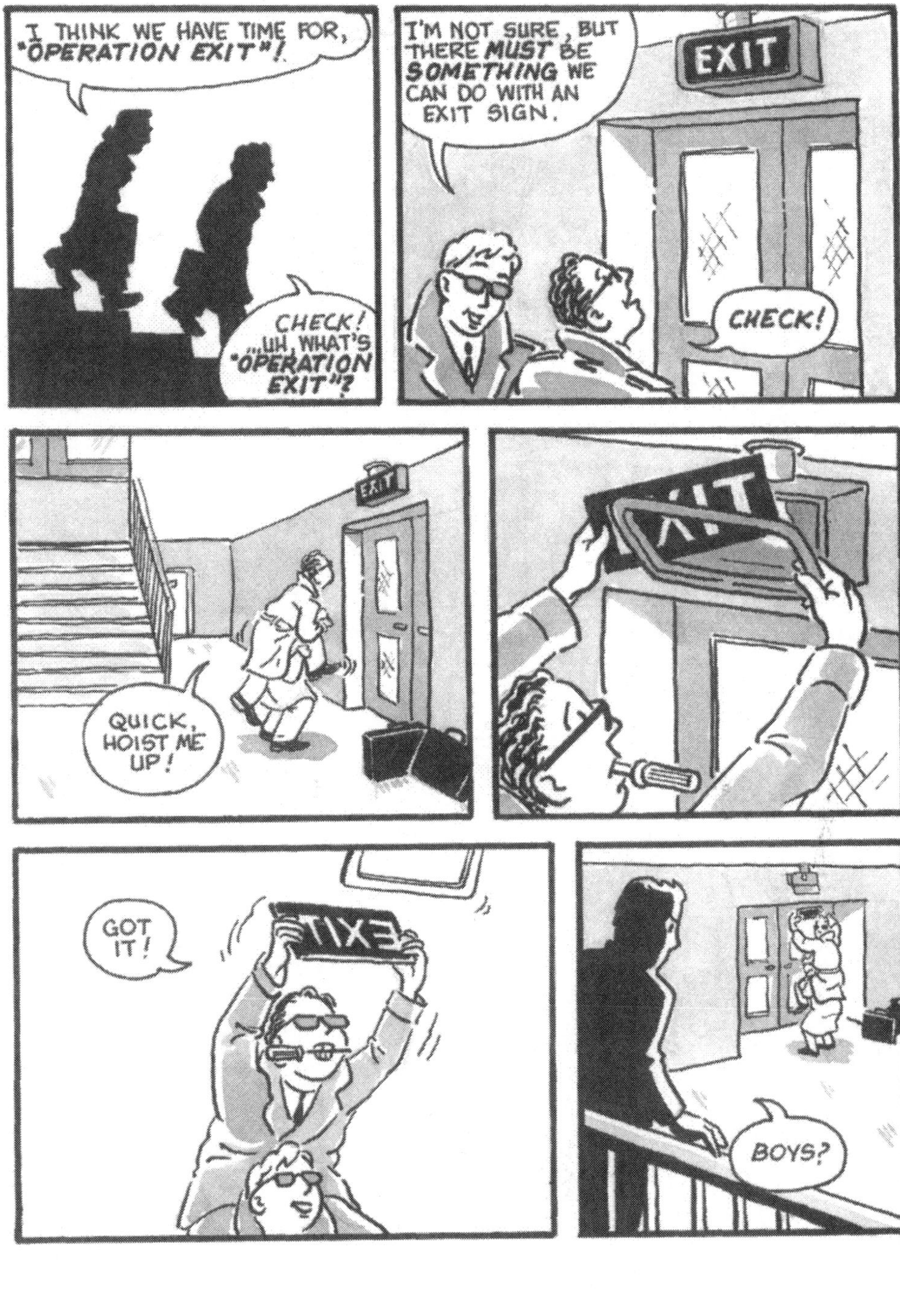
I THINK WE HAVE TIME FOR, "OPERATION EXIT"!
CHECK! ...UH, WHAT'S "OPERATION EXIT"?
I'M NOT SURE, BUT THERE MUST BE SOMETHING WE CAN DO WITH AN EXIT SIGN.
EXIT
CHECK!
EXIT
QUICK, HOIST ME UP!
GOT IT!
BOYS?

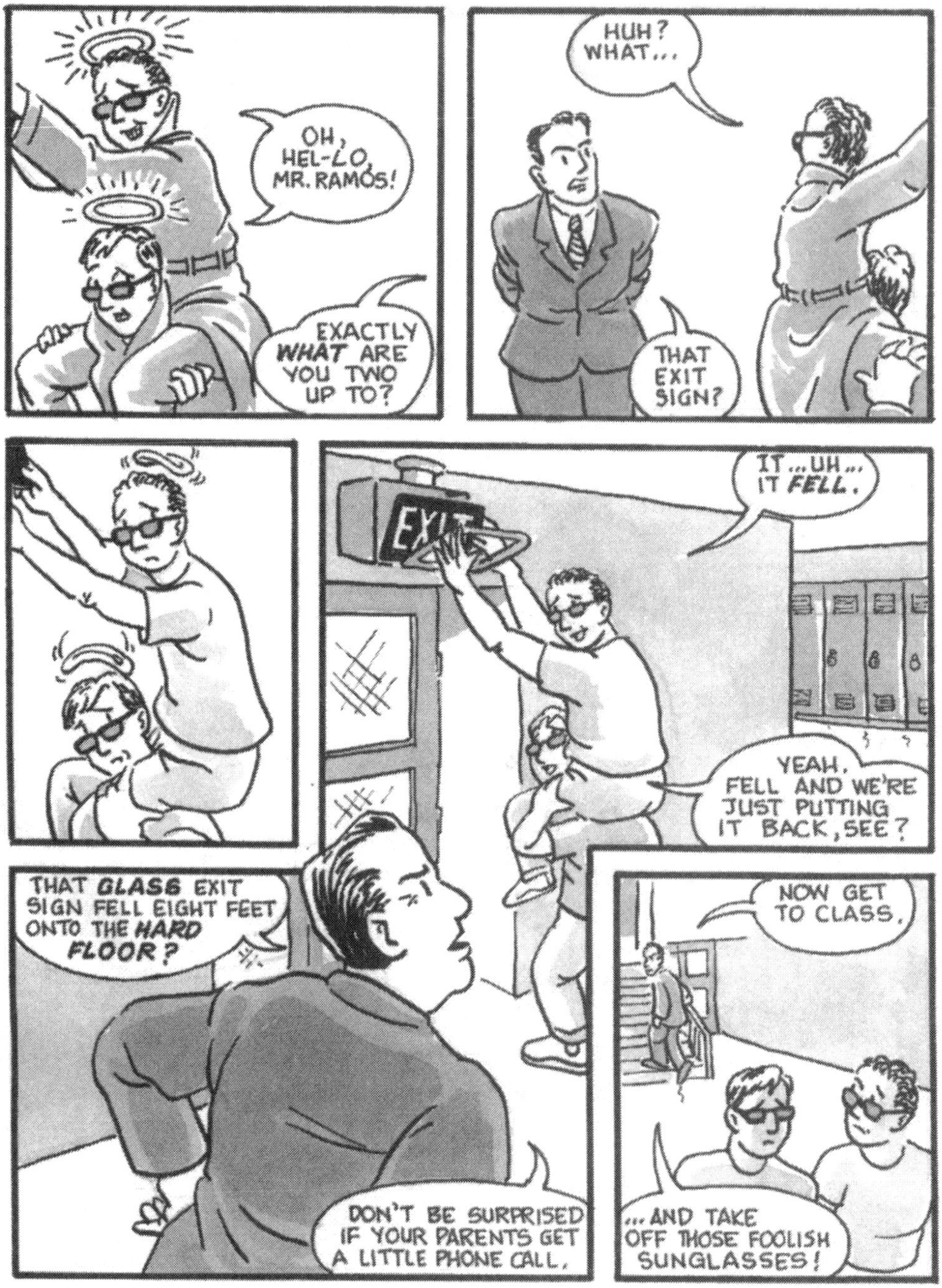
OH, HEL-LO, MR. RAMOS!
EXACTLY WHAT ARE YOU TWO UP TO?
HUH? WHAT...
THAT EXIT SIGN?
EXIT
IT...UH... IT FELL.
YEAH, FELL AND WE'RE JUST PUTTING IT BACK, SEE?
THAT GLASS EXIT SIGN FELL EIGHT FEET ONTO THE HARD FLOOR?
DON'T BE SURPRISED IF YOUR PARENTS GET A LITTLE PHONE CALL.
NOW GET TO CLASS.
...AND TAKE OFF THOSE FOOLISH SUNGLASSES!

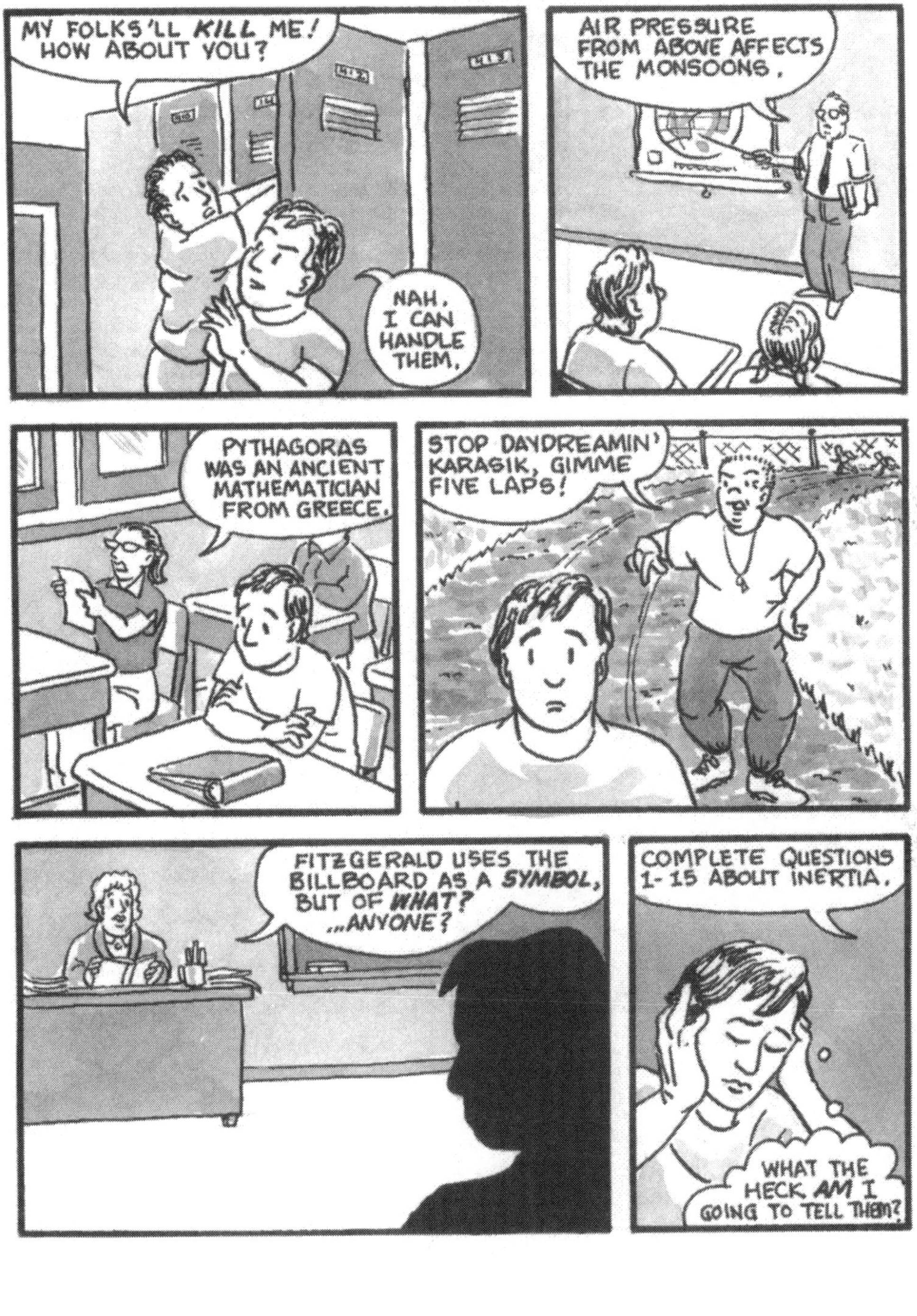
MY FOLKS'LL KILL ME! HOW ABOUT YOU?
NAH, I CAN HANDLE THEM.
AIR PRESSURE FROM ABOVE AFFECTS THE MONSOONS.
PYTHAGORAS WAS AN ANCIENT MATHEMATICIAN FROM GREECE.
STOP DAYDREAMIN' KARASIK, GIMME FIVE LAPS!
FITZGERALD USES THE BILLBOARD AS A SYMBOL, BUT OF WHAT? ...ANYONE?
COMPLETE QUESTIONS 1-15 ABOUT INERTIA.
WHAT THE HECK AM I GOING TO TELL THEM?

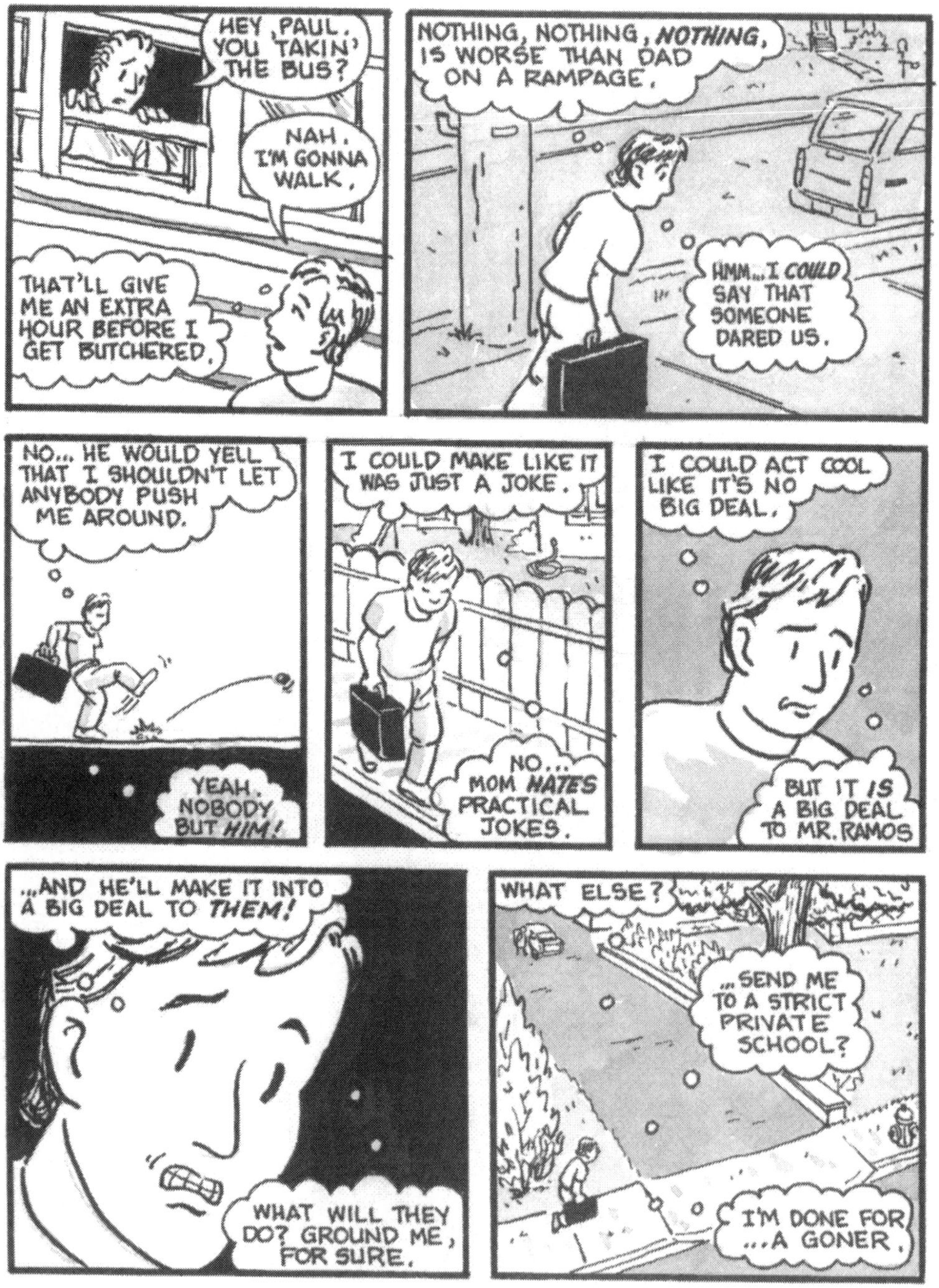
HEY, PAUL, YOU TAKIN' THE BUS?
NAH. I'M GONNA WALK.
THAT'LL GIVE ME AN EXTRA HOUR BEFORE I GET BUTCHERED.
NOTHING, NOTHING, NOTHING, IS WORSE THAN DAD ON A RAMPAGE.
HMM... I COULD SAY THAT SOMEONE DARED US.
NO... HE WOULD YELL THAT I SHOULDN'T LET ANYBODY PUSH ME AROUND.
YEAH. NOBODY BUT HIM!
I COULD MAKE LIKE IT WAS JUST A JOKE.
NO... MOM HATES PRACTICAL JOKES.
I COULD ACT COOL LIKE IT'S NO BIG DEAL.
BUT IT IS A BIG DEAL TO MR. RAMOS
...AND HE'LL MAKE IT INTO A BIG DEAL TO THEM!
WHAT WILL THEY DO? GROUND ME, FOR SURE.
WHAT ELSE?
...SEND ME TO A STRICT PRIVATE SCHOOL?
I'M DONE FOR ...A GONER.

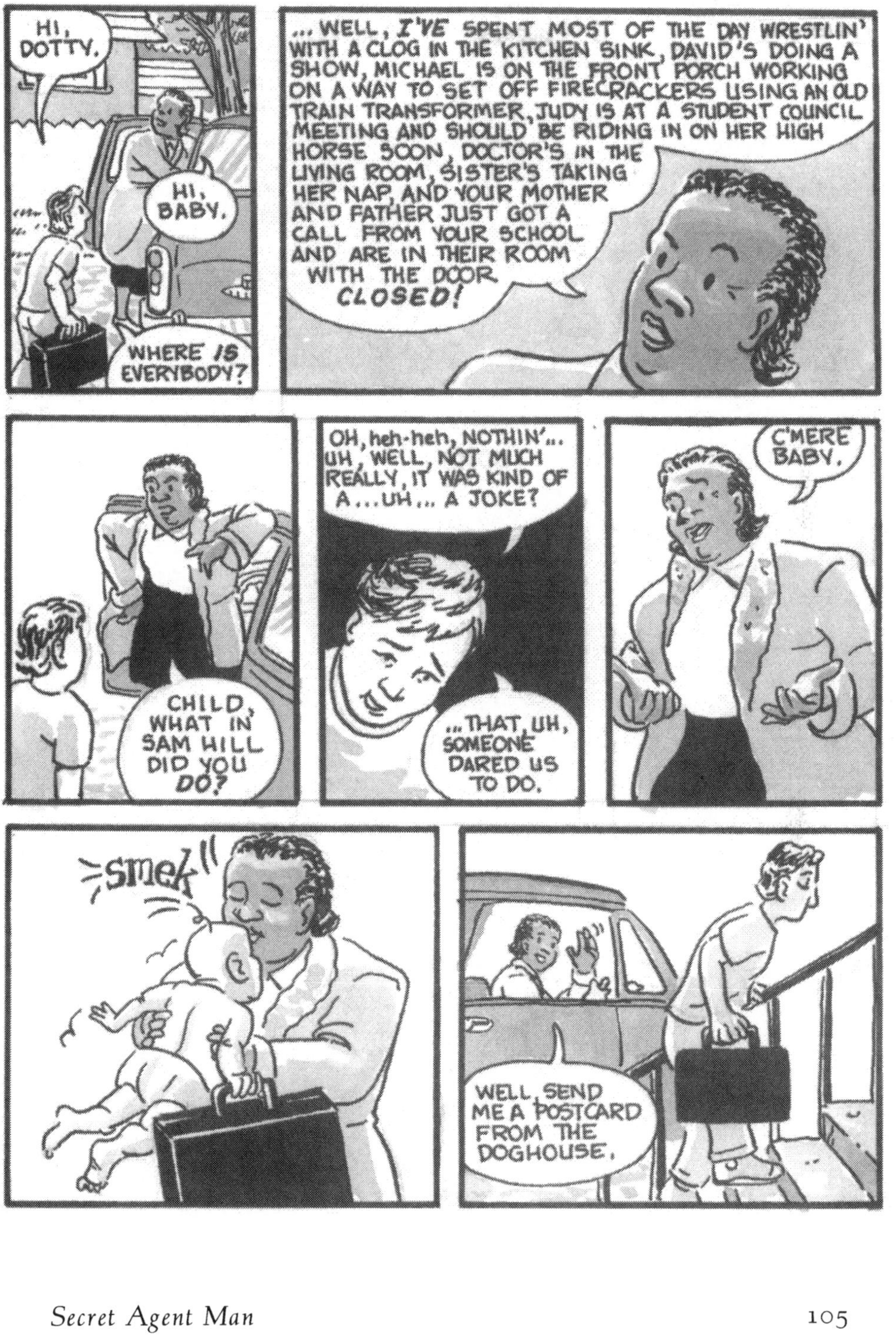
HI, DOTTY.
HI, BABY.
WHERE IS EVERYBODY?
... WELL, I'VE SPENT MOST OF THE DAY WRESTLIN' WITH A CLOG IN THE KITCHEN SINK, DAVID'S DOING A SHOW, MICHAEL IS ON THE FRONT PORCH WORKING ON A WAY TO SET OFF FIRECRACKERS USING AN OLD TRAIN TRANSFORMER, JUDY IS AT A STUDENT COUNCIL MEETING AND SHOULD BE RIDING IN ON HER HIGH HORSE SOON, DOCTOR'S IN THE LIVING ROOM, SISTER'S TAKING HER NAP, AND YOUR MOTHER AND FATHER JUST GOT A CALL FROM YOUR SCHOOL AND ARE IN THEIR ROOM WITH THE DOOR CLOSED!
CHILD, WHAT IN SAM HILL DID YOU DO?
OH, heh-heh, NOTHIN'... UH, WELL, NOT MUCH REALLY, IT WAS KIND OF A...UH... A JOKE?
...THAT, UH, SOMEONE DARED US TO DO.
C'MERE BABY.
SMEK
WELL, SEND ME A POSTCARD FROM THE DOGHOUSE.

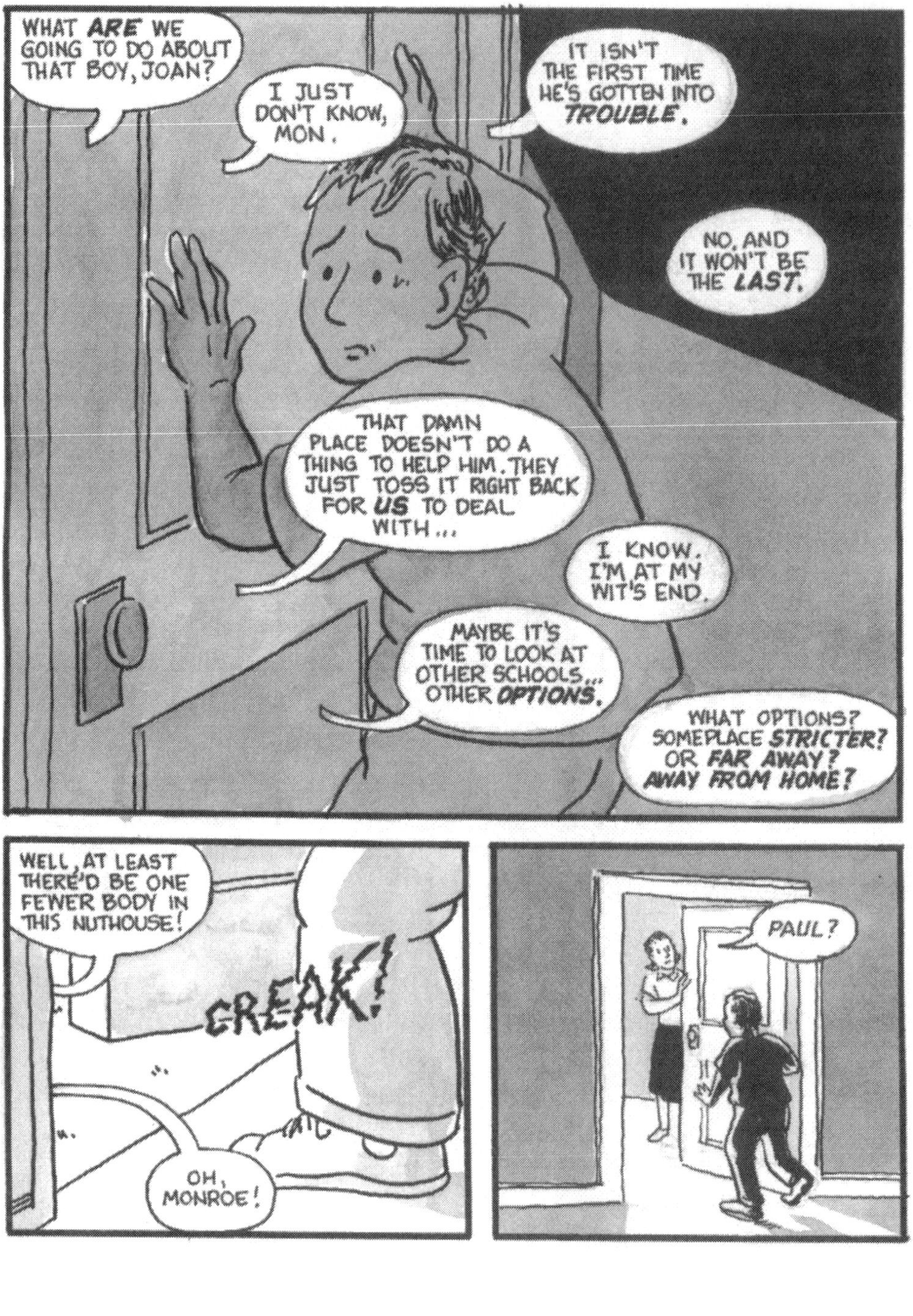

WHAT ARE WE GOING TO DO ABOUT THAT BOY, JOAN?
I JUST DON'T KNOW, MON.
IT ISN'T THE FIRST TIME HE'S GOTTEN INTO TROUBLE.
NO, AND IT WON'T BE THE LAST.
THAT DAMN PLACE DOESN'T DO A THING TO HELP HIM. THEY JUST TOSS IT RIGHT BACK FOR US TO DEAL WITH...
I KNOW. I'M AT MY WIT'S END.
MAYBE IT'S TIME TO LOOK AT OTHER SCHOOLS... OTHER OPTIONS.
WHAT OPTIONS? SOMEPLACE STRICTER? OR FAR AWAY? AWAY FROM HOME?
WELL, AT LEAST THERE'D BE ONE FEWER BODY IN THIS NUTHOUSE!
CREAK!
OH, MONROE!
PAUL?

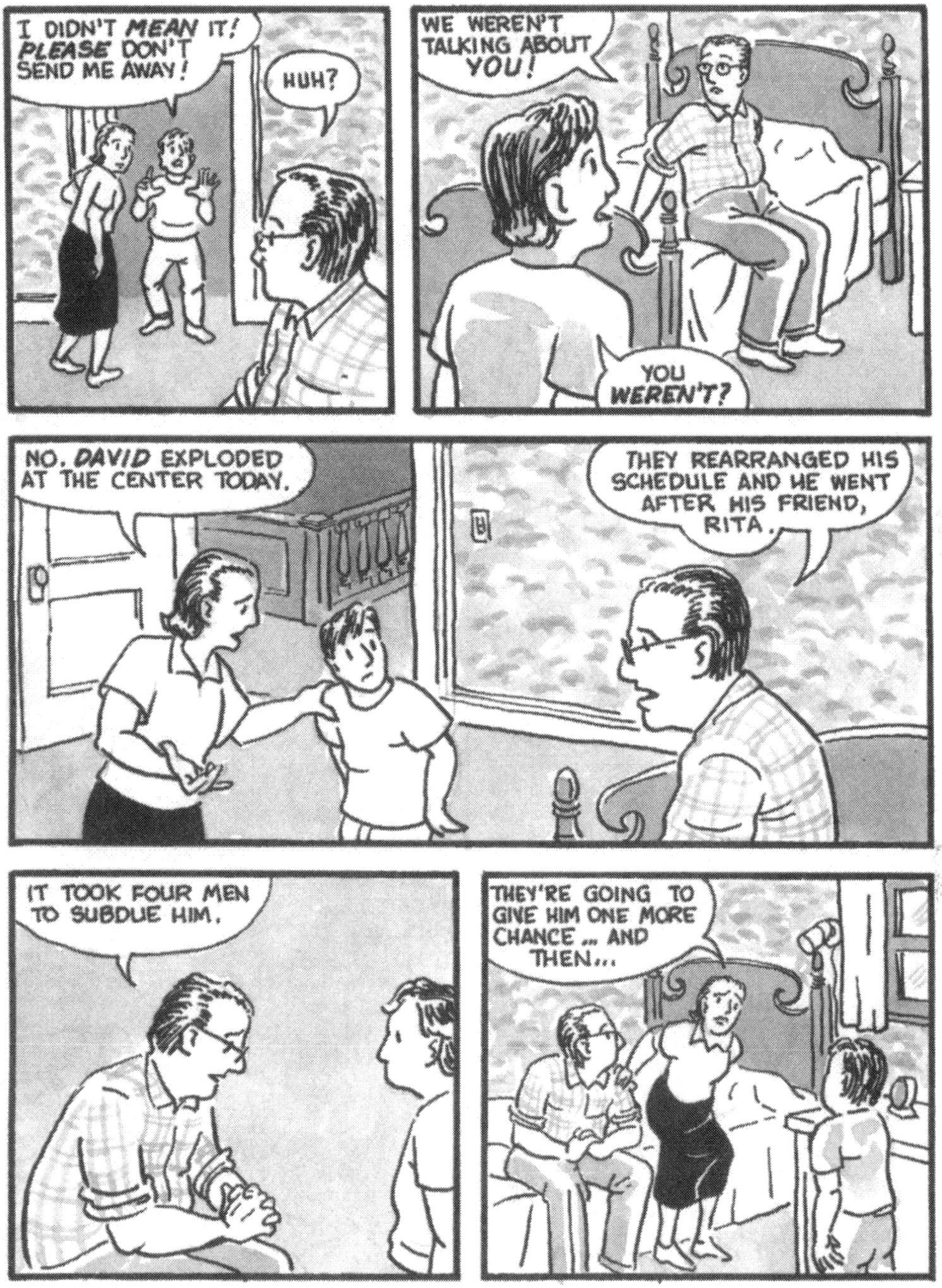
I DIDN'T MEAN IT! PLEASE DON'T SEND ME AWAY!
HUH?
WE WEREN'T TALKING ABOUT YOU!
YOU WEREN'T?
NO. DAVID EXPLODED AT THE CENTER TODAY.
THEY REARRANGED HIS SCHEDULE AND HE WENT AFTER HIS FRIEND, RITA.
IT TOOK FOUR MEN TO SUBDUE HIM.
THEY'RE GOING TO GIVE HIM ONE MORE CHANCE ... AND THEN...

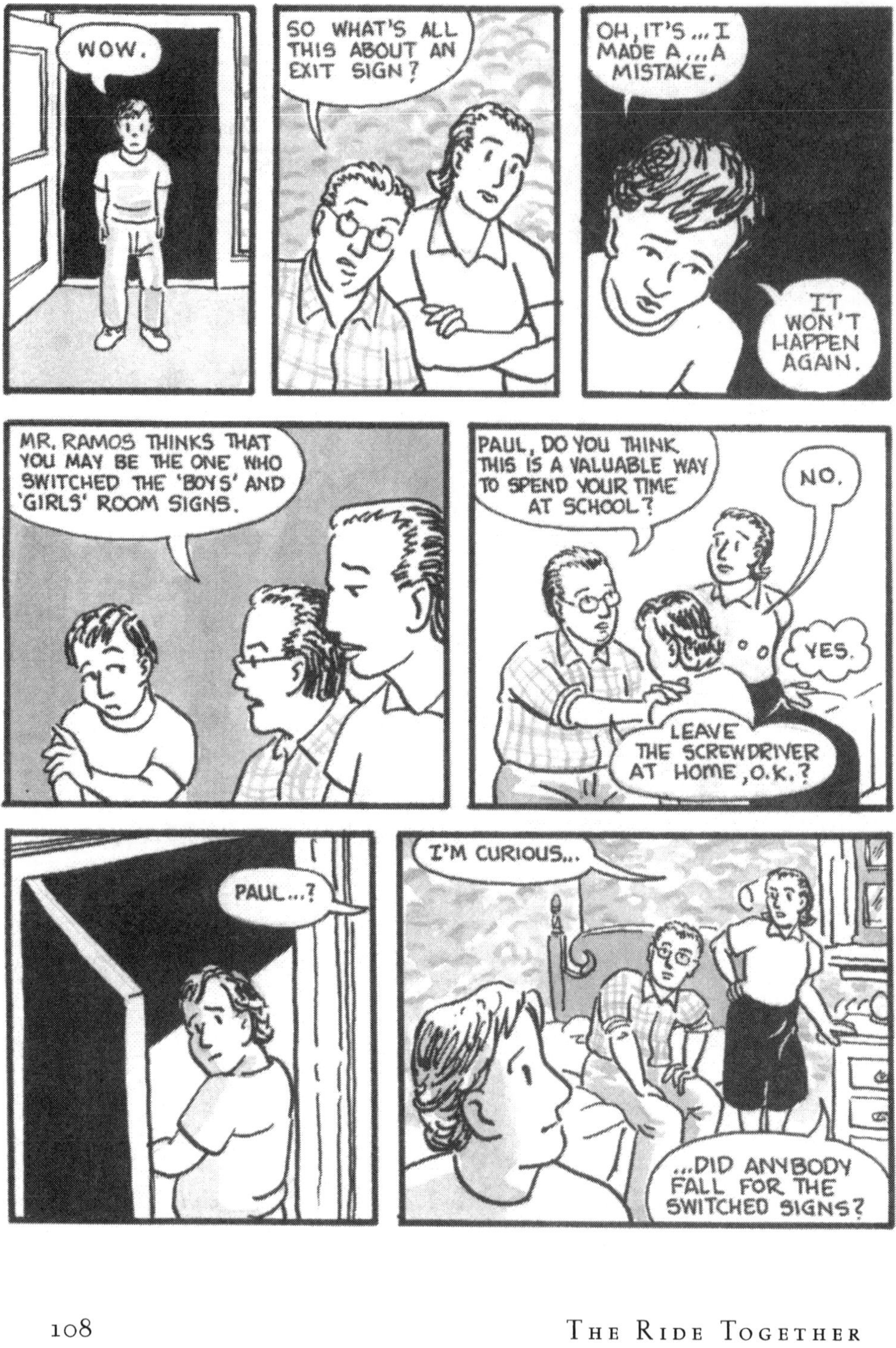
WOW.
SO WHAT'S ALL THIS ABOUT AN EXIT SIGN?
OH, IT'S ... I MADE A ... A MISTAKE.
IT WON'T HAPPEN AGAIN.
MR. RAMOS THINKS THAT YOU MAY BE THE ONE WHO SWITCHED THE 'BOYS' AND 'GIRLS' ROOM SIGNS.
PAUL, DO YOU THINK THIS IS A VALUABLE WAY TO SPEND YOUR TIME AT SCHOOL?
NO.
YES.
LEAVE THE SCREWDRIVER AT HOME, O.K.?
PAUL...?
I'M CURIOUS...
...DID ANYBODY FALL FOR THE SWITCHED SIGNS?

10 *The Fire*

Henry Pascal died in June 1971. After Grandpa's death, Joan considered whether it would be better to have Sister stay with us or put her in a nursing home. Dorothy, who had clearly been thinking about this for some time, immediately said there would be no nursing homes in Sister's future; instead, Sister would live with the Whites in their brick rowhouse on Allison Street.

Dorothy and her husband, Eddie, would enclose the sunporch at the back of the first floor and add a bath. Sister would be in the middle of the family action; there were always lots of people coming and going at Dorothy's house, unlike 9 West Lenox, which was increasingly quiet and empty.

Dorothy said of herself that she was getting too old to keep running over to another person's house to work and, besides, she had her cousin Flowree, who lived in the house, was completely blind from diabetes, and was a worry to everyone when left alone.

Dorothy put all of this forth as a suggestion. Joan and Monroe thought about the proposition and agreed. The way Joan put it, she knew that she herself would care for Sister as someone who needed to be taken care of, but the Whites would care for Sister as a member of the family. Joan drove over to Allison Street three times a week, which not only enabled Sister to see her, and she to see Sister, it also enabled our two families to stay linked. This arrangement lasted for nearly six years.

The night of the fire, by chance I had come home from New York, where I now lived, to see my parents.

I walked in the front door at 9 West Lenox Street around nine-thirty that evening. Only one or two lights were on. There, sitting on the living room floor, was Mom, surrounded by stacks of books.

She was dusting the books, as she did every few years. She had a cloth and was swiping their surfaces, one by one.

When I walked in she didn't say hello. She didn't need to. She had that expression on her face that tells you something bad has happened.

She said, "There's been a fire at Dorothy's. Sister is dead and Flowree is in the ICU and Eddie is in the hospital with bad burns. Mon's gone to identify Sister." The part of her face around the eyes looked very tired. "So I thought I'd dust the books," she added.

I said something, one of those collections of words that fills the space, then asked if she had called Michael. Paul and David were living at home, although our parents rarely saw Paul, who was doing a year at the community college and was rarely around except to sleep.

"It's late," Joan replied. "I figured I could do it tomorrow morning just as well."

We heard a noise on the stairs. On the landing David stood in his pajamas, sleepy, woken by my arrival and our talk.

"Mrs. Karasik?" he said. That was what he often called Mom. He saw me. "Hi, Judy, hi."

"Hi, Dave," I replied.

My mother went up the stairs. She stood on the step below him and told him the news. David nodded. Joan reached up to pat his shoulder.

"Okay, Dave?" she said. "We'll know more tomorrow."

"Where's Dad?" asked David, a remarkably direct question for David to ask.

"He'll be back soon," replied Joan. "He had to do something about what happened. Go on back to bed, Dave."

"Good night, Mrs. Karasik," said David.

"Good night, Dave," I called up the stairs.

"Good night, Judy," he replied.

"I'll see you in the morning," I called. I could barely hear his "Okay" in reply.

Monroe shortly returned from identifying what was left of Sister. She had been horribly burned. Although Pop had seen her only indirectly, through a video monitor, he could barely talk about what he had seen. He sat down on the low table in the living room and told Joan, still seated on the floor, that the task was done; his skin looked sick, like pale clay, or a hard rubber.

The next day Mom and I went to see Eddie over at Washington Hospital Center and he apologized to her for not succeeding in saving Sister. Joan would have none of it and we were all pretty close to tears at that moment. We all knew what he had done.

His bed was next to a window. The sun shone its light through the panes. His burns were all over his lower arms and probably other places I couldn't see.

It had been Belinda, Dorothy's adopted daughter, who had first seen the fire. She had needed something in the basement and as she came downstairs, she saw smoke coming from the direction of Sister's room at the back of the house. Belinda yelled "Fire," and everyone upstairs ran downstairs—Dorothy and Eddie and Flowree. As fast as they moved, the fire moved faster, from the back of the first floor to the front windows, crackling, making hot smoke and flame out of the carpet.

Dorothy shooed Flowree down the stairs. Belinda was already out.

Eddie did not walk out. At the bottom of the stairs, without hesitating, he walked toward the flames and then he walked through them. He walked through the fire.

Sister, however, was already dead from smoke inhalation by the time he touched her.

Eddie turned around and the fire was everywhere. Somehow he got out to the street. People surrounded him.

Flowree made it halfway down the stairs but she turned back. She remembered the money she had collected for the church and she went back to get it. She died late the next day. As with Sister, it wasn't the heat that killed her, it was the smoke.

Dorothy stood wrapped in a blanket as the ambulance took away her husband and her cousin and the fire engines roared.

Here was a woman whose work and whose genius was caring for the helpless, and she lost two of them that night, in her own home.

That next morning, before Joan and I went to the hospital, my parents and I drove over to Allison Street to walk through the house. Belinda went with us, but not Dorothy. It was a long time before Dorothy would go back inside that house.

The fire marshal said that the blaze had been caused by a short from the television next to Sister's bed.

In addition to the charred ruins of the first floor and much of the second, there were small fascinating pieces of destruction, evidence of a violent power: Dorothy's nightgowns, all made of synthetics, were ruined, not only from smoke but from the heat, the fibers partially melted. I remember a row of medicine bottles—those little plastic ones you get prescription drugs in—leaning over on

Dorothy and Ed's bureau, half melted. The sliding shower door upstairs melted, too, bowed out of its frame as though it were a sail filled with wind. Of course it wasn't a sail—by the time I touched its billows and bulges they were hard as glass—and it hadn't been wind that pushed it into those shapes, but air and smoke at terrifically high temperatures, blasting out of the floor vent.

The rooms were empty, quiet. Something had been here and gone, it didn't matter what you called it: a wind, a dragon's tongue, a great hand that had entered the house, twisted the walls and floors, and clutched the family by their throats.

The next week, my mother mailed out the following note to family and friends:

> My sister, Cornelia Pascal, died last Friday, on March 11. She was pro-
> foundly retarded and physically incapacitated from birth. At this time,
> Monroe and I wish to express our gratitude for those who loved and cared
> for her throughout her life, particularly my parents, Irene and Henry
> Pascal, who devoted so much of themselves to her while they lived, and the
> White family, Dorothy and Eddie White and their children, who took
> Sister into the warmth of their home and gave her six wonderful years.
>
> Let us also give a thought to Sister, an independent-minded person all of
> her days, who enjoyed and suffered the pleasures and pains of existence
> within the small area of life permitted to her.

Sister didn't have a funeral. Several months later Joan took her ashes to the hill in Connecticut where Grandpa Henry's ashes had been laid, a woodsy slope overlooking the former site of his vegetable garden.

Flowree did have a funeral, however.

I thought I would stay down in Washington for it, that since Flowree had died on Saturday and they wanted an open casket it would have to be held early in the week, but my mother told me to go back to New York and return the following Friday. Relatives of the Whites were coming in from North Carolina, she explained, and many of the people coming didn't have jobs where they were allowed to take off for a funeral, so the service would be held the following weekend.

We all were there. Michael and I came in from out of town to join Paul and David and Joan and Monroe.

Collecting like that in public made the four of us kids seem more of a unit than it felt like we really were. We all had separate lives. David was at home in the day program, Michael was working in a community action center in New Jersey, Paul was nominally at 9 West Lenox but AWOL most of the time, and I had an apartment in Manhattan and worked at a literary agency. Each of our lives was filled with people whose names the rest of us didn't know. That morning, however, we huddled together.

The pews in the church the Whites belonged to curved around the altar area; it was a wide church, not one of those long, narrow ones. We sat toward the middle of the congregation. Dorothy, Eddie, and their immediate family came in through another entrance and were seated in the front row. Eddie had on a suit but you could see the bandages underneath, stretching the arms of the jacket, peering out from beneath his cuffs.

The casket was open and Flowree was lying right there.

Soon after the service had begun, a tall man in a dark suit found Monroe and asked him in a whisper if he wanted to say a few words. Monroe, who was, I think, profoundly frightened by death and almost physically uncomfortable at funerals, politely declined, but in a way that established his respect and ours for the family and the setting.

We didn't know what the ceremony would be like, what would happen. At one point, we saw the second row rise and file out of the pews, and soon it became clear that, as part of this ceremony, the entire congregation would walk by Flowree's open coffin to pay last respects. Some people spoke, some cried, some reached out to touch her hand or her powdered face. I was terrified but I knew what was expected of me.

David, Michael, Paul, and I each looked down briefly as we walked by the coffin—that was part of paying respects, it was clear. Flowree's face hadn't been damaged in the fire, so even though she had been dead for more than a few days and she was wearing a lot of makeup, there was no denying that this was sweet old Flowree. She had died in a fire, and she was gone forever.

After the entire congregation had walked by and were back in their pews, two men laid hands on the coffin, which was on wheels, and rolled it toward where the Whites were seated. They rolled it slowly past each member of the family, stopping when any one of them wanted to touch Flowree, kiss her, or place something next to her.

When they rolled Flowree in front of Dorothy, Dorothy let out a scream of grief that was a sound I had never heard before. It came from deep inside, it was both low and high, and it was a sound of terrible, terrible pain.

We milled around the outside of the church for a while after the funeral. Monroe and Joan were approached by the Whites' family and friends to exchange handshakes and words of mutual consolation. It was clear who we were, the only white faces present, clear that we didn't know most of the crowd, and courtesy, as well as ritual, demanded that we be included and welcomed.

Michael and Paul and David and I hung on the railing of the church steps.

"Luke!" said David, urgently. " 'This old man, he played one!' " I figured this meant he wanted to get going.

"We're going over to Mrs. Vaughn Hinton's, Dave," I replied. "For the wake. There'll be people there and food and we'll stay for a while."

"Come on, Luke!" he said again. I took his hand to calm him.

Michael shook his head. "I can't believe the minister let the whole thing get so out of hand," he said.

"Out of hand?" Paul asked. "What are you talking about, Michael?"

"When they rolled Flowree right up against Dorothy. When he hurt her. He hurt her, Paul. That's not right."

Paul looked flustered. He didn't want to say that hurting Dorothy was right. "Well, maybe that's just the way it is. Maybe that's what they always do."

"Well they shouldn't do it to Dorothy," Michael replied. "You heard her. It's outrageous."

"Clem!" David said.

"We'll be going soon," I told Dave. "Mom and Dad just need to say hello to some people."

"The Catholics do it, too," said Paul, regaining his composure. "At least I think so. What do Jews do, anyway?" We were allegedly Jews but since Monroe had an aversion to the social aspects of membership in a congregation and Joan was cheerfully incapable of connecting to any religion in any form, we had been raised ignorant of the most ordinary details of the faith. We picked up bits and pieces of information at random.

"Jews have the sense to cremate really soon," Michael explained. "Ashes to ashes."

There was nothing I could say to either one of them. In my opinion, Dorothy had needed to make that sound. In some ways, it was the best part of the whole thing. But I didn't have the energy to get into it. I was already fearing the immense amount of handshaking with strangers there would be at the wake.

The wake was back on Allison Street, in Mrs. Vaughn Hinton's house next door to Dorothy and Ed's. It was just what I'd expected, glistening piles of food, crowds, people approaching me whom I barely recognized, and brief interactions with the few people I did know—including Dorothy and Ed's sons, James and Eddie-Lane, whom I hadn't seen in years.

I came in with David but he soon disappeared into the crowd. Maybe he was headed for a television. I hid behind a plate of food on a chair in the corner.

Mom located me and sat down with her own plate. "These croquettes are amazing," she said. "I won't have to eat for days."

"I missed them," I replied.

She held out her fork and I had a bite. Perfectly breaded, slightly soggy underneath the crisp fried surface, with a delicate, salty flavor.

"It's weird to be in this house," I said. "The floor plan is just like Dorothy's."

"A few differences," Joan replied. "It's interesting. Dorothy and Ed could make some improvements when they remodel."

"Do you think they'll keep the little room at the back?"

"I would," said Joan. "It's handy."

I remembered Sister sitting on her bed in that small insulated sunporch, stiffly pulling up her chin as I walked in to say hello, almost looking down her nose at me. She regarded me quizzically and sniffed. Sometimes, when I was there with Joan or Dorothy, and one of us ruffled her head or gave her a special treat to eat, Sister smiled.

"Mom," I said, "do you think Sister would have had a different life if she'd been born forty or fifty years later?"

"Oh sure," Joan replied. "Therapies have changed. The whole attitude toward people like her has changed."

"Did anybody ever try any physical therapy with her?"

Joan leaned back.

"As a matter of fact, I tried once. I had her on the floor once. I was trying to see if she could crawl."

"What was she able to do?"

"Well, Grandpa stopped me. He didn't think it was right."

"He thought you'd hurt her?"

"No, he thought it was disrespectful. She wasn't a toy, she was a human being—that's how he would have put it. I was using a cookie or a carrot to see if she would try to move by herself. Anyway, I stopped. I never tried it again."

"He didn't think exercise like that was a good idea?" I asked.

Joan paused.

"You know, once, when Sister was still a child, Grandpa took her to a medical convention at Atlantic City. He wanted to know if there was a cure."

"A cure? No offense, Mom, but that's somewhat grotesque."

"Well, you know, he was a surgeon. A surgeon looks for a cure."

I thought of Sister in the fire. She didn't have a chance, not a chance.

Just then David appeared in my field of vision, working the crowd. It made me realize I hadn't seen Michael or Paul since we'd gotten there.

Dave was shaking hands like he got paid by the greeting, like someone running for office. This kind of quick encounter was perfect for him. He remembered the name and face of every person he ever met. Hello, shake hands, I'm Dave, how are you, I'm fine, so long. To me this was like jumping into cold water over and over.

A woman who I think was Dorothy's cousin smiled at him and leaned over the table, reaching to cut a fat slice of a triple-layer yellow cake, handing it to Dave.

"About time to get going, don't you think?" said Joan. "I'll just see if I can find Dorothy and Ed and tell them I'll be by next week to help out with the insurance."

Shortly thereafter, we left, using the family excuse that David was getting restless.

When the six of us came down the flight of steps from Mrs. Vaughn Hinton's to Pop's car, I looked back at Dorothy and Ed's house, boarded up, the shattered windows removed, but slices of coal-black ruin still visible here and there through the boards.

As much as it would be good to spend the night with my brothers and my parents, I thought, I would be relieved when I got on the train and headed back to New York, back to where my life really was.

11 *The Stooges*

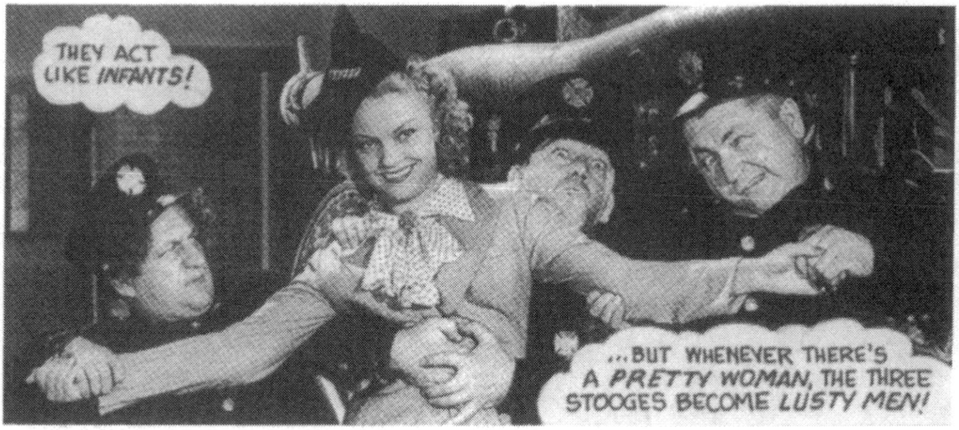
THEY ACT LIKE INFANTS!
...BUT WHENEVER THERE'S A PRETTY WOMAN, THE THREE STOOGES BECOME LUSTY MEN!

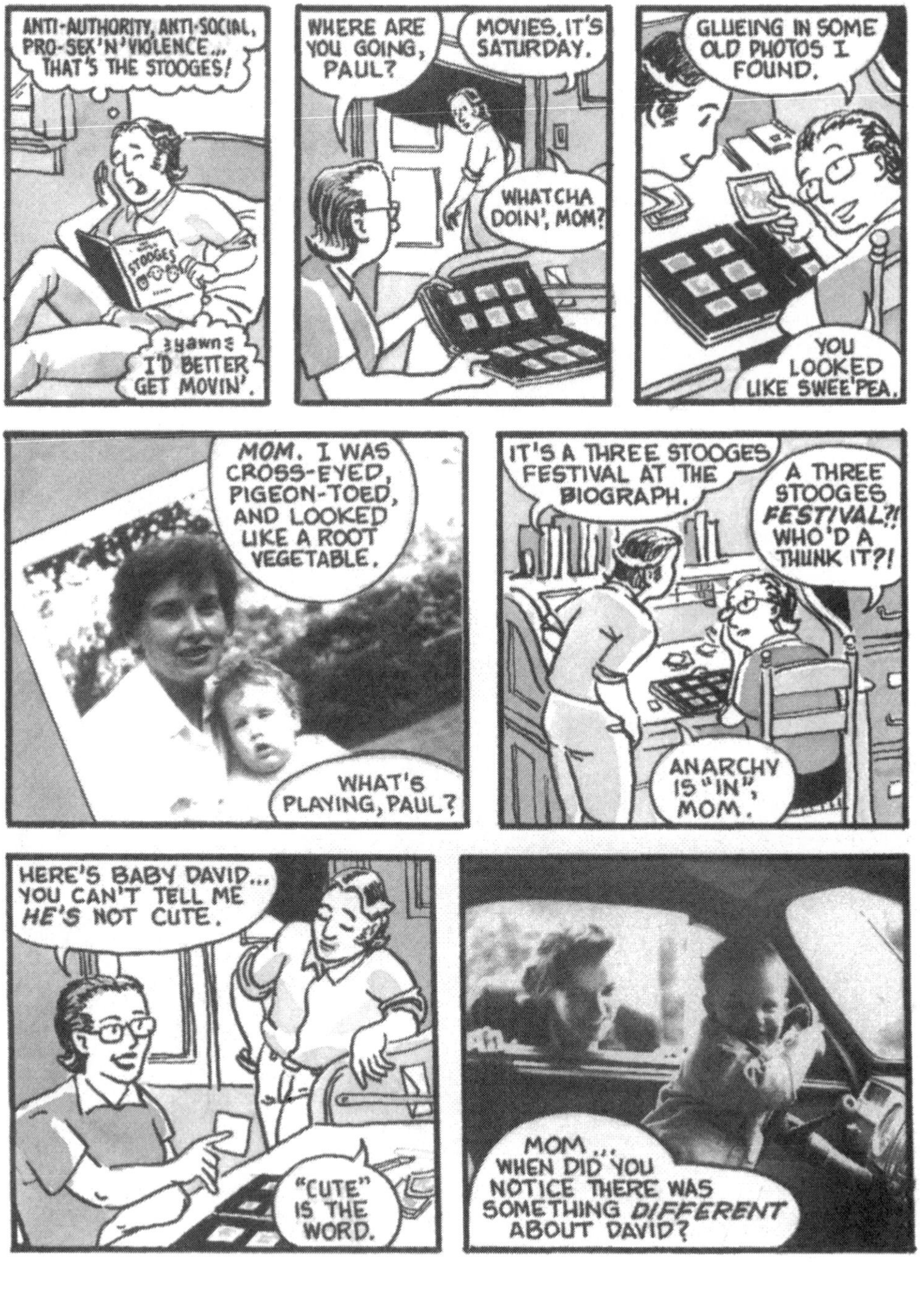
ANTI-AUTHORITY, ANTI-SOCIAL, PRO-SEX'N'VIOLENCE... THAT'S THE STOOGES!
STOOGES
yawn
I'D BETTER GET MOVIN'.
WHERE ARE YOU GOING, PAUL?
MOVIES, IT'S SATURDAY.
WHATCHA DOIN', MOM?
GLUEING IN SOME OLD PHOTOS I FOUND.
YOU LOOKED LIKE SWEE'PEA.
MOM. I WAS CROSS-EYED, PIGEON-TOED, AND LOOKED LIKE A ROOT VEGETABLE.
WHAT'S PLAYING, PAUL?
IT'S A THREE STOOGES FESTIVAL AT THE BIOGRAPH.
A THREE STOOGES FESTIVAL?! WHO'D A THINK IT?!
ANARCHY IS "IN", MOM.
HERE'S BABY DAVID... YOU CAN'T TELL ME HE'S NOT CUTE.
"CUTE" IS THE WORD.
MOM... WHEN DID YOU NOTICE THERE WAS SOMETHING DIFFERENT ABOUT DAVID?

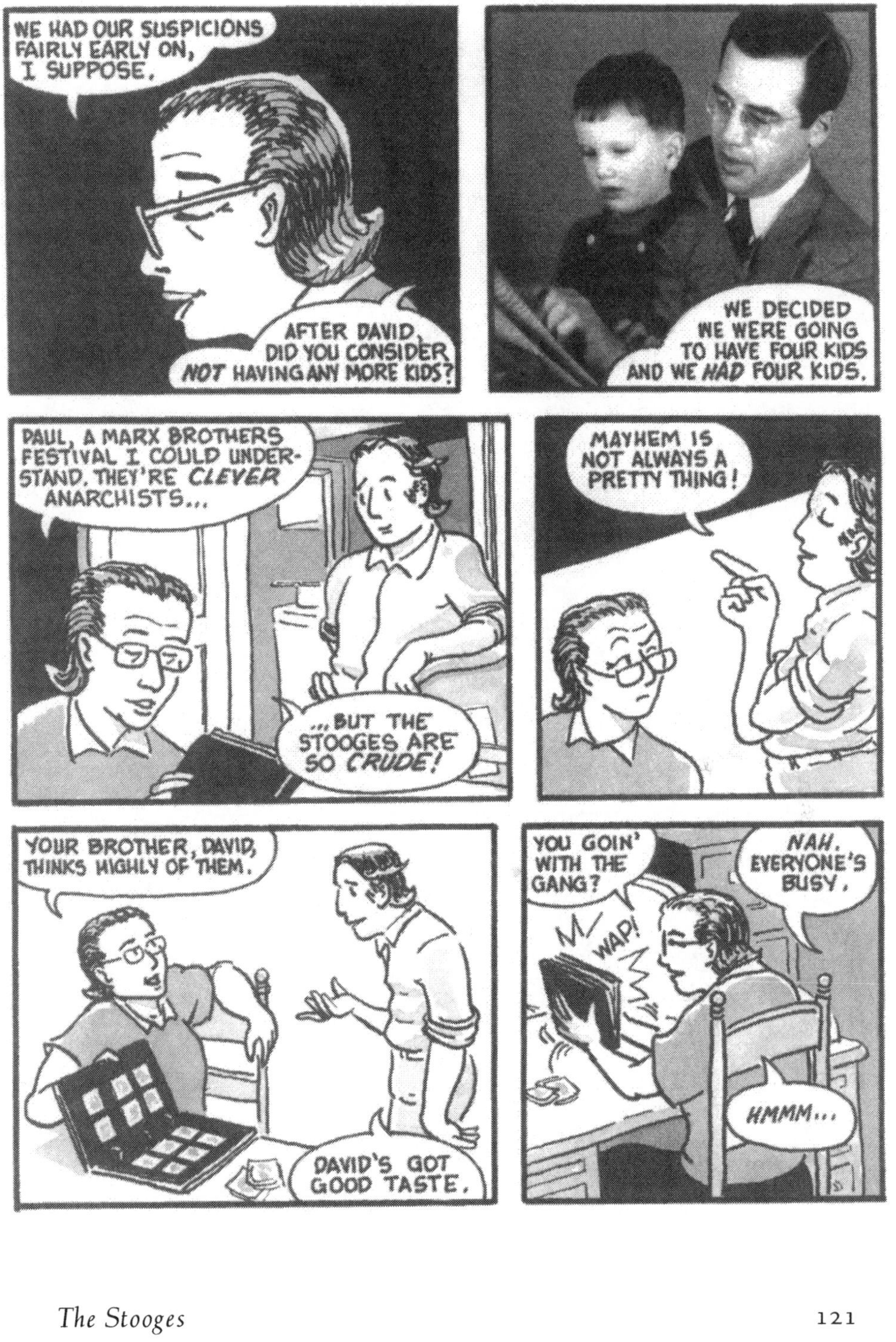
WE HAD OUR SUSPICIONS FAIRLY EARLY ON, I SUPPOSE.
AFTER DAVID, DID YOU CONSIDER *NOT* HAVING ANY MORE KIDS?
WE DECIDED WE WERE GOING TO HAVE FOUR KIDS AND WE *HAD* FOUR KIDS.
PAUL, A MARX BROTHERS FESTIVAL I COULD UNDERSTAND. THEY'RE *CLEVER* ANARCHISTS...
...BUT THE STOOGES ARE SO *CRUDE*!
MAYHEM IS NOT ALWAYS A PRETTY THING!
YOUR BROTHER, DAVID, THINKS HIGHLY OF THEM.
DAVID'S GOT GOOD TASTE.
YOU GOIN' WITH THE GANG?
NAH. EVERYONE'S BUSY.
WAP!
HMMM...

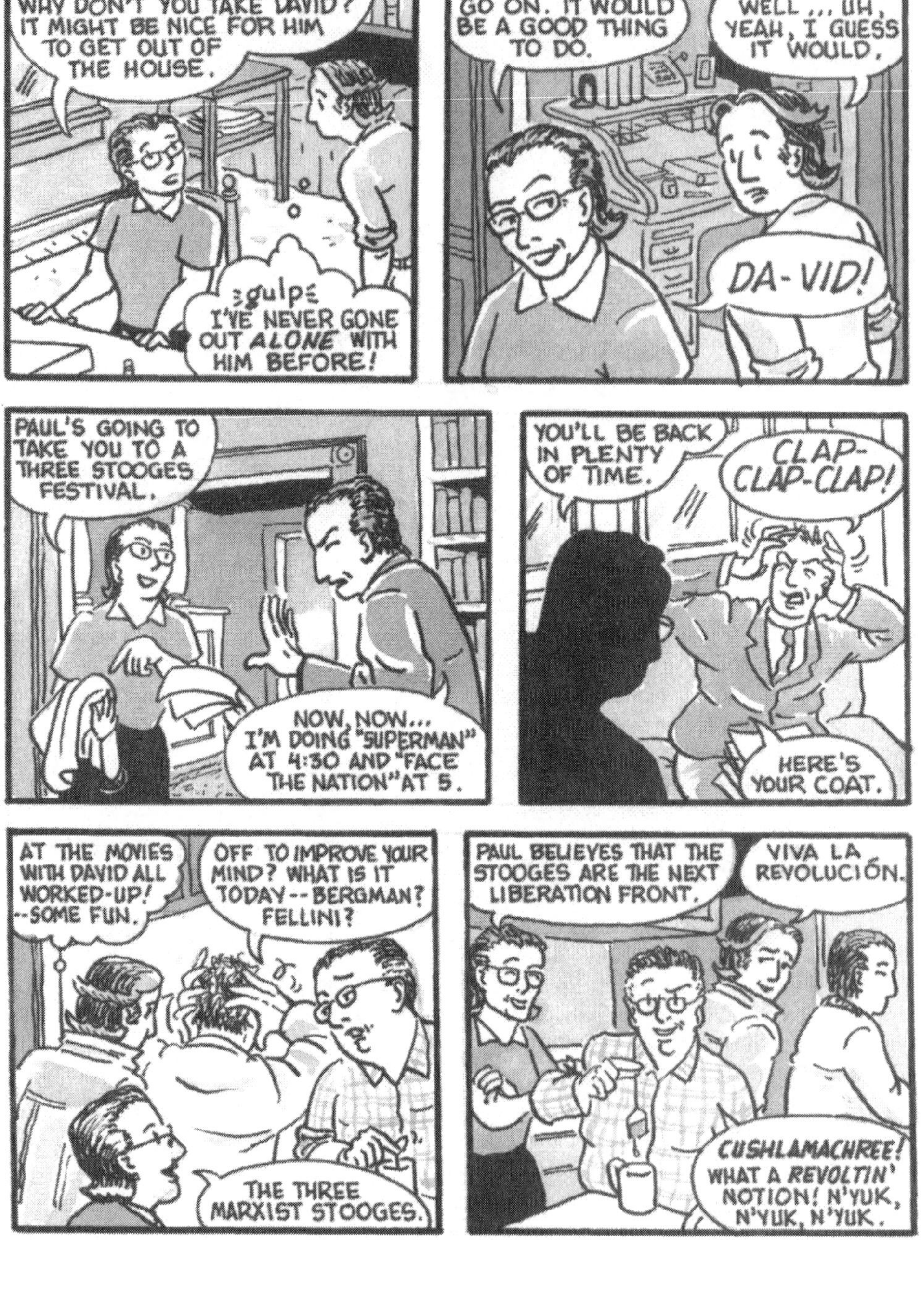

WHY DON'T YOU TAKE DAVID? IT MIGHT BE NICE FOR HIM TO GET OUT OF THE HOUSE.
gulp
I'VE NEVER GONE OUT ALONE WITH HIM BEFORE!
GO ON. IT WOULD BE A GOOD THING TO DO.
WELL ... UH, YEAH, I GUESS IT WOULD.
DA-VID!
PAUL'S GOING TO TAKE YOU TO A THREE STOOGES FESTIVAL.
NOW, NOW... I'M DOING "SUPERMAN" AT 4:30 AND "FACE THE NATION" AT 5.
YOU'LL BE BACK IN PLENTY OF TIME.
CLAP-CLAP-CLAP!
HERE'S YOUR COAT.
AT THE MOVIES WITH DAVID ALL WORKED-UP! --SOME FUN.
OFF TO IMPROVE YOUR MIND? WHAT IS IT TODAY--BERGMAN? FELLINI?
THE THREE MARXIST STOOGES.
PAUL BELIEVES THAT THE STOOGES ARE THE NEXT LIBERATION FRONT.
VIVA LA REVOLUCIÓN.
CUSHLAMACHREE! WHAT A REVOLTIN' NOTION! N'YUK, N'YUK, N'YUK.

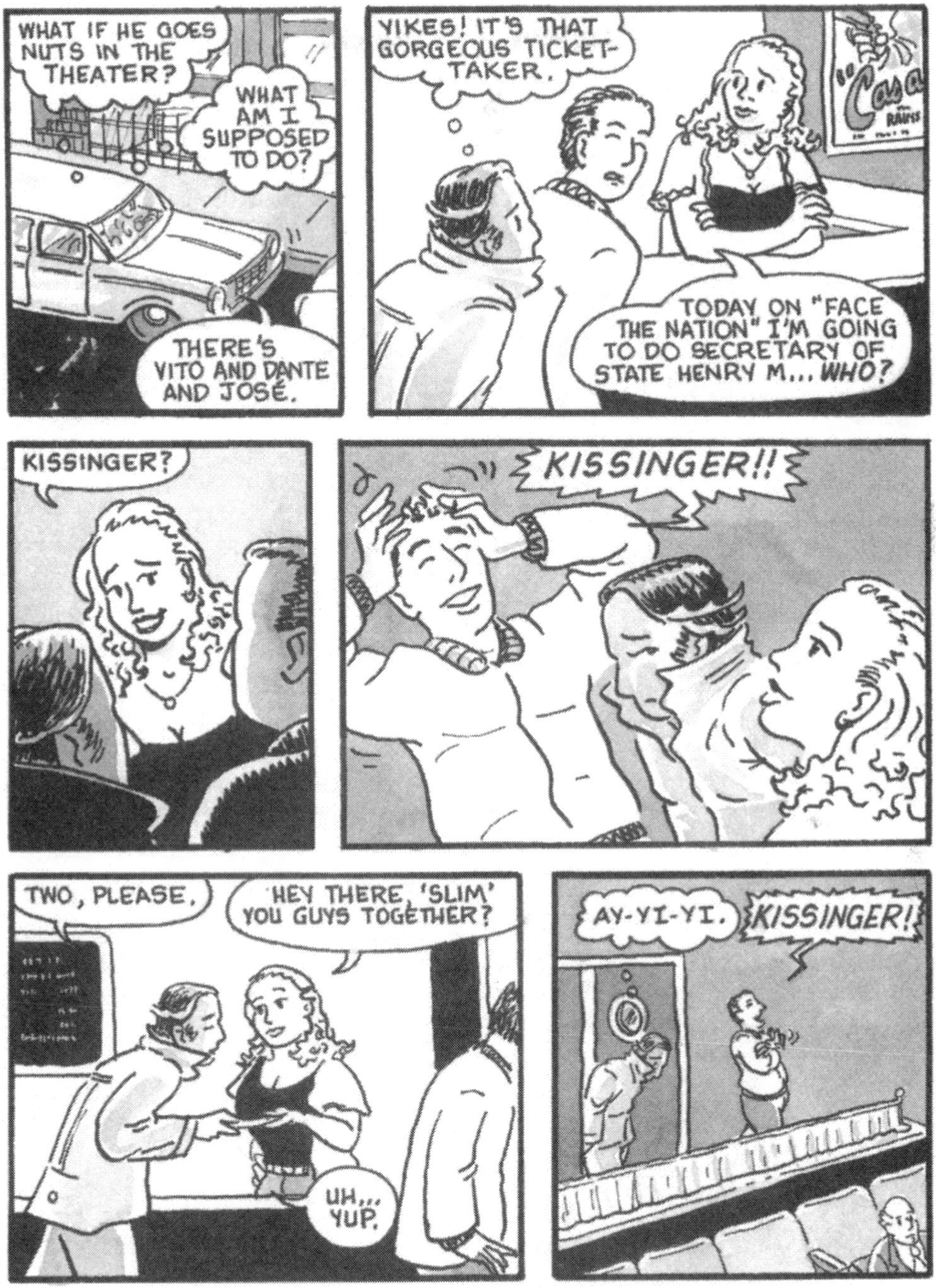
WHAT IF HE GOES NUTS IN THE THEATER?
WHAT AM I SUPPOSED TO DO?
THERE'S VITO AND DANTE AND JOSÉ.
YIKES! IT'S THAT GORGEOUS TICKET-TAKER.
TODAY ON "FACE THE NATION" I'M GOING TO DO SECRETARY OF STATE HENRY M... WHO?
KISSINGER?
KISSINGER!!
TWO, PLEASE.
HEY THERE, 'SLIM' YOU GUYS TOGETHER?
UH,... YUP.
AY-YI-YI.
KISSINGER!

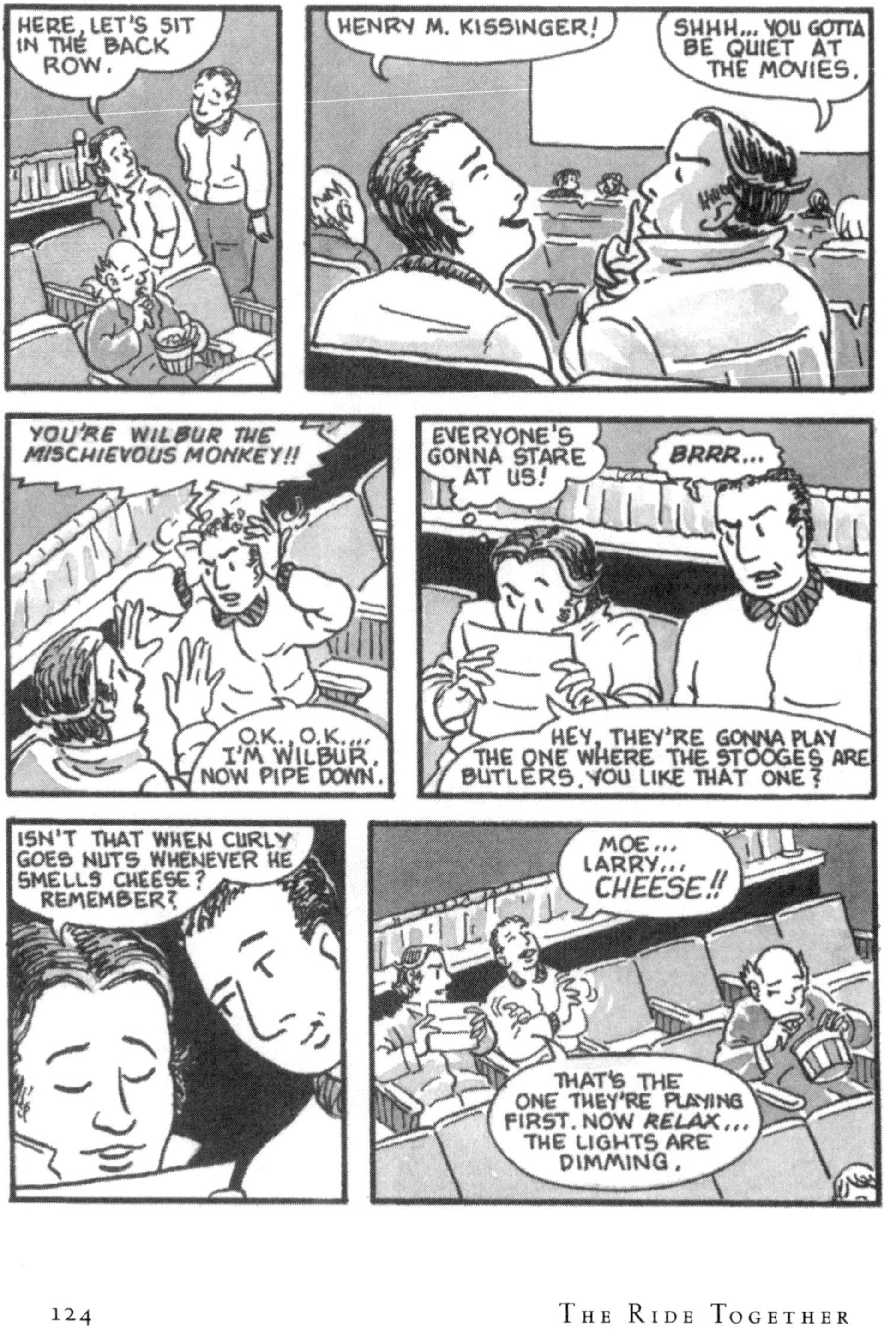
HERE, LET'S SIT IN THE BACK ROW.
HENRY M. KISSINGER!
SHHH... YOU GOTTA BE QUIET AT THE MOVIES.
YOU'RE WILBUR THE MISCHIEVOUS MONKEY!!
O.K., O.K..., I'M WILBUR, NOW PIPE DOWN.
EVERYONE'S GONNA STARE AT US!
BRRR...
HEY, THEY'RE GONNA PLAY THE ONE WHERE THE STOOGES ARE BUTLERS. YOU LIKE THAT ONE?
ISN'T THAT WHEN CURLY GOES NUTS WHENEVER HE SMELLS CHEESE? REMEMBER?
MOE... LARRY... CHEESE!!
THAT'S THE ONE THEY'RE PLAYING FIRST. NOW RELAX... THE LIGHTS ARE DIMMING.

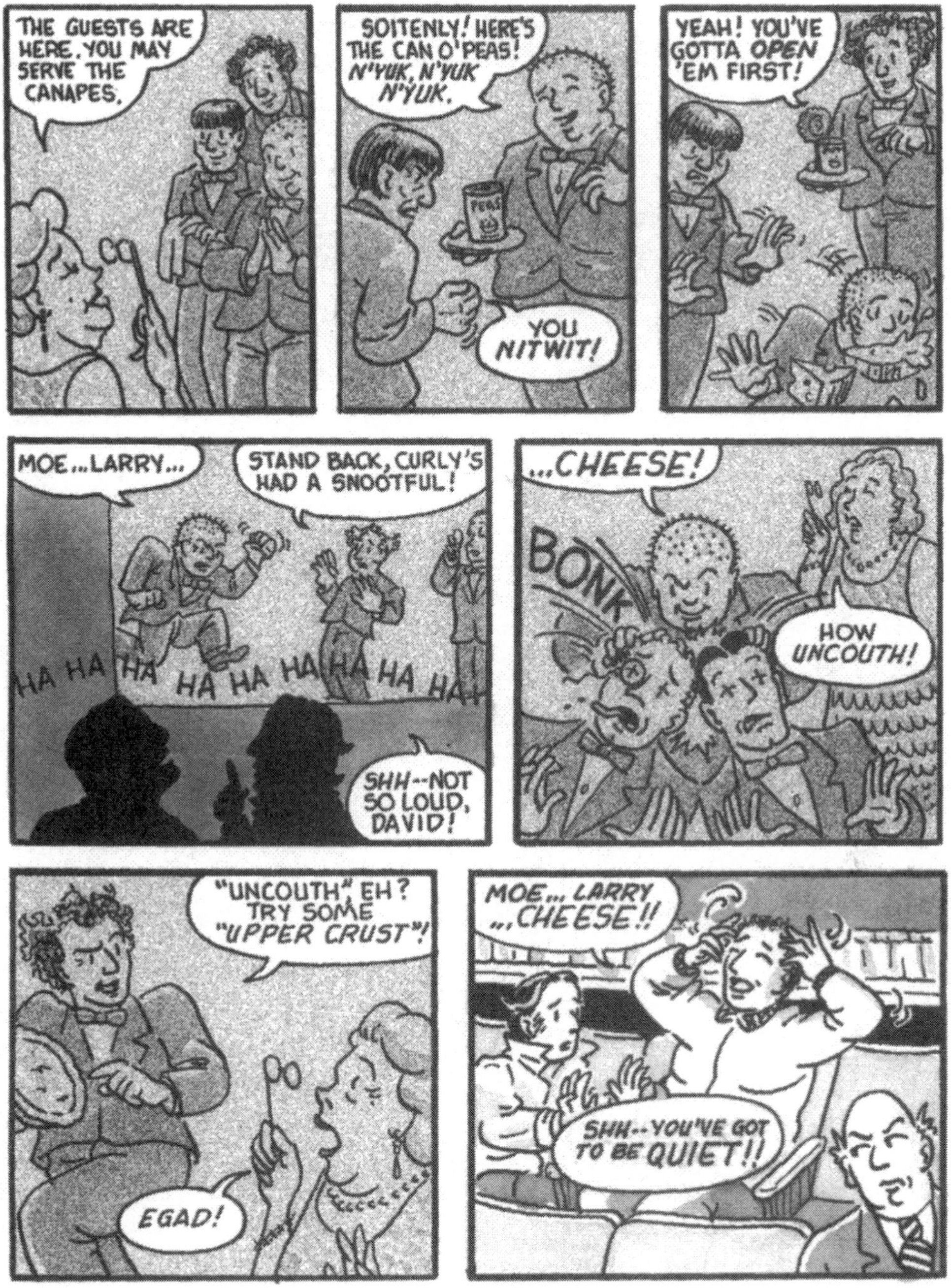
THE GUESTS ARE HERE. YOU MAY SERVE THE CANAPES.
SOITENLY! HERE'S THE CAN O' PEAS! N'YUK, N'YUK N'YUK.
PEAS
YOU NITWIT!
YEAH! YOU'VE GOTTA OPEN 'EM FIRST!
MOE...LARRY...
STAND BACK, CURLY'S HAD A SNOOTFUL!
HA HA HA HA HA HA HA HA HA
SHH--NOT SO LOUD, DAVID!
...CHEESE!
BONK
HOW UNCOUTH!
"UNCOUTH," EH? TRY SOME "UPPER CRUST"!
EGAD!
MOE... LARRY ...CHEESE!!
SHH--YOU'VE GOT TO BE QUIET!!

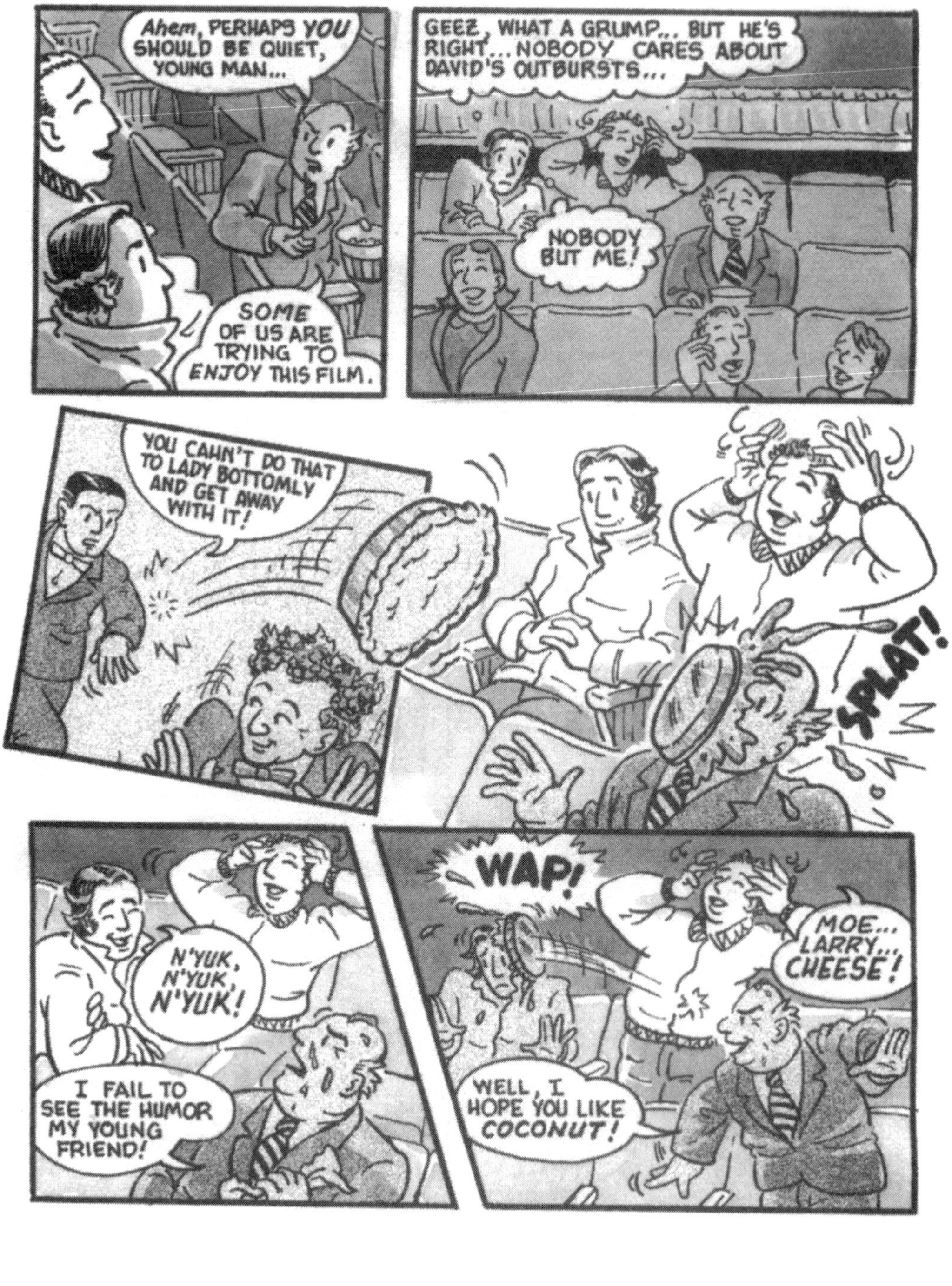
Ahem, PERHAPS YOU SHOULD BE QUIET, YOUNG MAN...
SOME OF US ARE TRYING TO ENJOY THIS FILM.
GEEZ, WHAT A GRUMP... BUT HE'S RIGHT... NOBODY CARES ABOUT DAVID'S OUTBURSTS...
NOBODY BUT ME!
YOU CAHN'T DO THAT TO LADY BOTTOMLY AND GET AWAY WITH IT!
SPLAT!
N'YUK, N'YUK, N'YUK!
I FAIL TO SEE THE HUMOR MY YOUNG FRIEND!
WAP!
MOE... LARRY... CHEESE!
WELL, I HOPE YOU LIKE COCONUT!

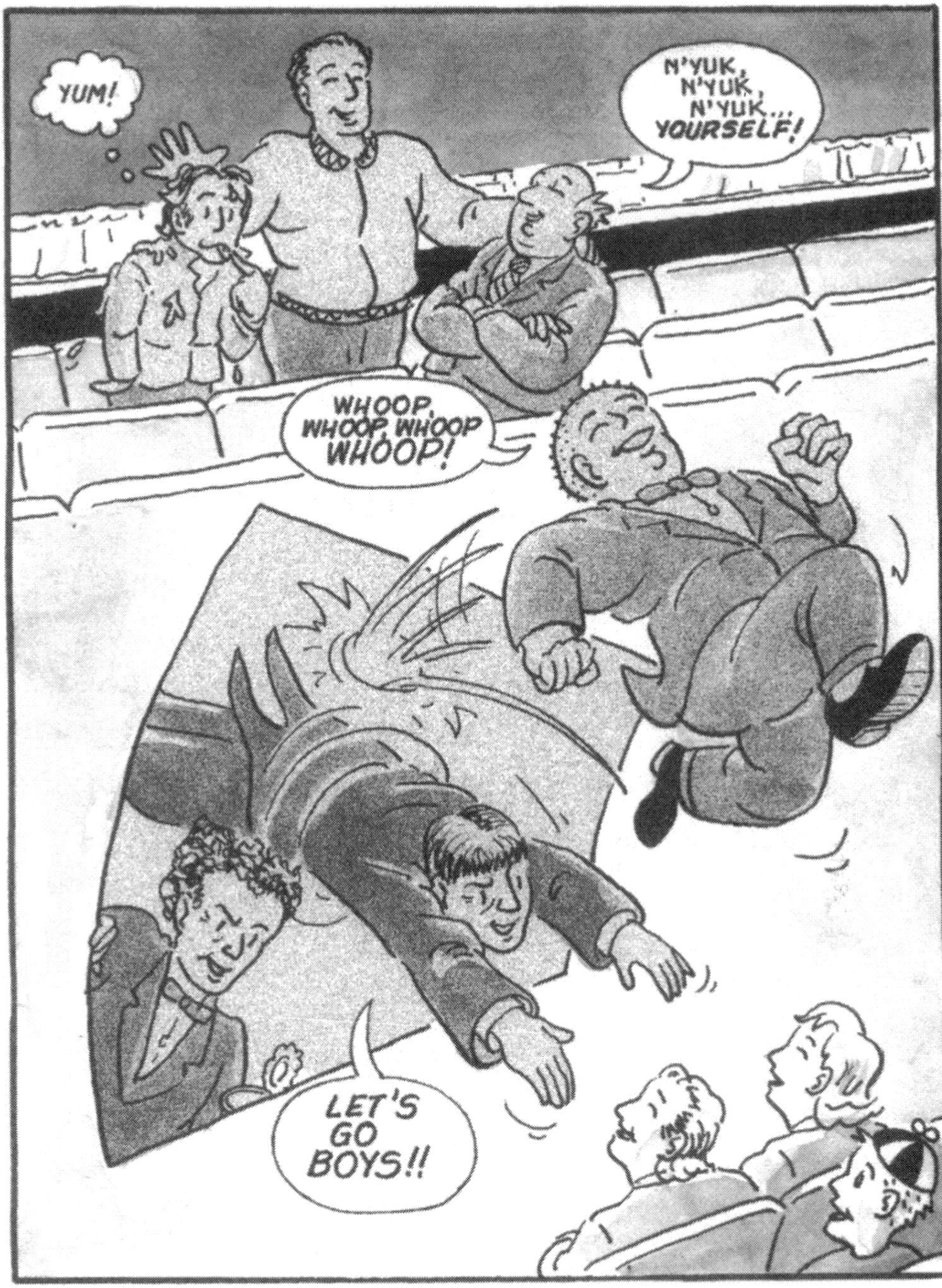
YUM!
N'YUK, N'YUK, N'YUK... YOURSELF!
WHOOP, WHOOP, WHOOP WHOOP!
LET'S GO BOYS!!

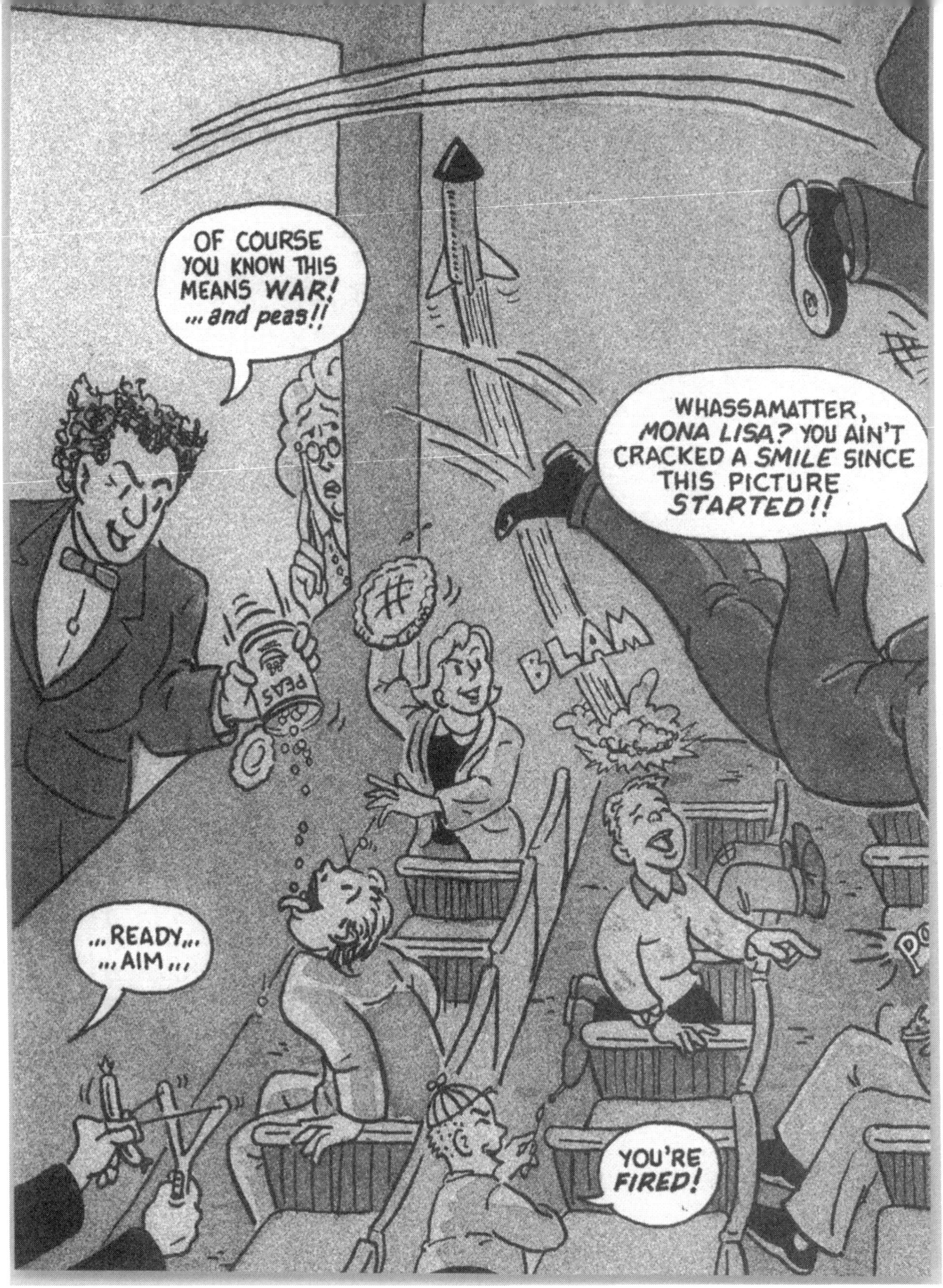
OF COURSE YOU KNOW THIS MEANS WAR! ...and peas!!
WHASSAMATTER, MONA LISA? YOU AIN'T CRACKED A SMILE SINCE THIS PICTURE STARTED!!
PEAS
BLAM
...READY,... ...AIM...
YOU'RE FIRED!

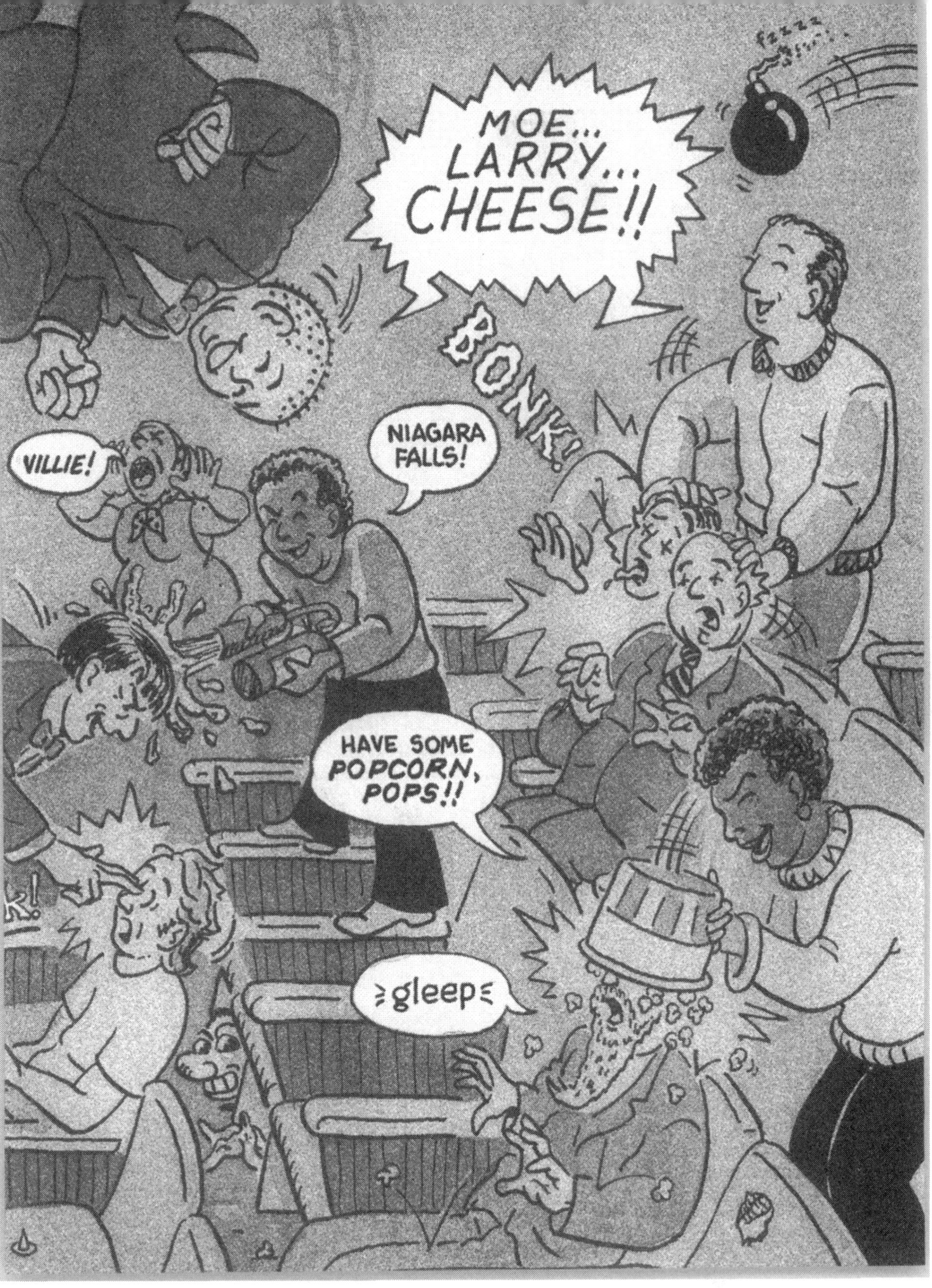
MOE... LARRY... CHEESE!!
BONK!
VILLIE!
NIAGARA FALLS!
HAVE SOME POPCORN, POPS!!
gleep

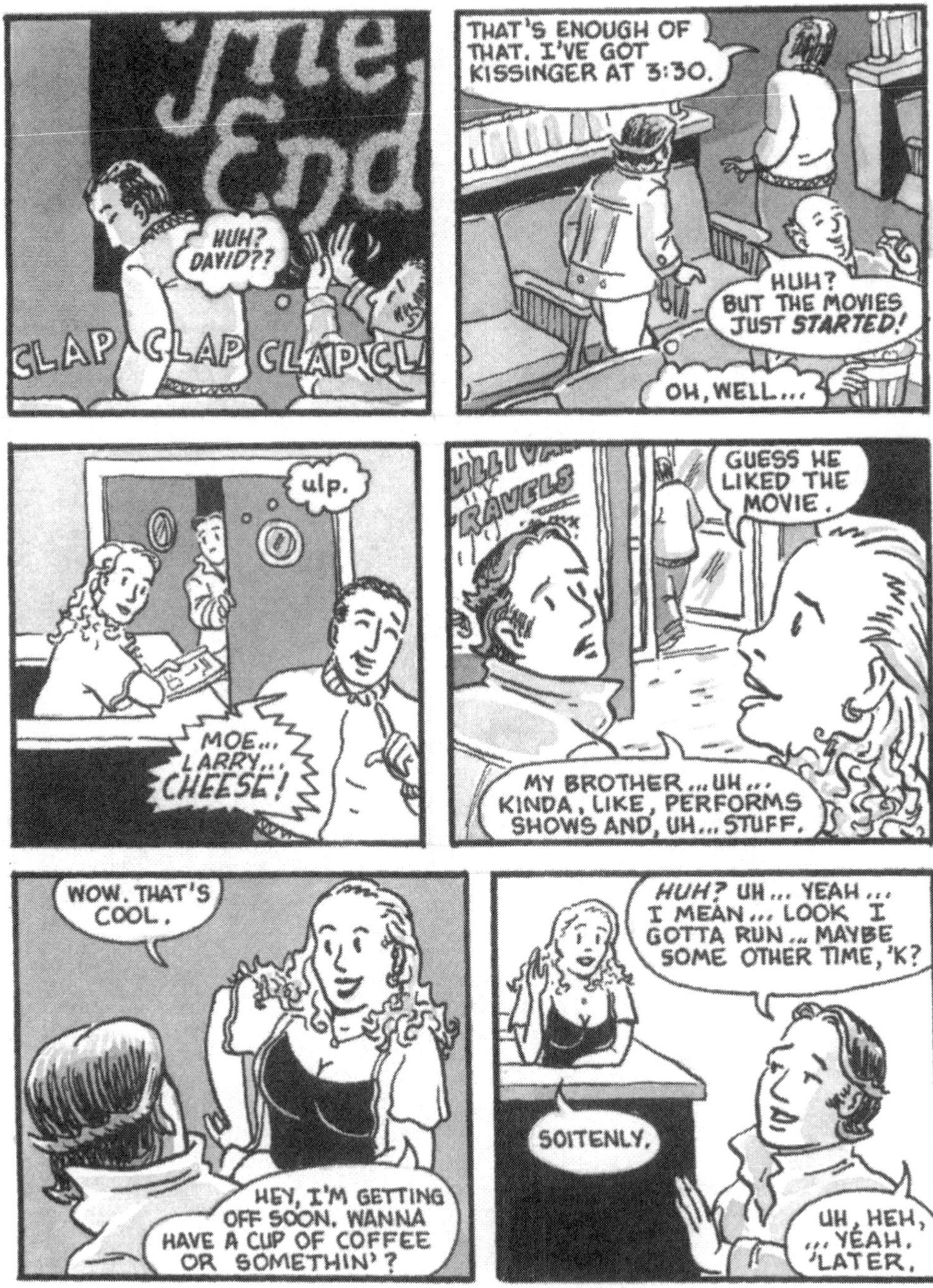
The End
HUH? DAVID??
CLAP CLAP CLAP CL
THAT'S ENOUGH OF THAT. I'VE GOT KISSINGER AT 3:30.
HUH? BUT THE MOVIES JUST STARTED!
OH, WELL...
ulp.
MOE... LARRY... CHEESE!
GUESS HE LIKED THE MOVIE.
MY BROTHER ... UH ... KINDA, LIKE, PERFORMS SHOWS AND, UH... STUFF.
WOW. THAT'S COOL.
HEY, I'M GETTING OFF SOON. WANNA HAVE A CUP OF COFFEE OR SOMETHIN'?
HUH? UH ... YEAH ... I MEAN ... LOOK I GOTTA RUN ... MAYBE SOME OTHER TIME, 'K?
SOITENLY.
UH, HEH, ... YEAH. 'LATER.

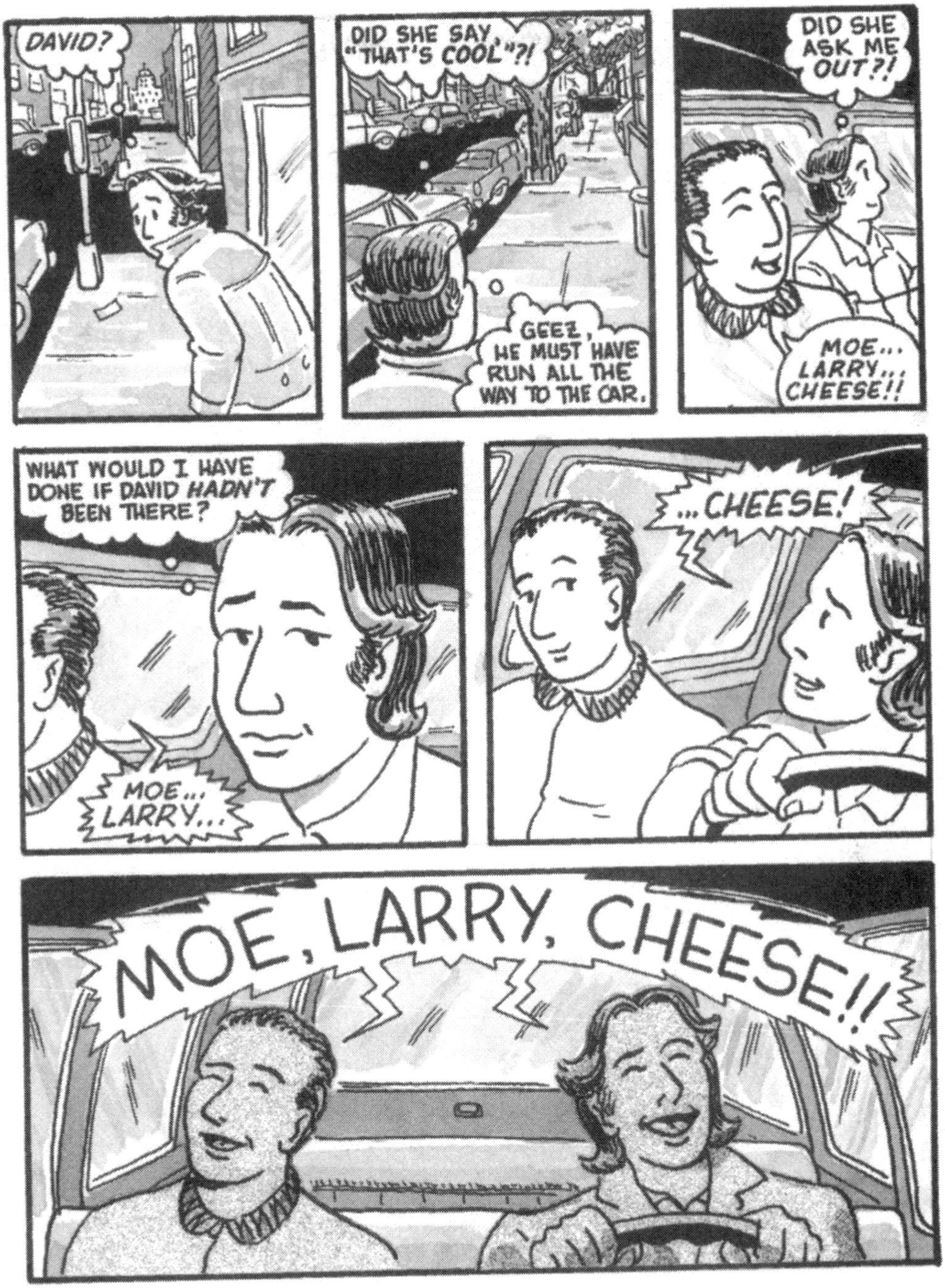
DAVID?
DID SHE SAY, "THAT'S COOL"?!
GEEZ, HE MUST HAVE RUN ALL THE WAY TO THE CAR.
DID SHE ASK ME OUT?!
MOE... LARRY... CHEESE!!
WHAT WOULD I HAVE DONE IF DAVID HADN'T BEEN THERE?
MOE... LARRY...
...CHEESE!
MOE, LARRY, CHEESE!!

12   *The Big Yellow Balloon*

The first time David was ever in my charge I was twenty-seven years old and he was thirty-two. One Friday in September I came down from New York, where I now worked as a book editor, to cover for my parents while they took a week's vacation on the Vineyard.

Pop was in a good mood that Friday night. He was looking forward to a holiday and he and Joan had finally found a place for David. The place wouldn't be ready until the following spring, as soon as construction was completed on a new residential hall—but this looked like a long-term solution.

It was a place in western Pennsylvania called Brook Farm, run by a couple named Rudolph and Diane Zarek.

The Zareks had known David from a day program he'd been in that Diane had run years back. When Joan reminded them of David's condition the Zareks said, "No problem; that's exactly the kind of person we want to help." They had a big piece of land in the countryside and gotten a good staff together and trained and the place was up and running. Brook Farm was not as close to the family as my parents would have liked—a good two-hour drive each way—and it took a large chunk of our capital, but the distance wasn't impossible and, Monroe explained, considering what it was buying, neither was the money. David would have the possibility of a better life, more to do, more people to be friendly with, more people who would help him to develop better control over the things that agitated and hurt him so much.

Michael and Paul and I had all left home and now our oldest brother would, too.

"Have I got something to show you, Judy," said my father. We were sitting in the study. Pop put out his cigarette tidily—Monroe had boasted for years that he could quit smoking whenever he felt like it; apparently he also believed that possessing the ability to quit was an acceptable substitute for actually doing it—and picked up a newspaper clipping he had kept to show me.

A woman had written in to a helpful household-hints column explaining that she had found a time saver—instead of wasting precious time slicing banana into chunks for the family's morning cereal, she now used a potato masher. With one stroke the job was done!

"I tried it," said Monroe, smiling like a well-fed cat. "It does not cut the banana. It *flattens* the banana. The most outrageous thing about this pinheaded little female is that she truly believes that she is too busy to slice a banana in the morning. Who in the world is too busy to slice a banana?"

Finding Brook Farm was a lucky break, because David had been discharged from his day program the year before. Joan, in her early sixties, and Monroe, nearly seventy, were watching out for him at home.

Despite the fact that in the last few years the people working with David had observed that he was making strong efforts to better control his outbursts, in his final six months in the program those violent attacks increased. The staff at the day program were well trained to work with most people in the program but they couldn't handle my six-foot-two, 175-pound brother when he went out of control. Because of what they called his "dual diagnosis" of mental retardation and emotional disturbance, Dave sometimes hurt others in the program as well as staff.

"Underneath these problems," the discharge letter read, "many have found David to be a warm and wonderful person. David can and does learn, he likes to be with other people, and he generally enjoys most program activities. The problem, then, has been to find a program which could adequately serve David's 'dual handicaps,' when in fact no such programs have existed."

In the day program he'd had friends, people he talked about still. He'd had work; Dave was on the landscaping crew, where, according to his supervisor, not only did he do his share but also kept busy telling his coworkers when they were goldbricking. Now, unless Joan took him shopping or on other expeditions or to the occasional family party, David had no social contacts beyond us. Our parents had looked into many other options until they heard about Brook Farm, but other places had been too restrictive or not restrictive enough, or too far away.

So until the spring rolled around, David roamed upstairs and downstairs doing shows, he watched television, he listened to his records in his room, and he wrote his papers.

Monroe was retired by this time and Joan's domestic responsibilities had lightened as most of us left home, so both our parents had more time for the work that they had always done on the side: advocating on behalf of people with disabilities. They spent most of their time in Grandpa's bedroom, once again a study, the smallest space in the house if you didn't count the bathrooms and closets.

The two of them worked for hours in silence, except for the occasional phone call or until one of them asked what their position was supposed to be on an issue the other one covered. Joan kept the house and covered the meetings in the county seat. Also, she was part of a team assessing how the federal laws that now integrated children with disabilities into the school system were actually being applied. Monroe worked the state legislature in Annapolis and, when he had the chance, the feds on Capitol Hill. After all those years as an attorney, he knew how to persuade, cut deals, and write laws. On top of the bookshelf piles of plaques and trophies accumulated.

The house, which had accommodated so much action, now echoed emptily the perpetual orbit of three satellites, each in a different rotation.

Monroe and Joan always rose before dawn to start the long drive north to Martha's Vineyard, so I woke up Saturday morning to a big empty house containing only David. Coming down for breakfast, I stood in the stairwell landing and observed my responsibility.

He was watching television in the kids' living room, sitting in a trapezoidal splash of light on the couch. A stack of paper and a book lay on the table near him. David often wrote with his papers on his lap, using a large book as a writing board.

"Just you and me, Dave," I told him, descending, entering the living room, bending to kiss him hello on his cheek, not quite knowing what to say. "We going to do okay this week? A little break, huh?"

He replied, "Yes, ma'am!" and twiddled his fingers on his head in happiness.

The papers were covered with television show synopses, in his typical style, sprinkling uppercase letters within words, underlining a letter here or there, as though for emphasis, or according to some private code or some hidden rhythm. The book was a children's hardcover, flat, tall, wide, and thin, just the right shape for a tablet. On its front Babar and Celeste, the King and Queen of the Elephants, rose into the sky in a basket attached to a big yellow balloon, waving good-bye with their royal handkerchiefs and cheerfully paying no attention to the fact that the balloon was about twelve times too small to lift their weight. A snapshot from the world of David.

I headed into the kitchen. All was in order.

David had left his cereal bowl in the sink several hours earlier, a few bright gold cornflakes stuck to the inside, staggered toward the bowl's rim as though they were trying to crawl out. David never understood that you had to wash the bowl right after you used it or the flakes would stick as though the milk were glue. I filled up the bowl with water, figuring the stuff would be soaked free by the time I had to wash my coffee cup.

He'd already put his hot dogs in water in a saucepan on the stove; he always had hot dogs for lunch. There were four in the pot; he was allowed three. I removed one, demonstrating that I knew the rules. David had placed his plate, with a big dollop of ballpark mustard and a fork, on the counter, ready for his lunch at ten-thirty. I needed to keep an eye on the kitchen from about ten on, because when Dave cooked his hot dogs he often turned up the heat as high as possible; this burned out the bottoms of pans.

After making up a pot of espresso and laying it on the burner, I went outside to retrieve the *Washington Post* from the corner of the front steps, where *Post* carriers had been throwing it for the previous twenty-four years.

On my way back with the paper, as I walked through the dining room a wide glint of light hit my eye. All of the glass tumblers in the house, from the small juice glasses to the crystal highball set, had been filled with water and set in a long row on the sideboard. In several, tiny bubbles sparkled.

I figured David had done this, but I didn't know why. I decided to leave it as it was for the time being.

Late Tuesday afternoon, David finished a session of *Meet the Press*, where he interviewed Prime Minister Ben-Gurion. I had listened with one ear as I sat reading in the next room. Our dog, Maia, a Siberian husky, lay on the couch next to me.

"Good show, Dave," I said. "What's next?"

David nodded his head thoughtfully and patted his forehead. Then, bending the long fingers of one hand with the other, as though counting, he rattled off about fifteen names of political figures, ending up with the current secretary of state.

"You doing Mike Mansfield this week?" I asked. He had told me before that the former senator from Montana was slated for an appearance while I was going to be home, but although David scheduled the man regularly his air dates always slipped into the future.

"No," David corrected me. "Mansfield is on for Thanksgiving. Thanksgiving." His fingers spread out again and again he ticked off names. "At Thanksgiving there'll be Mike Mansfield on *Issues and Answers*, Senator Henry M. 'Scoop' Jackson on *Meet the Press*, and, on *Face the Nation*, General Curtis E. LeMay."

I would never hear Mansfield, not in this life. One David chased the Mike Mansfield interview through eternity and another David pushed it eternally further into the future.

Dave rubbed Maia gently on her furry back and walked away. I listened to where he walked. I heard the sound of a drawer opening in the living room. I didn't have to worry, I told myself, since that was where David kept a stash of his papers. He wasn't making off with paper that wasn't his—all paper in the house needed to be completely hidden, certainly blank paper, which he felt was his right to take if he found it, but documents too, since sometimes David was compelled to steal paper that had been written on and write all over the backs.

I heard the sound of pages flipping as he rearranged his papers according to schemes and in service of purposes known only to David. It didn't sound any faster than usual. It didn't sound as though he was getting upset. Everything was fine.

All that week, even though my brother and I rarely spoke, and when we did it was in the code of David, I was aware of him all the time. Whether I was on the porch, or in the living room, or cooking supper, I knew exactly where David was inside the great block of the house and what he was doing. It felt something like a hangover, a minor, slightly painful distracting all-day headache.

On Thursday morning I was organizing my thoughts about which trade paperbacks I could manage to get together to make next year's fall list when I discovered that David had put an entire gallon of laundry detergent in a single wash. The empty jug, tossed into the trash bucket, evidence of David's compulsive action, seemed like the aftermath of a small hurricane, a hole blown through ordinary polite behavior. I twisted the washer's knob to On, punched it in, heard the water start to fill the machine to run the clothes through a second time and rinse off the rest of the soap, went upstairs, and said good morning to David. Just to check.

David was furiously attacking his head with his fingers and completely wound up in his rage but managed to let me know what the problem was: I had forgotten to get him paper. I made a very quick drive to the drugstore, hoping he wouldn't do anything awful while I was gone, hoping that the paper would calm him and not stir up the agitation. I considered giving him two pads, to make up for my mistake, then decided against it. Too much could be worse than too little. I pictured David writing and writing and flipping the pages into a stack and speeding up and writing some more and flipping and flipping and writing, faster and faster in an unimaginably endless task.

It was my fault. I should have gotten him what we both knew he expected and needed.

At the back door David took the pad from me, raced through the house in his long stiff stride, sat on the couch, and started right in. He didn't waste time being angry—getting the paper was the important thing. And although part of David was annoyed with me for being so stupid, another part of him knew that I was the person who had gotten him what he wanted and could continue to do so in the future.

I made sure he had his lunch—the three hot dogs with mustard and a glass of milk—when he wanted it. When he came into the kitchen with the empty plate and glass, I asked him what shows he was doing. We talked.

He was calming down. Slowly, the autism let go of the frustration. The autism stopped battering my brother with the frustration and went back to its usual habit, which was fascinating David with the patterns and images and ideas inside his head. I never got back to thinking about next fall's paperback list, not that day.

Our household had it easy. Some people with autism banged their heads repetitively with their hands, or they banged their heads against walls; some threw things—one family we knew had put Plexiglas over the windows because otherwise there would have been broken glass all over the place; some ran, ran anyplace, around the house, outside, across streets, who knew where.

For these families every day was a workout, a physical workout.

An hour later I put down my book and checked on my brother. He was upstairs in his room. On the record player the Mitch Miller Singers, who had been popular on television in the early 1960s, crooned the folk song "Listen to the Mockingbird." David walked back and forth along the oriental carpet at a moderate and calm pace, waving his arms to the music.

The next afternoon, David went into the dining room. I looked up from where I was reading on the living room couch.

Our parents would be home Saturday, in time for dinner, the four of us together.

David wore his suit jacket and tie. He wore dark glasses. He took a tumbler of water from the sideboard and sat down at his place at the foot of the table.

Three glasses were left.

He had marked out the week with the glasses. Each interview had its own assigned tumbler. When the glasses were gone, our week together would be done. Once you understood it, it seemed obvious.

He had hundreds of tricks that we didn't understand to organize the world.

David sat down, cleared his throat, and announced the appearance of Ambassador Covey T. Oliver—a friend of Monroe's from his time many years back in the State Department. Oliver actually had been an ambassador at one point, but David routinely reassigned him to new postings—on *Face the Nation.*

As it turned out, the four of us did not have dinner together the next evening.

Less than an hour after our parents had arrived at the house, at the end of a carefully paced ten-hour journey down the East Coast during which they traded off driving duty every two hours, Monroe was lying on the floor of the study, telling Joan to call an ambulance.

He felt pains in his chest and along his arm, he said.

The rescue squad arrived within six minutes, walking in the front door with a stretcher and boxes of tools.

From then I saw no more. My job was to keep the dog and David out of the way.

David and Maia and I sat on the porch until the medics carried Pop, cocooned in white sheets, on a stretcher to the van, where they quickly, gently, loaded him in and snapped shut the doors.

My father had suddenly become a fragile thing.

The ambulance's sirens screamed down the street until they were absorbed by distance. Joan's car followed. She would call later, from the hospital.

The process of whatever was going to happen had begun.

When I called David to dinner, he was sitting in the living room, wearing his pajamas but hard at work nonetheless. He had a pile of paper, from heaven knows where, and I knew that he would not stop writing until he had covered every page.

I went back into the kitchen and turned down everything on the stove, just to keep it warm and came back to keep David company.

He did not write as rapidly as usual but in a steady slower rhythm. He methodically flipped each written sheet onto the waiting pile and immediately started a new page, his mind so full of what needed to be written that he did not pause for a moment.

As it turned out, Monroe's heart attack, while serious, was not fatal. There was even some good that came of it—Pop stopped smoking, and, after a couple of months, cut out the hard liquor.

At that moment, however, David and I didn't know anything except that Pop was gone.

Sitting there, watching my brother, I didn't ask him what he felt. After a week together that really wasn't necessary.

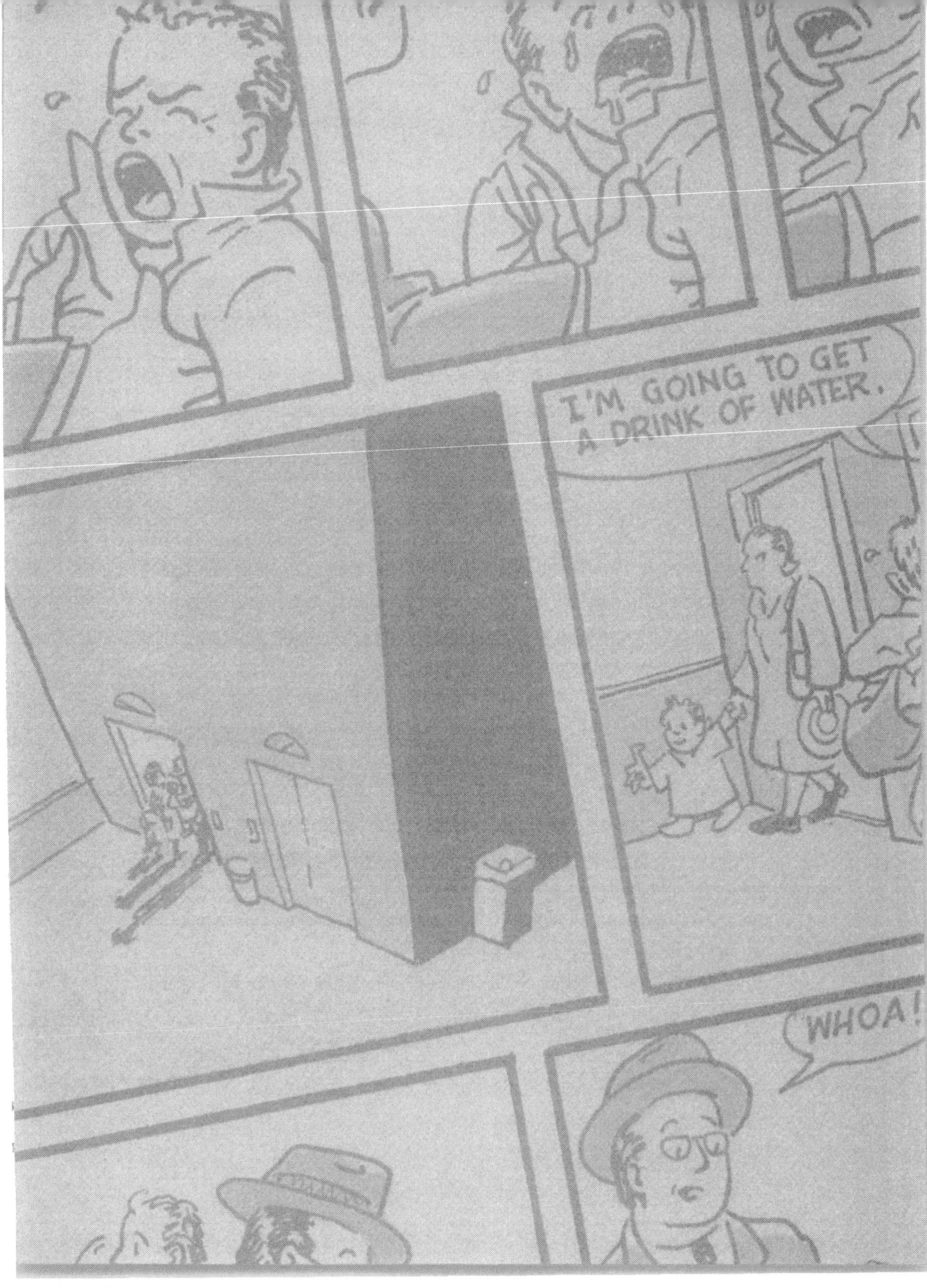
I'M GOING TO GET A DRINK OF WATER.
WHOA!

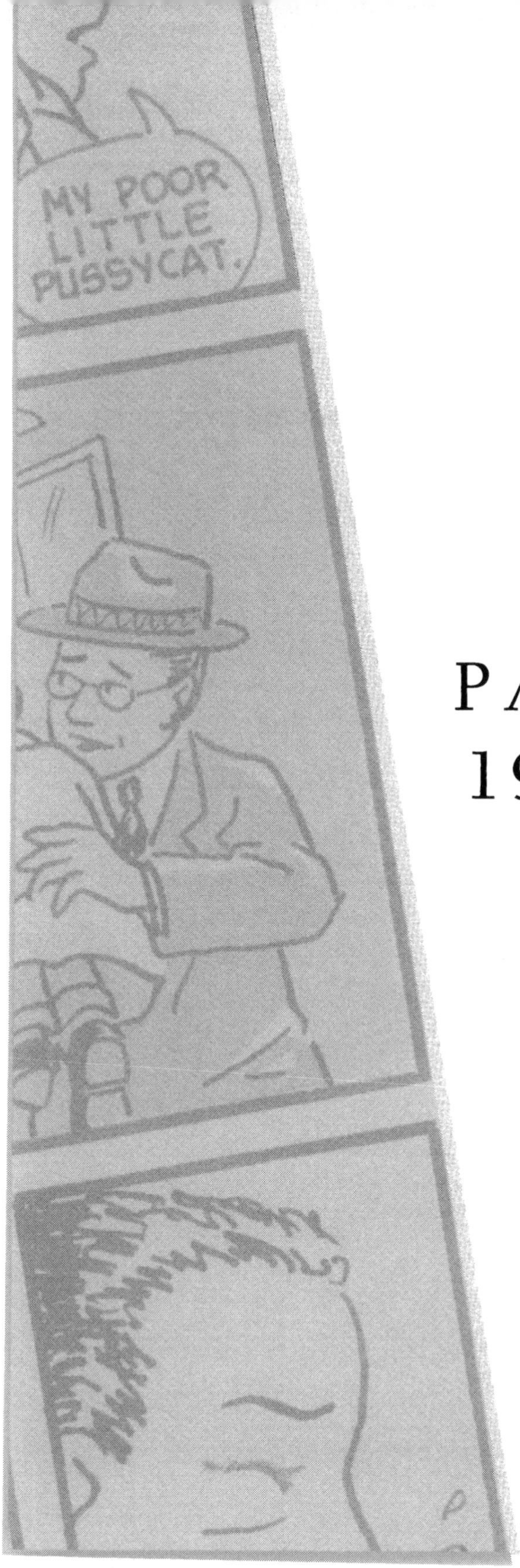
MY POOR LITTLE PUSSYCAT.

PART FOUR
1990—1996

13 My Real Brother

Ten years later, David had graduated from the central campus at Brook Farm to a small supervised house in the nearby town. David and the two other residents there lived on an ordinary street. They walked to the grocery store in the afternoons and got coffee and doughnuts. We hadn't expected that he'd be able to handle so much freedom, but all reports on Dave were good ones, and his talk was full of happy references to his house counselor.

The way the setup worked, David came home regularly. There, nothing was demanded of him: he could relax and do as many shows as he liked, he was not being improved by work or by counselors, he was just with his parents and whatever siblings were home. Family vacations, in short, just like the rest of us took.

He had holidays in February, Easter, summer vacation (at the end of May into early June), his birthday in August, Thanksgiving, and Christmas.

The February holiday happened over the Presidents' Day weekend but our version of it didn't have to do with presidents. We had invented an event to warm up that cold and dark month. As many of us as possible came home and we celebrated our dog's birthday. Michael baked Maia a birthday cake, which she didn't eat but we did, and we invited friends over. We had drinks at six-thirty and dinner around seven and sang "Happy Birthday" to Maia over the cake, candles blazing. That past winter, however, and unfortunately, the dog had died, so the weekend had had a hole in it where the party used to be.

All the other holidays continued as usual, all of them set down, dates and days of the week cemented in place for years in advance, double-checked regularly in David's head.

That year I added something to David's schedule of departures and arrivals. In March I took him out for a short road trip, one day out and one day back.

This was a coda to a journey I had made alone from September to February, driving twenty-six thousand miles across, back, and around the United States—from New England where I'd lived for four years, to my parents' house in Maryland, where I figured I would roost for a while until I found work. Every morning I had woken up, looked at the map, and chosen a road, usually a back road. I was interested in small places, local places, overlooked details. By the end of the journey I'd snapped a shoe box full of photographs that later filled four photo albums: grasslands in North Dakota, racks of sunglasses in California, churches in Alabama. The world only failed me one day out of 156, on January 24, when I drove from Tallahassee to Jacksonville and nothing happened to my brain.

There were more than enough reasons to add my brother to this road trip. Since what I had been doing for more than five months, day after day sitting inside my head, was pure David behavior, it would have been weird if I hadn't associated David and the trip. Second, the fit was good between the two of us: I love long drives and David doesn't mind them, and he loves motels and I don't mind them. Third, the trip had been a colossal liberty, and I'd had plenty of time to reflect on the fact that it wasn't fair that I got so much and David got none; at least I could give him a taste of it. Finally, David himself was a part of the country I needed to see. After a very long young adulthood, I was beginning to understand that my life would always include David and that getting to know him better might be a smart idea.

I was nervous, in the back of my mind, about what David would do in public, so I proposed a short trip, most of it with us hidden behind a windshield, and that was fine with Dave. We were going to head south from Brook Farm, drive all day, and stop at a place for the night. The next day we'd get up and have breakfast and take some different roads back.

As we drove along, down the soft green hills of western Virginia toward the Blue Ridge, cows grazed aimlessly over knobby meadows, filling up enough to make milk. We passed big old sheds cluttered with stained tractors, the tractors studded with rows of steel knives. We never saw anyone working, unless you count what a cow does as work.

We talked that day—when we talked, which wasn't much of the time—about Paul's upcoming wedding to Marsha, set for June on the Vineyard, where the two of them lived. Dave and I were going up together with our parents.

The conversation with David about the wedding, although it was a David conversation, was much like the conversation I'd had with my parents on the subject. Because everyone in the family agreed that it was absolutely wonderful that Paul and Marsha were getting married, we wanted to talk about it when we saw one another. But because we all agreed about it, there really wasn't much to say. What do you say after you say you're happy?

Being talkers, we found ways to get past the problem.

Joan and Monroe had discussed the event entirely in terms of food. Dorothy and Eddie White were coming and Dorothy and Joan were planning to do a big pot of beans. Eddie was packing secret ingredients for his special barbecue, and Monroe had chartered a fishing boat for himself and Ed, believing that the two of them could feed the entire crowd on stripers after a day on the ocean.

David discussed the wedding entirely in terms of Gorilla Watson, who had been a character on the *Superman* television show and whom David had transformed, over the years, into a general but potent threat lurking outside the family tent.

"If Gorilla Watson comes to Paul and Marsha's wedding party, what will you do?" Dave asked me.

I replied, "I'll call the police and have them drag away that thug!"

"Who?" David asked.

"Gorilla Watson," I replied.

David smiled. "He's a real rotter," added my brother, pleasurably rolling the insult around on his tongue, "isn't he?"

"Yes," I agreed, "he's a creep."

"He's an idiot," declared David.

"He sure is," I said.

"Where will you send him?" David asked me.

"Who?" I replied, pausing for a moment. "You mean Gorilla Watson?"

"Yes," he replied. "Gorilla Watson."

"Where do you think I should send him?" I asked.

David's response was quick. "To the slammer," he cried happily.

"Where?" I asked.

"The hoosegow," my brother added.

"You are suggesting, perhaps, the *calabozo*?" I said.

"Yeah," David replied, "send him right into the pokey."

David smiled and so did I.

In the early evening we found a motel and nearby, one of those country cooking warehouses, a big hall of picnic tables buzzing with large-sized people methodically loading up on platters of hot home-style food, meat crunchy on the outside and wet on the inside, potatoes doused in salty red-brown gravy, fried okra, and hush puppies, delectable but dense.

David ate what seemed like an entire fried chicken.

"Do you want more, Dave?" I asked toward the end of the chicken. "More meat? More soda?"

"More soda!" he replied, loading mashed potatoes into his mouth.

I waved to the waitress, who cheerfully brought more soda. I sat, watching my brother. I was satisfied—all the women in my family love to see men consume at the dinner table. In this place everybody ate fast.

The motel was a franchise; I was accustomed to franchises. Although initially I had felt intimidated by motels on my trip across the country, after a week I'd realized that the transaction was nothing personal. The price was fixed by market conditions that had iced in over the years, and standard was standard: a solid lock on a flimsy door, wall-to-wall carpeting, plenty of hot water, a minimum of two bleached towels, and a color television with a remote.

Back in the room David was completely at his ease. It didn't take him a week to get comfortable with standard. He watched a little television and was in his pajamas and ready for his meds by eight, his normal bedtime.

I sorted through the bouquet of small sealed envelopes they'd given me when I'd checked David out at Brook Farm. Each envelope was marked with the day of the week, time of day—there were both morning and evening meds—and the names of the drugs: phenobarbital (David was prone to grand mal seizures) and something for his asthma. David didn't keep the envelopes himself. He could get anxious about outstanding tasks and in that frame of mind might take them all at once, ripping open envelope after envelope, emptying each one down his throat.

It was a strange thought to me, after five months wandering this great nation at random and alone, that every night of David's life someone appeared at his bedroom door to count out his meds, which David then swallowed.

"Good night, Judy," said my tired brother, burrowing under his industrially clean sheets.

" 'Night, Dave," I replied.

I read a little and turned the motel TV back on, keeping the sound low and the other lights in the room off, so the TV was the only light in the room.

A movie came on, a film I had loved when I had seen it in a theater.

What good luck, I thought. There's actually a good movie on a motel TV.

I had cried the whole way through this movie when I had seen it before, wept and wept—and because of David. One of the main characters in the film, the hero's brother, an institutionalized adult with autism, had mannerisms that were almost exactly like David's. The character demanded that certain things happen at certain times; he had an almost physical attraction to the drama of television, just like David. He lived in a place that was chosen for him; he lived watched over by people who were supposed to make sure he didn't get into dangerous situations, or do anything that would cause trouble.

There were some differences. The character in the movie counted so fast that he could tell how many matches there were in a spilled box before the matches hit the floor. My brother lacked those kinds of plot devices.

The movie moved past its credits. David slept, breathing gently through his mouth.

In the movie, the character with autism is kidnapped by his brother, taken out of that safe place, a home way out in the countryside, and together they drive away, into America.

I had cried so much when I'd seen it, I'd felt so sorry for the character and so sorry for David, but I didn't start crying in the motel room that night. My eyes were dry. I kept watching. It was still a good movie—it just didn't seem as sad or as powerful as it had before. I was watching the movie but at the same time I was also watching me watching with David in the next bed, asleep.

At that moment, David turned over.

I thought he might wake up. I thought he might see the movie. I didn't want him to, and this was exceptionally bizarre because when I'd seen it, I'd thought, thank God now I don't have to explain David to everyone I meet. There's a movie that tells a story that does it for me.

David turned over again. I turned the movie off with a little click of the remote, and then my hand sat there, on the remote, frozen. I could not move.

I didn't want David to see the film.

I didn't want him to see the brother with autism, how the camera showed his strangeness.

No, that wasn't it. He'd been with people with autism and people without autism his whole life—he knew the difference.

I didn't want him to see the other characters in the movie, how they looked at the brother as though he was strange.

No, that wasn't it. He knew how people without autism looked at people with autism.

I didn't want him to see a film where the person without autism was the hero, not the person with autism.

No, that wasn't it. A person could easily think the brother with autism was the real hero in the movie. Lots of people had.

The problem wasn't what David could take, but what I could. I couldn't be with the movie, the movie that I had used to make a neat package out of David, and be with David at the same time.

I turned my head slightly to look at David asleep. My real brother. The television screen was blank in the darkness.

Back in the hall of picnic tables the next morning I was still a little shaky from the revelations of the previous night, but I did not let that get between me and a nice big plate of eggs over easy with link sausage and home fries on the side. David, who was himself and not somebody in a movie, ate pancakes like he hadn't been fed in three days.

Four hours later, when the car stopped in the visitors' parking area at Brook Farm, David jumped out of the car with his bag and headed into the main building. With much less energy and purpose I followed him to check in at the front desk.

"Well, he's back," I said to a slim blond woman I knew only as Priscilla. I fished out the final envelopes of meds—they had provided one or two extra in case we were delayed coming back.

"Did you have a nice time?" she asked brightly.

"Very nice," I said. "I think he did too." She smiled and bent over the envelopes to check that they were all there.

I called down the hall where David had disappeared and he came running back.

"Will you be home for Christmas this year, Judy?" he asked.

I wasn't surprised by David's first question, since his schedule runs so far ahead of everyone else's. I said, "Sure I'll be home for Christmas."

"And New Year's?" he asked.

I said, "Sure. Sure I'll be home for New Year's."

Then David, without skipping a beat, asked me, "And the Late Maia's Birthday? Will you be home for that?"

Maia was not alive, but that was no reason to stop celebrating her birthday. We still loved her, after all. And later, I realized that Washington and Lincoln weren't alive, either, but people didn't think it was abnormal to celebrate their birthdays.

So I said, "Yes. Of course, David." I said this like it had been my idea or everybody's idea. "Of course I'm coming home for the Late Maia's Birthday. I always come home for that."

"And if Gorilla Watson shows up at the Late Maia's Birthday, Judy," asked David, "what will you do?"

"I'll throw him in the clink," I replied.

"In the what?" he asked.

"In the *calabozo*," I answered.

"Who?" asked my brother.

"Gorilla Watson, David," I replied. "That rat."

David smiled.

He kissed me on the top of my head, mumbled a good-bye, and hurried away toward rooms I'd never entered.

He was so smooth. I'd thought I was running the show, but it was David who had been managing me.

It didn't matter to my brother what we'd done together on our trip—but it did matter to him that we had been together. In fact, being together was really all that counted. So he made sure we'd be together, the family would be together, in the future.

He'd had it figured all along.

I felt strange, leaving David behind, even though he was in good hands, even though my duty, my boring duty, was done and it was time for me to get into the car and go. Something felt unfinished, like a piece of uneven writing you put into a drawer. Because you can't figure it out, you move on to something else. You'll have to come back to it later.

That morning, just over the crest of a back road, about an hour after breakfast we had stopped to shoot a picture, so that on the final page of the final volume of the photos I took on my trip there is David in a beige hunter's cap standing in the sun with the Blue Ridge Mountains in the back.

14 Memory Believes

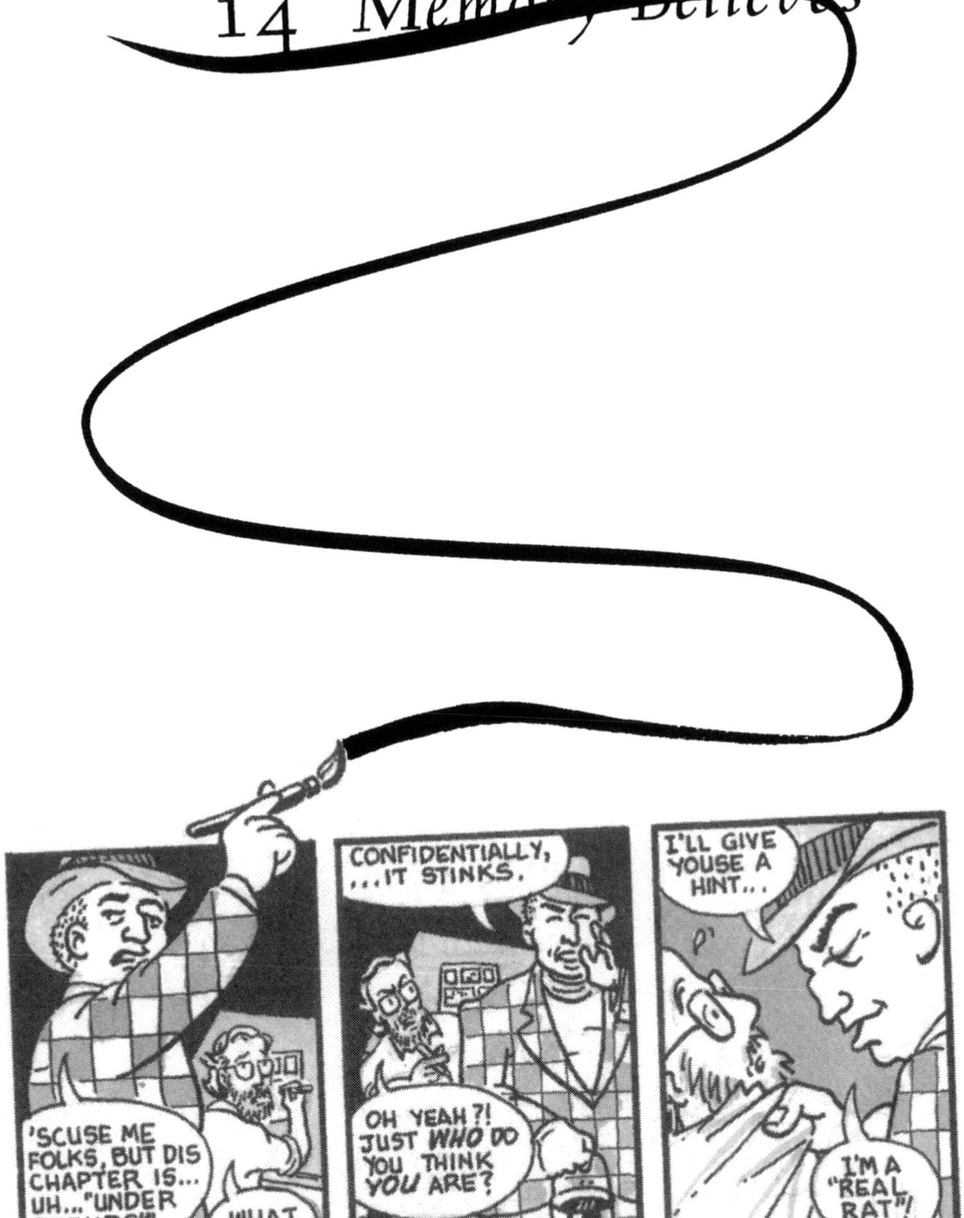
'SCUSE ME FOLKS, BUT DIS CHAPTER IS... UH..."UNDER REPAIRS."
WHAT TH...?
CONFIDENTIALLY, ...IT STINKS.
OH YEAH?! JUST WHO DO YOU THINK YOU ARE?
I'LL GIVE YOUSE A HINT...
I'M A "REAL RAT"!

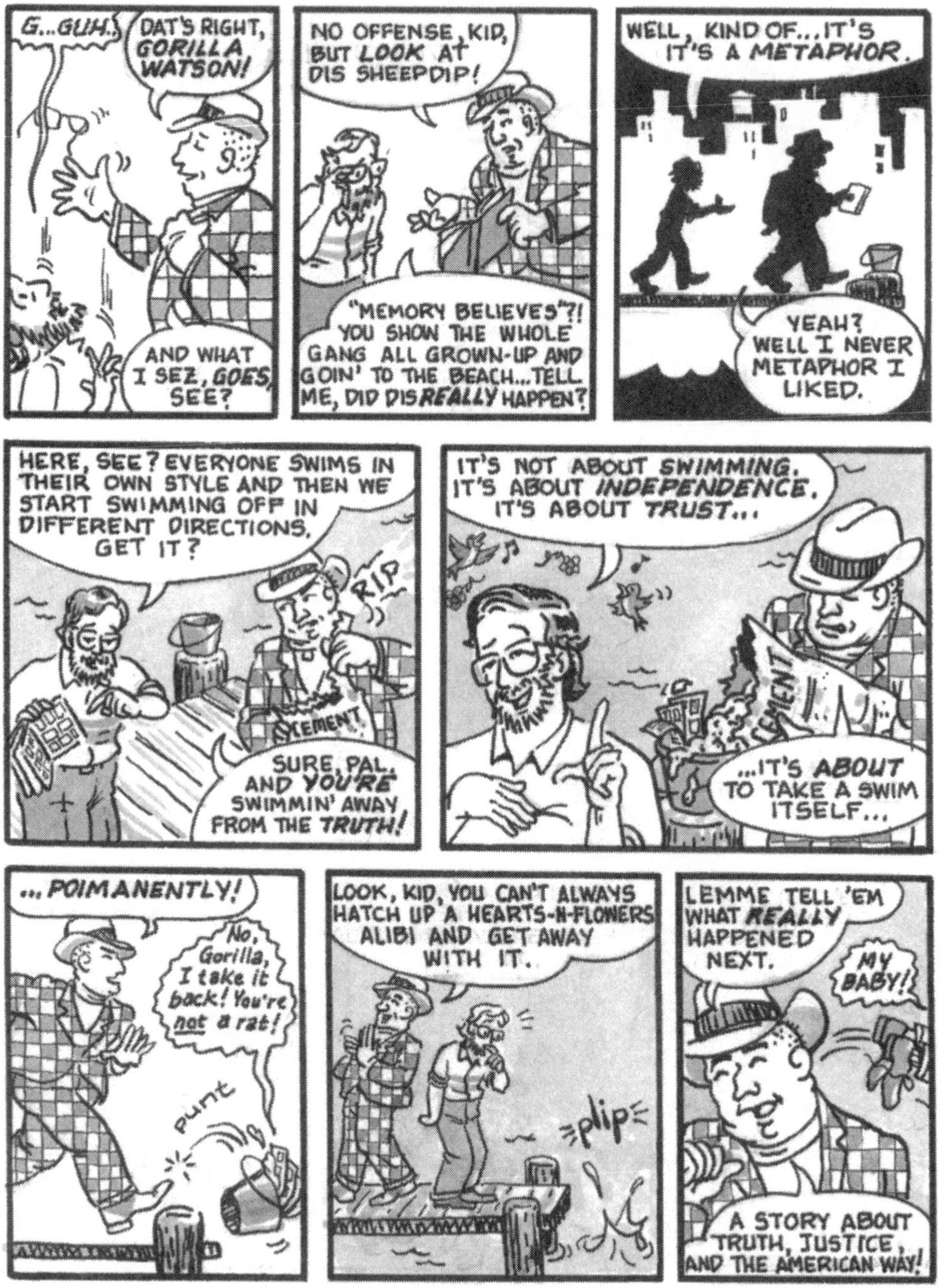
G...GUH.
DAT'S RIGHT, GORILLA WATSON!
AND WHAT I SEZ, GOES, SEE?
NO OFFENSE, KID, BUT LOOK AT DIS SHEEPDIP!
"MEMORY BELIEVES"?! YOU SHOW THE WHOLE GANG ALL GROWN-UP AND GOIN' TO THE BEACH... TELL ME, DID DIS REALLY HAPPEN?
WELL, KIND OF... IT'S IT'S A METAPHOR.
YEAH? WELL I NEVER METAPHOR I LIKED.
HERE, SEE? EVERYONE SWIMS IN THEIR OWN STYLE AND THEN WE START SWIMMING OFF IN DIFFERENT DIRECTIONS. GET IT?
RIP
CEMENT
SURE, PAL, AND YOU'RE SWIMMIN' AWAY FROM THE TRUTH!
IT'S NOT ABOUT SWIMMING. IT'S ABOUT INDEPENDENCE. IT'S ABOUT TRUST...
CEMENT
...IT'S ABOUT TO TAKE A SWIM ITSELF...
...POIMANENTLY!
No, Gorilla, I take it back! You're not a rat!
punt
LOOK, KID, YOU CAN'T ALWAYS HATCH UP A HEARTS-N-FLOWERS ALIBI AND GET AWAY WITH IT.
plip
LEMME TELL 'EM WHAT REALLY HAPPENED NEXT.
MY BABY!
A STORY ABOUT TRUTH, JUSTICE, AND THE AMERICAN WAY!

14 *The Adventures of Superman*

FACE IT, "THE ADVENTURES OF SUPERMAN " WAS NEVER BORING.

ACTION AND LAFFS... ...HARDBOILED JOES AND WISE-CRACKIN' DAMES.

BASICALLY IT HAD EVERYTHING GOIN' FOR IT ... ...TO ATTRACT THE MIND OF DAVID P. KARASIK.

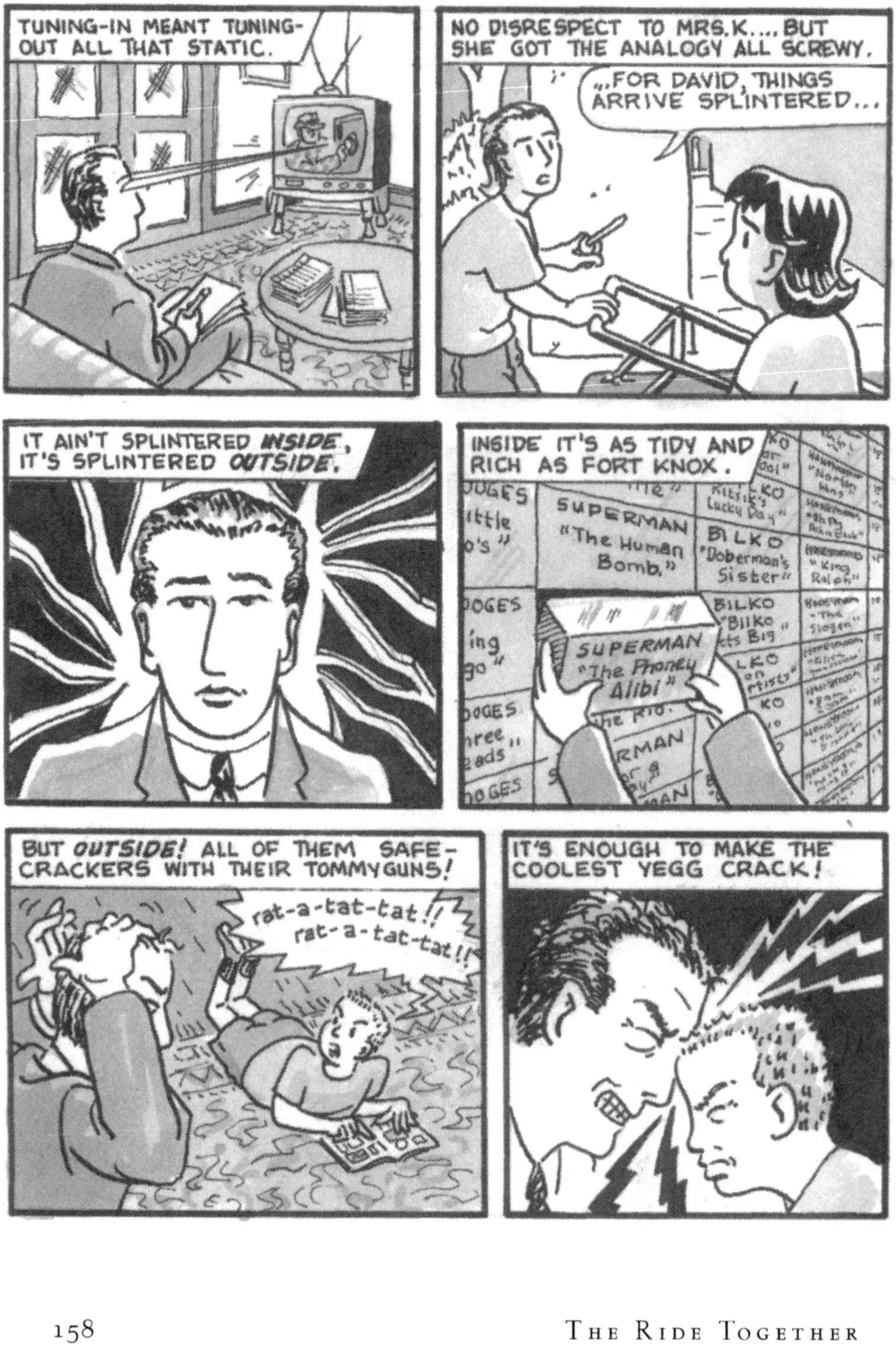
TUNING-IN MEANT TUNING-OUT ALL THAT STATIC.
NO DISRESPECT TO MRS.K...., BUT SHE GOT THE ANALOGY ALL SCREWY.
...FOR DAVID, THINGS ARRIVE SPLINTERED...
IT AIN'T SPLINTERED INSIDE, IT'S SPLINTERED OUTSIDE.
INSIDE IT'S AS TIDY AND RICH AS FORT KNOX.
SUPERMAN "The Human Bomb."
BILKO "Doberman's Sister"
SUPERMAN "The Phoney Alibi"
BUT OUTSIDE! ALL OF THEM SAFE-CRACKERS WITH THEIR TOMMYGUNS!
rat-a-tat-tat!!
rat-a-tat-tat!!
IT'S ENOUGH TO MAKE THE COOLEST YEGG CRACK!

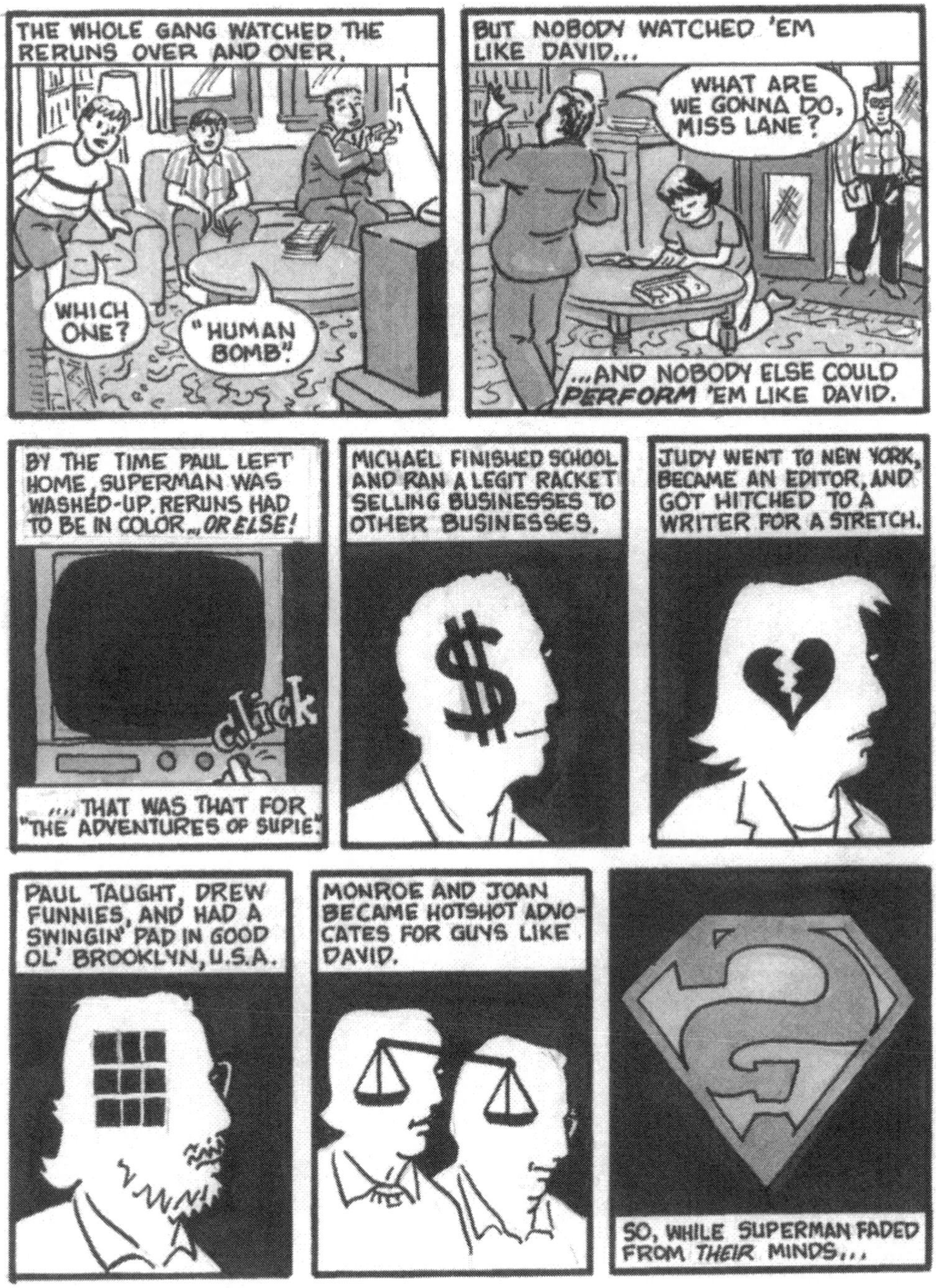
THE WHOLE GANG WATCHED THE RERUNS OVER AND OVER.
WHICH ONE?
"HUMAN BOMB".
BUT NOBODY WATCHED 'EM LIKE DAVID...
WHAT ARE WE GONNA DO, MISS LANE?
...AND NOBODY ELSE COULD *PERFORM* 'EM LIKE DAVID.
BY THE TIME PAUL LEFT HOME, SUPERMAN WAS WASHED-UP. RERUNS HAD TO BE IN COLOR...*OR ELSE!*
click
....THAT WAS THAT FOR "THE ADVENTURES OF SUPIE."
MICHAEL FINISHED SCHOOL AND RAN A LEGIT RACKET SELLING BUSINESSES TO OTHER BUSINESSES.
JUDY WENT TO NEW YORK, BECAME AN EDITOR, AND GOT HITCHED TO A WRITER FOR A STRETCH.
PAUL TAUGHT, DREW FUNNIES, AND HAD A SWINGIN' PAD IN GOOD OL' BROOKLYN, U.S.A.
MONROE AND JOAN BECAME HOTSHOT ADVOCATES FOR GUYS LIKE DAVID.
SO, WHILE SUPERMAN FADED FROM *THEIR* MINDS...

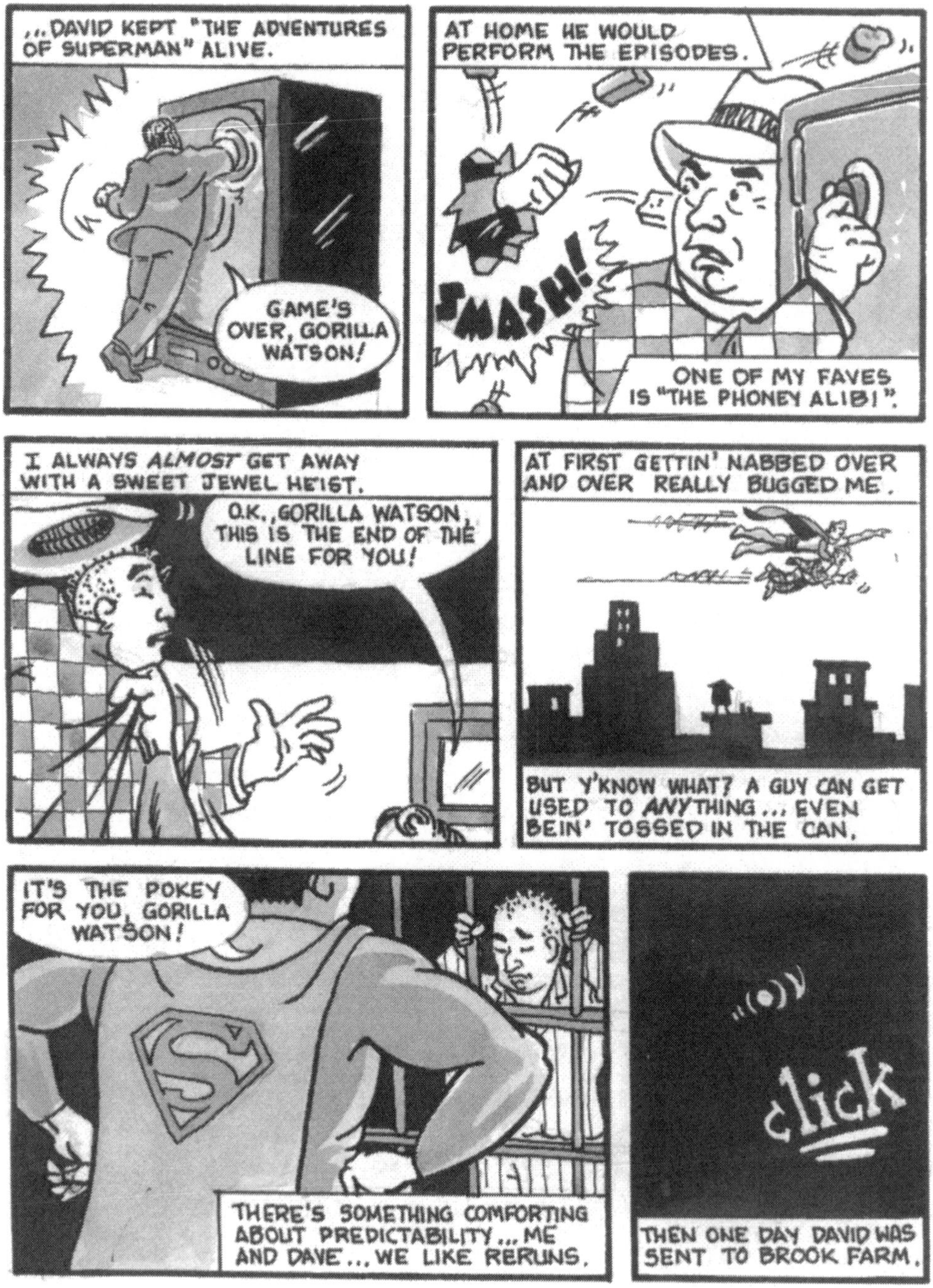
...DAVID KEPT "THE ADVENTURES OF SUPERMAN" ALIVE.
GAME'S OVER, GORILLA WATSON!
AT HOME HE WOULD PERFORM THE EPISODES.
SMASH!
ONE OF MY FAVES IS "THE PHONEY ALIBI".
I ALWAYS ALMOST GET AWAY WITH A SWEET JEWEL HEIST.
O.K., GORILLA WATSON, THIS IS THE END OF THE LINE FOR YOU!
AT FIRST GETTIN' NABBED OVER AND OVER REALLY BUGGED ME.
BUT Y'KNOW WHAT? A GUY CAN GET USED TO ANYTHING... EVEN BEIN' TOSSED IN THE CAN.
IT'S THE POKEY FOR YOU, GORILLA WATSON!
THERE'S SOMETHING COMFORTING ABOUT PREDICTABILITY... ME AND DAVE... WE LIKE RERUNS.
click
THEN ONE DAY DAVID WAS SENT TO BROOK FARM.

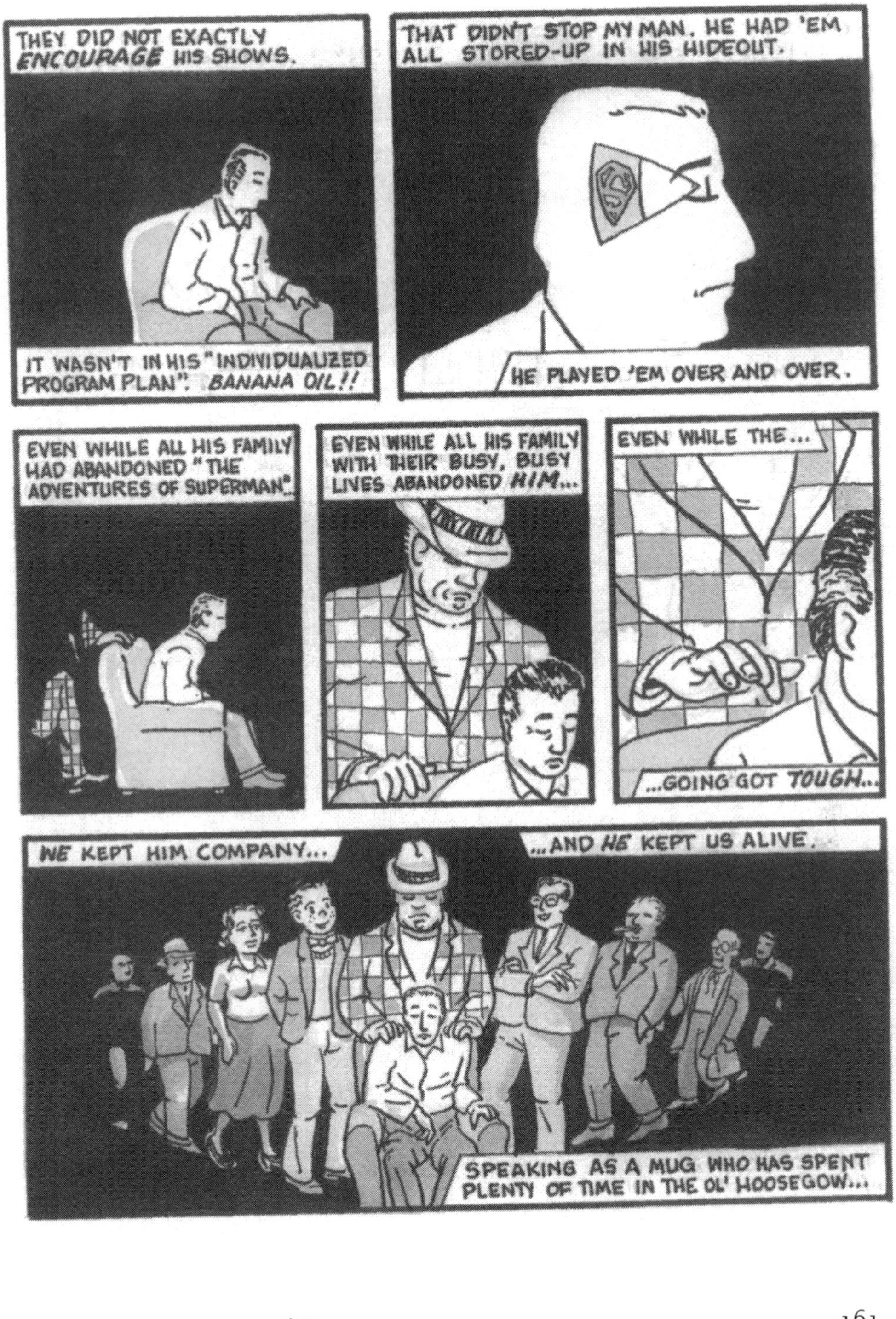
THEY DID NOT EXACTLY ENCOURAGE HIS SHOWS.
IT WASN'T IN HIS "INDIVIDUALIZED PROGRAM PLAN". BANANA OIL!!
THAT DIDN'T STOP MY MAN. HE HAD 'EM ALL STORED-UP IN HIS HIDEOUT.
HE PLAYED 'EM OVER AND OVER.
EVEN WHILE ALL HIS FAMILY HAD ABANDONED "THE ADVENTURES OF SUPERMAN"...
EVEN WHILE ALL HIS FAMILY WITH THEIR BUSY, BUSY LIVES ABANDONED HIM...
EVEN WHILE THE...
...GOING GOT TOUGH...
WE KEPT HIM COMPANY...
...AND HE KEPT US ALIVE.
SPEAKING AS A MUG WHO HAS SPENT PLENTY OF TIME IN THE OL' HOOSEGOW...

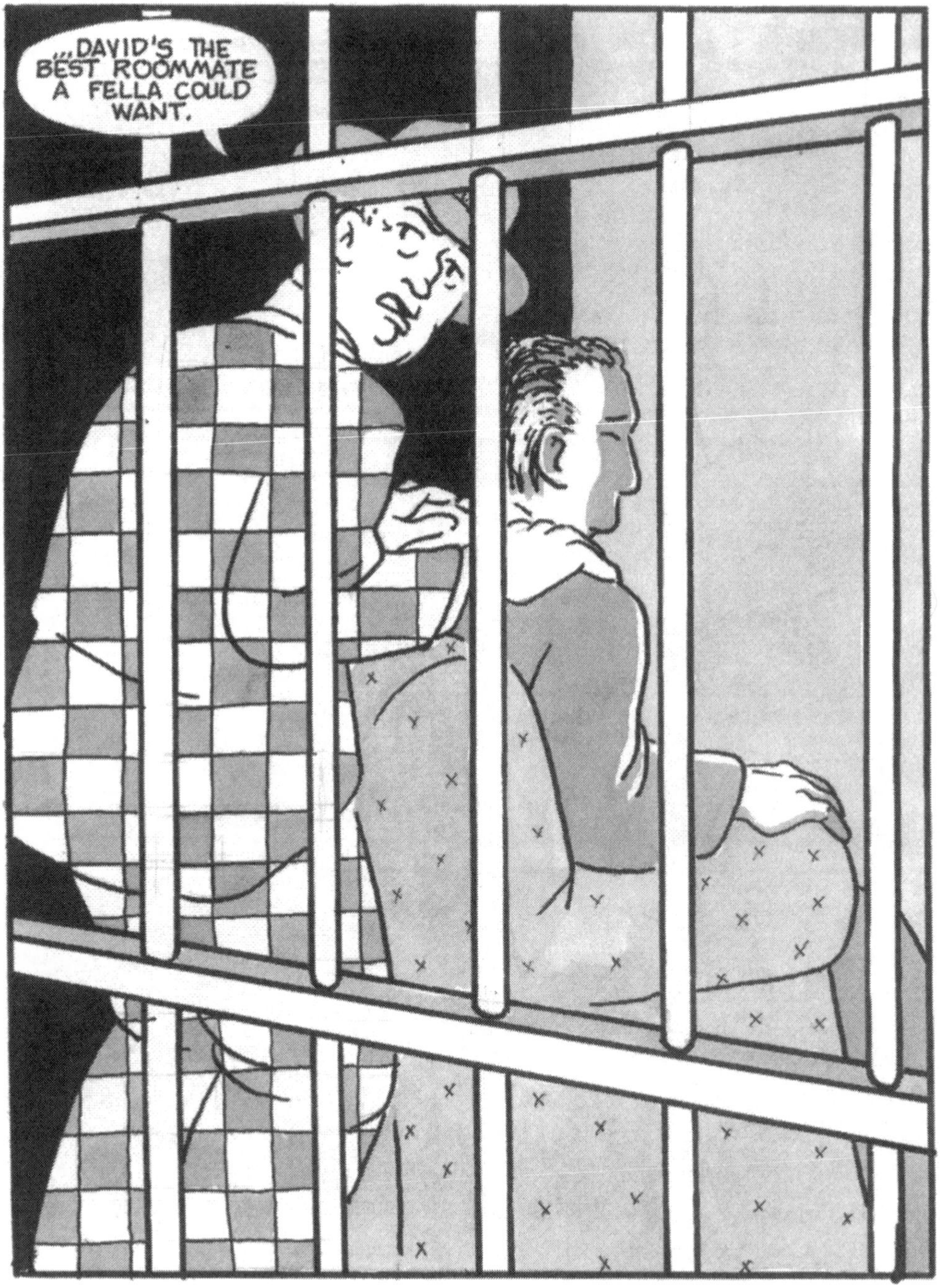
...DAVID'S THE BEST ROOMMATE A FELLA COULD WANT.

15 *Haircut*

Davíd was not only my father's first child, but his first son, and so David was the first one my father took to Vito Cortese, the man who cut Pop's hair. All three boys went, David first, then Michael, and finally Paul, down to Vito's, in the right order, at appointed times.

David knows all the barbers' names. "Vito," he says, "and Dante and José and Robert and Armando." He knows them all—and they know him.

When David was eight or nine years old, back in the mid-1950s, before we moved to Lenox Street, when we lived in the District, one day he disappeared. My mother thought he was upstairs. She had four children by then and having one of them out of eyesight was not a calamity.

An hour or so later, before anyone had a chance to miss David, the phone rang.

It was Vito. David had gone to get a haircut.

We never knew how it happened exactly, just that he'd taken the bus. David had no money, but he can be determined on a goal, and in our family a trip to Vito's for a haircut is a worthy goal. As for the bus driver, all we could guess was that he was more interested in getting past Albemarle Street and farther down Connecticut Avenue than in arguing with some difficult little boy.

David knew where to get off, and they knew him at the barbershop. He got his haircut from Vito.

"Vito," David says, counting on his long, elegant fingers, "Dante, José, Robert—and who?"

"Armando," we say, to make the list complete.

"Armando," he replies, with satisfaction. He loves the name Armando; he loves all the names.

My father spent the first half of 1992 enduring the trials of the flesh. Piece by piece, his body went bad and broke down; finally it killed him.

The sickness started with a nasty touch of sciatica, a small nerve whose irritation set off six months of firecrackers. For the sciatica, Pop took anti-inflammatories, which cut up his stomach, and painkillers, which made him strangely high. He took too much of both. A week after starting the regime, he threw up blood and, about eight hours after arriving in the hospital, he became delirious. All that vomiting pushed the painkillers into the wrong places in his nervous system. After a day and a half of delirium, including long intervals when he seemed to be completely blind but nonetheless full of ferocious energy—he pulled all the sheets off the hospital bed, and all of the clothes off his stout body, and as many as possible of the intravenous lines out of his arms, and even managed to yank the catheter out of his penis, and also socked me in the nose when I tried to get a sheet back on him—we got him out of the regular hospital ward and into the intensive care unit. There, he went into a coma.

He came out of the coma slowly, frightening us a little less each day. At the beginning, we thought he had lost his mind, and worried about whether we'd have to kill him, and if we did, how we could, but then it became clear that he hadn't lost all of his mind. He eventually recognized people again. He had lost pieces of his mind, however. For example, he came out of the coma incapable of reading; that was tough. Later, other parts of his mind got lost. He stopped being able to eat. He looked at food and said no. So, against my mother's better judgment, we put in a feeding tube, and Pop's meals went through a funnel and a line of rubber hose straight into his stomach.

He couldn't walk without assistance. He had a hard time sleeping. Someone needed to adjust the pillow, or move his legs, every few hours. He grew thin and weak, and the hits kept coming. He'd be home for a week, sleeping downstairs in the living room where we'd brought his big bed, and then something else would snap and he'd be back in the hospital. He found ways to retreat, dodge, and come back from the assaults, but each time he lost ground.

Monroe knew what was happening. Fairly early on during those six months, he gave Paul the keys to his car. The Volvo's a sturdy car, said Pop, good for navigating the ruts of the island roads, good for carrying children. I won't be driving again, he said, so why don't you take it.

For the most part, however, it wasn't possible for Pop to be the person he had been his whole life. He was just an old man in desperation, plotting his next breathing space.

Wherever he was, he didn't want visitors. He didn't have time to disappoint people and he didn't have time to be on the receiving end of pity. When people asked if they could come, Pop said no. Except for Dorothy, because nobody in our family ever says no to Dorothy, and except for Odell Kominers. Pop tried to say no to Odell, but Odie had known him too long for that. He had been Pop's roommate in Washington when both of them were young bachelors and when Pop said no, Odie replied, "Oh be quiet, Monnie, you're a sick man. I'll be downtown anyway, I'll just stay for a minute." Odie was a regular in that hospital room, and Pop accepted it.

Also, Pop did not say no to Vito Cortese. When Vito called the hospital to ask if he could visit, my father said, "Yes. Please come." To Vito, Pop was even polite.

When Vito walked into the hospital room, my father looked through his foggy glasses with his foggy eyes and saw Vito standing there and said, "Welcome, old friend. I am so glad to see you."

A haircut is a simple thing, but it can seem very important. Vito smiled at my father. Pop sat up carefully in the bed and loosened the shawl of sickness and, for forty-five minutes, left the battle behind. He was in Vito's hands. Vito took out his scissors and cut my father's hair and he took out his other tools and gave him a shave.

A few months later, my father died.

He died on a Monday. That Thursday I was walking down the street near my parents' house and saw a neighbor walking her dog. I told her the house would be empty over the weekend since my mother and I were going to see David to tell him the news.

And the neighbor said, in the nicest way possible, the most sympathetic way possible, "Judy, does David understand these things?"

Meaning, did he understand death.

I had to laugh. I said, "Billie, do *I* understand?" I had just watched my father die for six months and, still, it made no sense to me.

But David understood. He talked about it just like we did. Not with our tone of voice, but he said the same words and they meant the same thing. He took it as well as any of us.

After my father died, the first big holiday was Thanksgiving. David came home to my parents' house just like always. The holiday was fine, and the big meal went fine, and everything went fine. It was the ordinary part when things got screwy.

The last three nights of his visit, when we didn't have a bunch of guests and ceremony—maybe David just missed our father, just like we all did. He got agitated.

He drummed on his scalp and his voice rose and he said urgent things over and over. His actions were violent, but only to himself. He wasn't violent to me or to our mother.

He needed to know what he would be doing in December and February and over Easter and June and for his birthday in August and for all the times he always comes home. He needed to know that everything was still going to happen in the right order and at the appointed times, probably because the world without Pop seems like a very disorderly and unreliable place. What would he be doing in the future?

Unfortunately, my mother didn't have all the answers. She just didn't. This made David feel terrible.

He said, "In February I'm getting my hair cut. Right?" he said.

We said, "Right."

And he said, "From who?"

Which is when things got worse.

Because my mother couldn't tell him all the usual names. Because David had grown up. And, although Vito was still there, some of the old gang had opened shops of their own and didn't work at Vito's Barbershop anymore.

David said, "Vito?" and my mother said, "Yes."

And he said, "Dante?"

My mother couldn't say Yes, because Dante had moved on. She said, "Vito and José, David." She said, "But I don't know who else works at Vito's."

David became very agitated.

I tried to make things better but I only made them even worse.

"There will be new guys there, David," I promised. "New barbers."

"Vito?" he asked.

I said, "Yes."

"And who?" he asked.

I couldn't say, past José.

And David shook his head and his face grew red and his long, elegant fingers played his skull like a drum.

"*I forbid it!*" he cried.

"I forbid it!" he cried.

We waited for him to calm down.

His fingers drummed. "I don't want to meet new people!" he screamed.

And who could blame him? Who could blame him for that.

When I think about the time when David was a little boy and took the bus downtown to Vito's, I often wonder how many people on that bus told David he was wrong to be there. I wonder how many people understood.

He was just a kid who needed a haircut. It's a simple thing, but sometimes it can seem very important.

16 *And Now, a Final Word from Monroe*

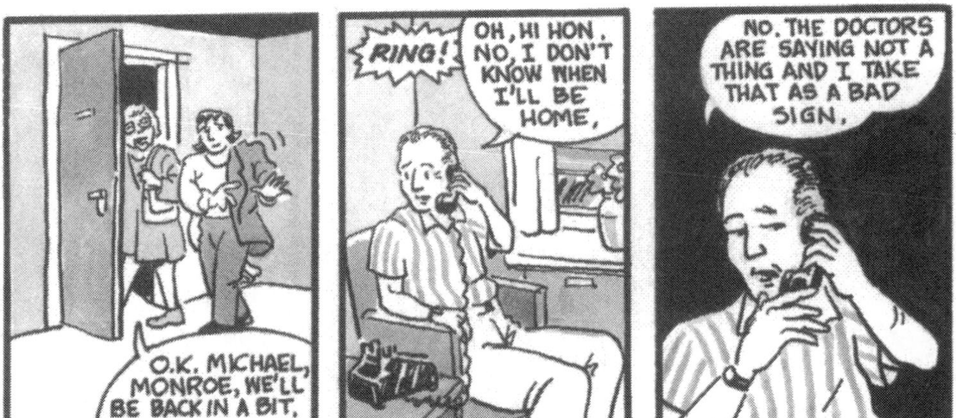

O.K. MICHAEL, MONROE, WE'LL BE BACK IN A BIT.
RING!
OH, HI HON. NO, I DON'T KNOW WHEN I'LL BE HOME.
NO. THE DOCTORS ARE SAYING NOT A THING AND I TAKE THAT AS A BAD SIGN.

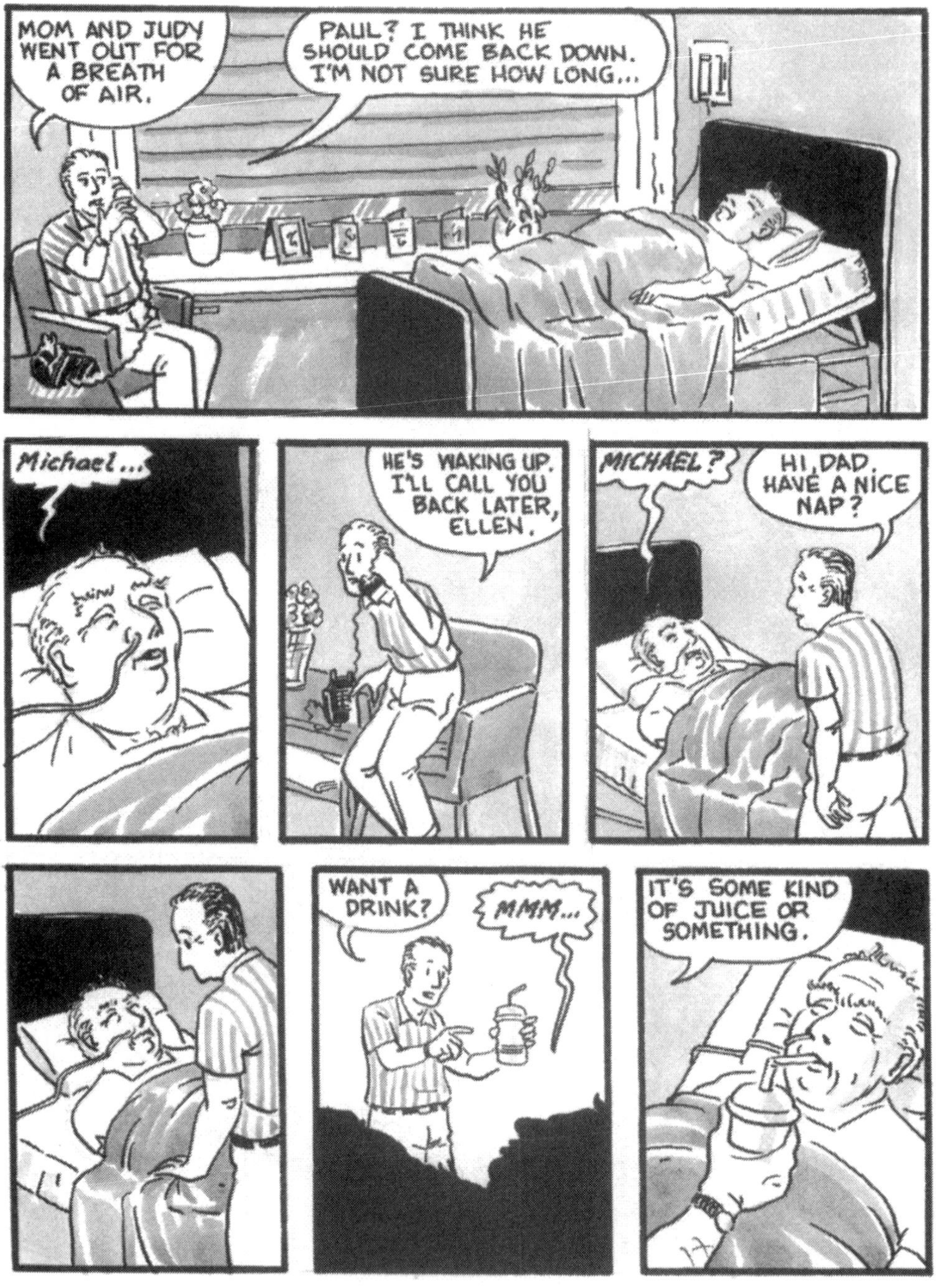
MOM AND JUDY WENT OUT FOR A BREATH OF AIR.
PAUL? I THINK HE SHOULD COME BACK DOWN. I'M NOT SURE HOW LONG...
Michael...
HE'S WAKING UP. I'LL CALL YOU BACK LATER, ELLEN.
MICHAEL?
HI, DAD. HAVE A NICE NAP?
WANT A DRINK?
MMM...
IT'S SOME KIND OF JUICE OR SOMETHING.

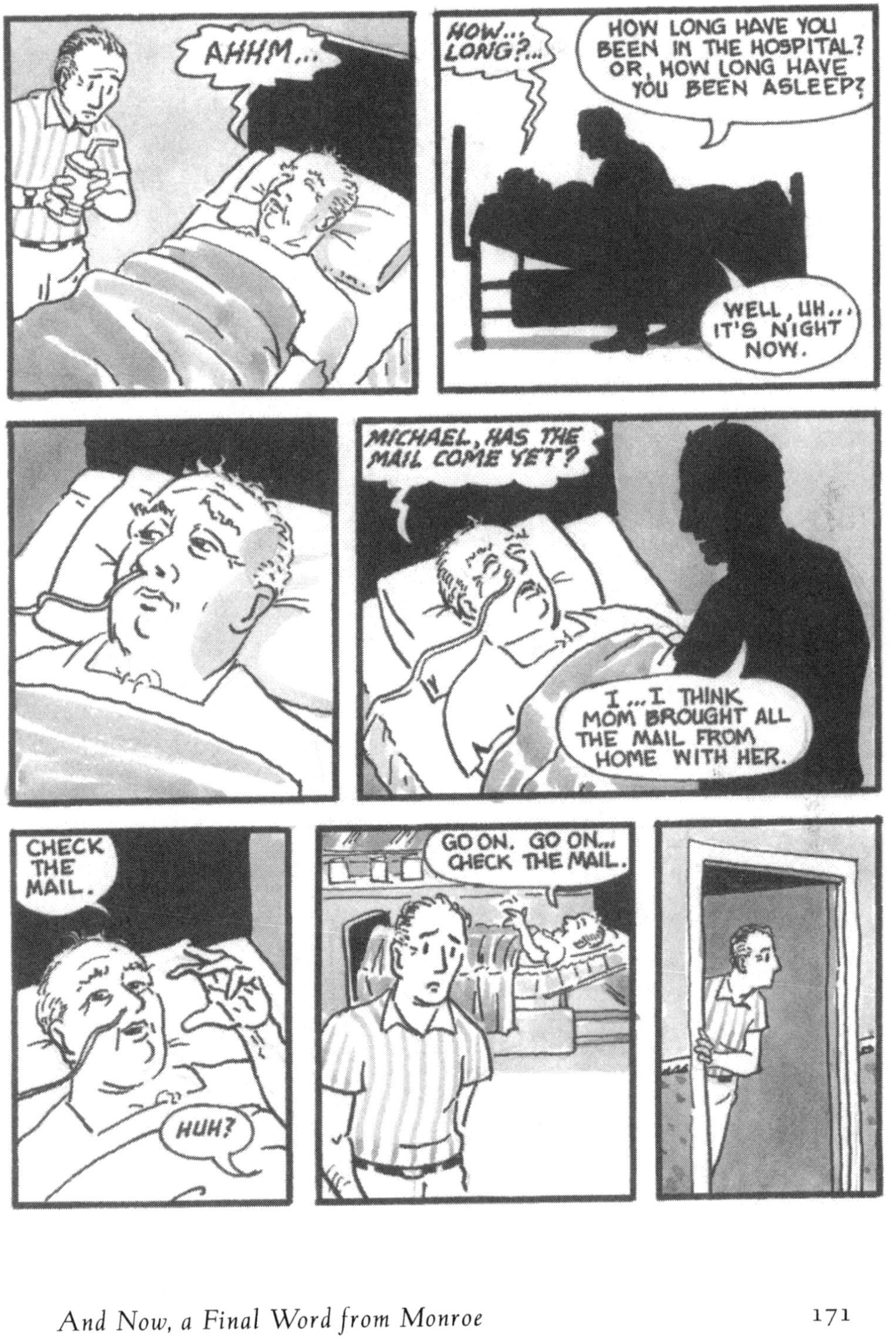
AHHM...
HOW... LONG?...
HOW LONG HAVE YOU BEEN IN THE HOSPITAL? OR, HOW LONG HAVE YOU BEEN ASLEEP?
WELL, UH... IT'S NIGHT NOW.
MICHAEL, HAS THE MAIL COME YET?
I... I THINK MOM BROUGHT ALL THE MAIL FROM HOME WITH HER.
CHECK THE MAIL.
HUH?
GO ON. GO ON... CHECK THE MAIL.

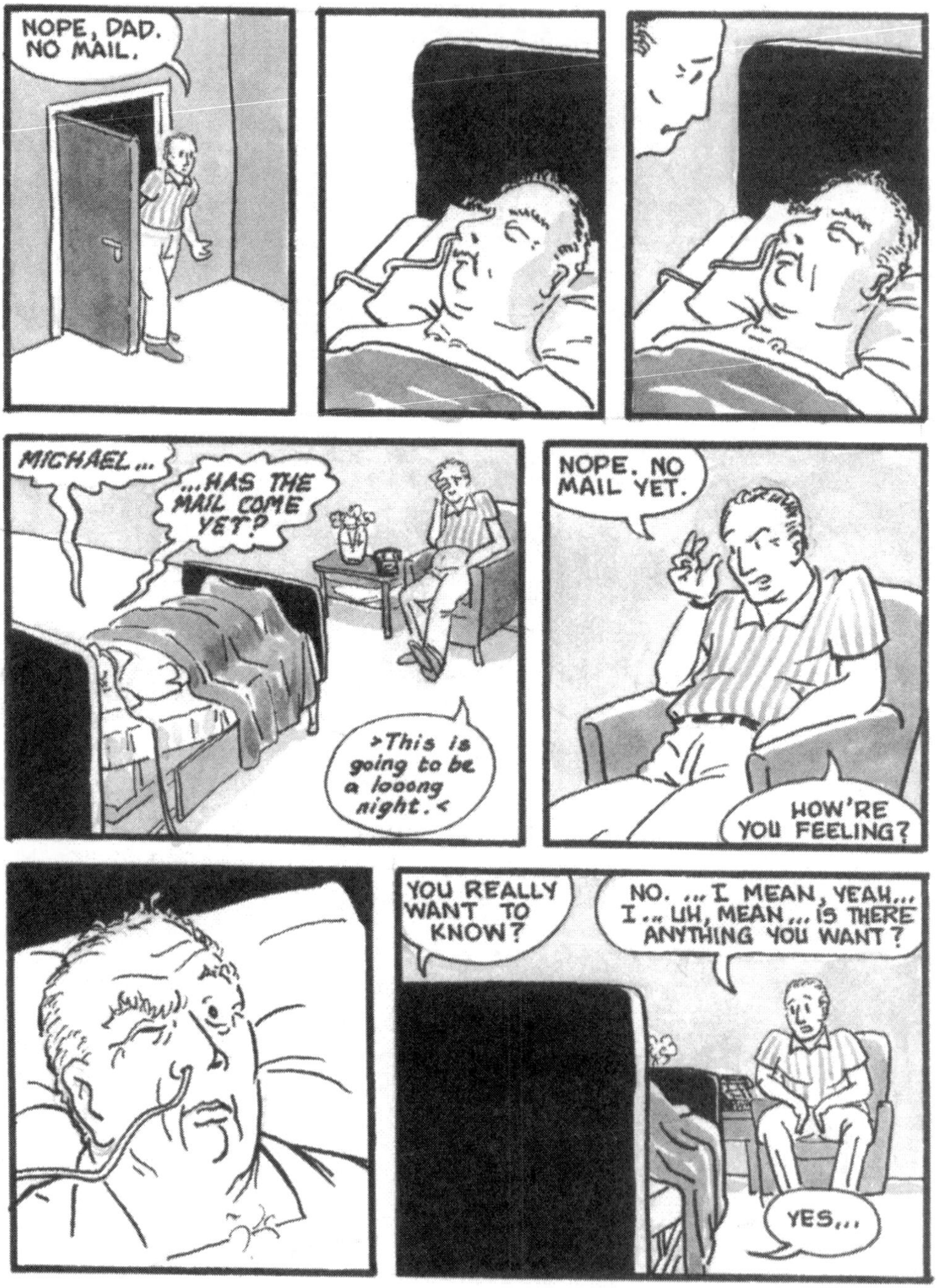
NOPE, DAD. NO MAIL.
MICHAEL...
...HAS THE MAIL COME YET?
>This is going to be a looong night.<
NOPE. NO MAIL YET.
HOW'RE YOU FEELING?
YOU REALLY WANT TO KNOW?
NO. ... I MEAN, YEAH... I.. UH, MEAN... IS THERE ANYTHING YOU WANT?
YES...

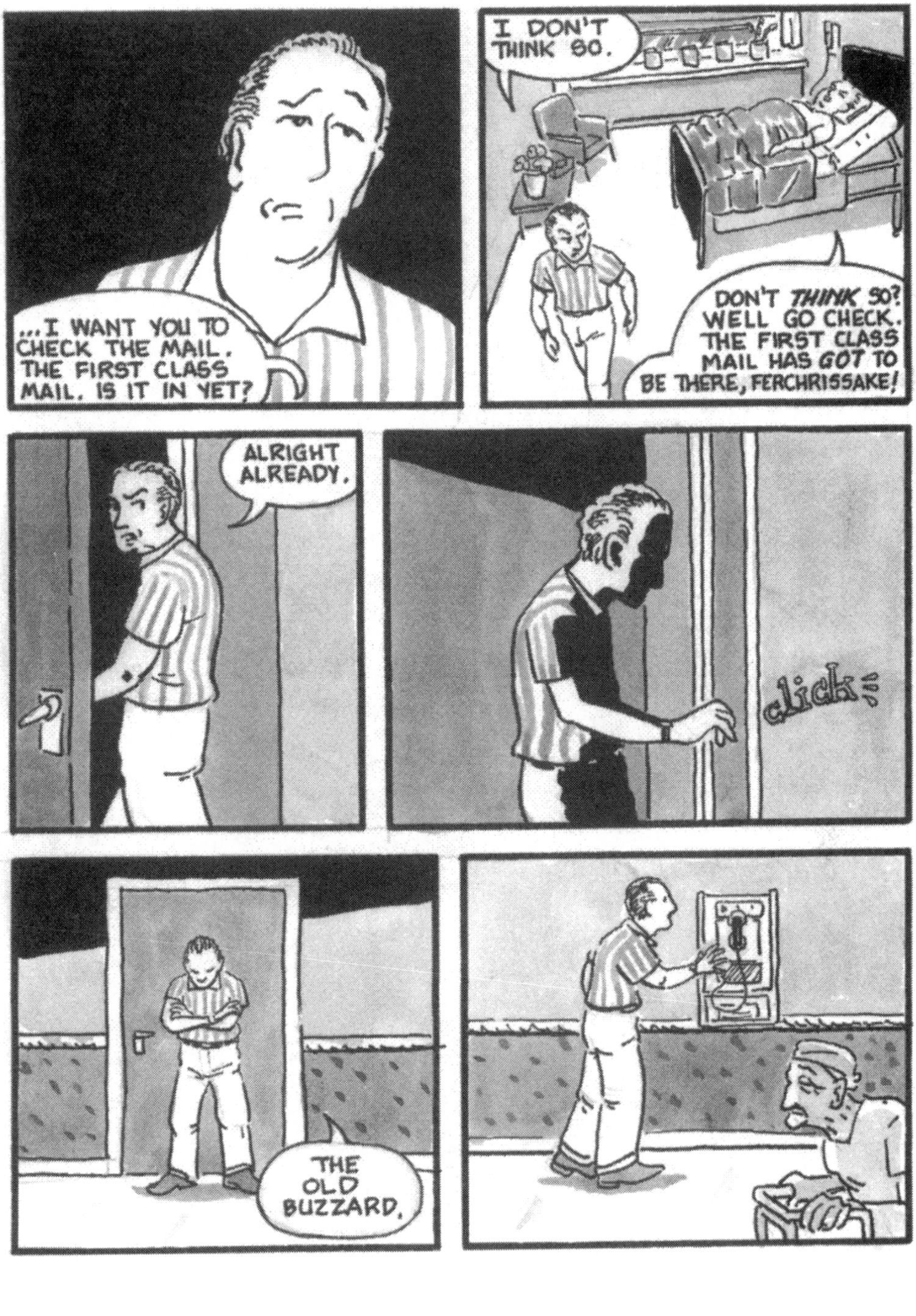
...I WANT YOU TO CHECK THE MAIL. THE FIRST CLASS MAIL. IS IT IN YET?
I DON'T THINK SO.
DON'T THINK SO? WELL GO CHECK. THE FIRST CLASS MAIL HAS GOT TO BE THERE, FERCHRISSAKE!
ALRIGHT ALREADY.
click
THE OLD BUZZARD.

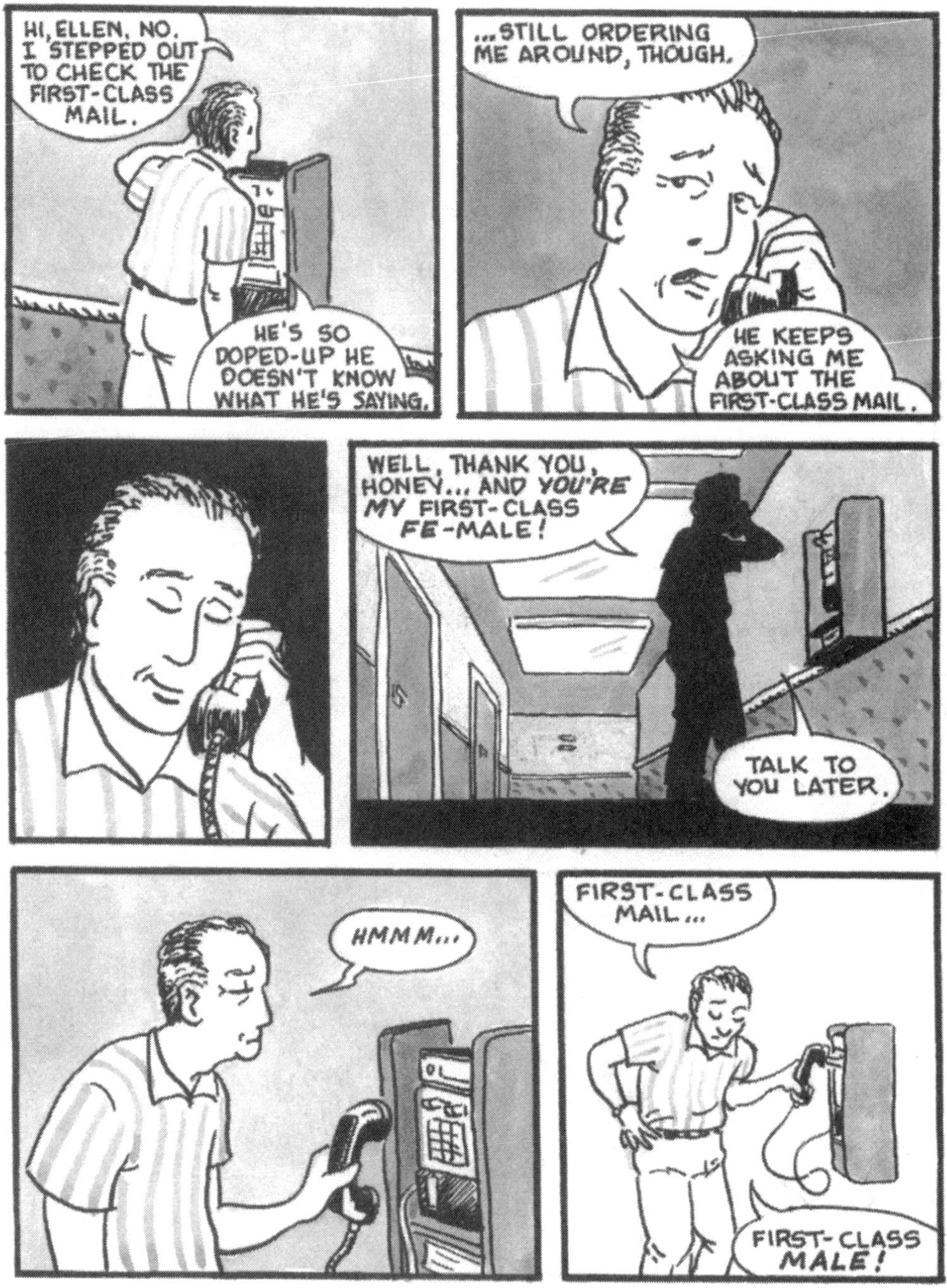
HI, ELLEN. NO. I STEPPED OUT TO CHECK THE FIRST-CLASS MAIL.
HE'S SO DOPED-UP HE DOESN'T KNOW WHAT HE'S SAYING.
...STILL ORDERING ME AROUND, THOUGH.
HE KEEPS ASKING ME ABOUT THE FIRST-CLASS MAIL.
WELL, THANK YOU, HONEY... AND YOU'RE MY FIRST-CLASS FE-MALE!
TALK TO YOU LATER.
HMMM...
FIRST-CLASS MAIL...
FIRST-CLASS MALE!

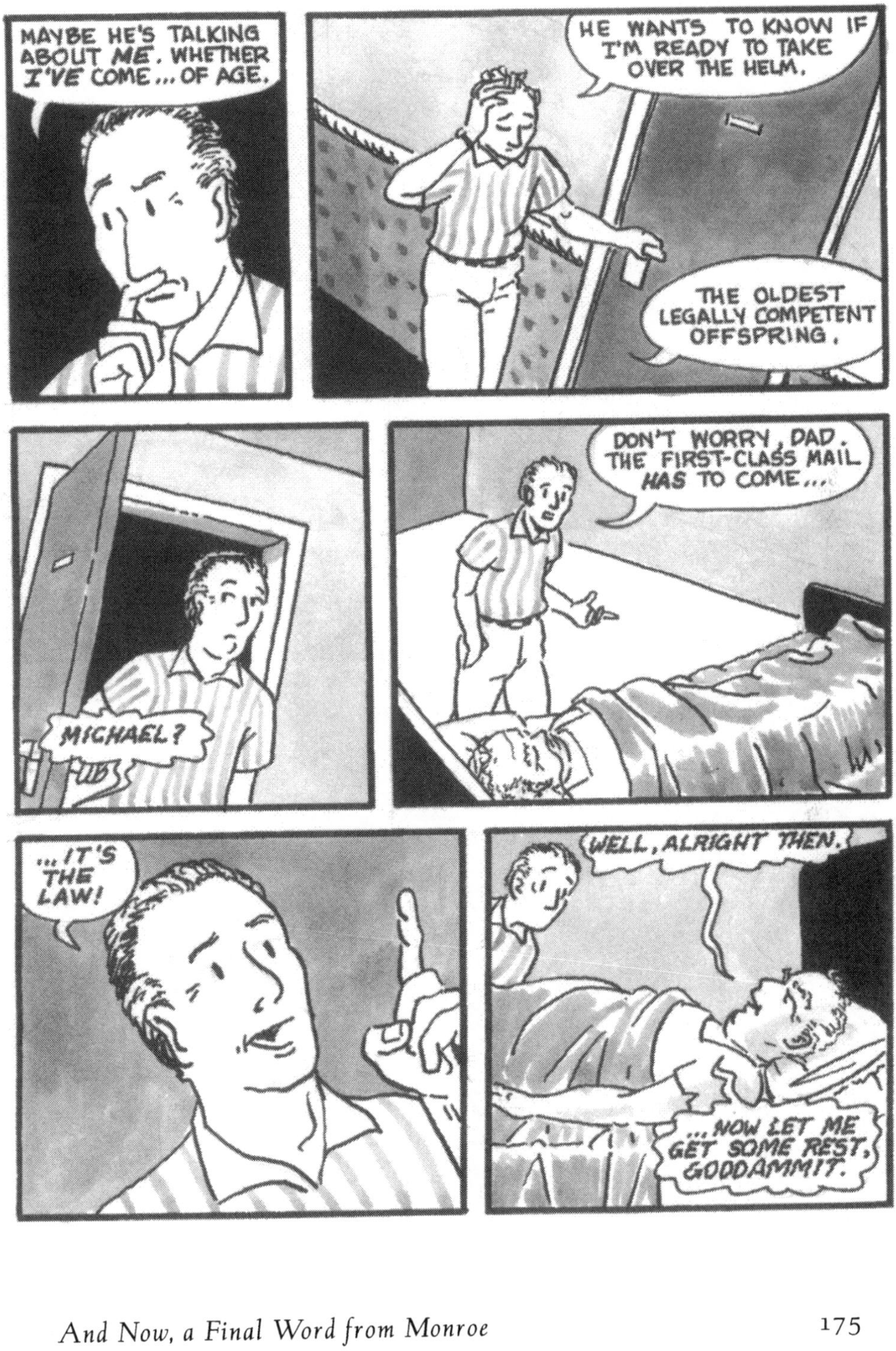
MAYBE HE'S TALKING ABOUT ME. WHETHER I'VE COME... OF AGE.
HE WANTS TO KNOW IF I'M READY TO TAKE OVER THE HELM.
THE OLDEST LEGALLY COMPETENT OFFSPRING.
MICHAEL?
DON'T WORRY, DAD. THE FIRST-CLASS MAIL HAS TO COME...
...IT'S THE LAW!
WELL, ALRIGHT THEN.
...NOW LET ME GET SOME REST, GODDAMMIT.

17 Rudolph's Airplane

It was a dazzlingly sunny day in western Pennsylvania. Mom and I had driven out to the celebration of Brook Farm's twentieth anniversary at the 1995 Open House.

On the broad, slightly curved lawn behind the main building, families, residents, and counselors wandered. Parents squinted into the noon light, trying to identify their adult children.

Dave appeared from nowhere, running toward us in his long strides, a strange run that had its own kind of gracefulness. He grabbed me by my shoulders and kissed me on the head, as usual, then kissed Mom on her head.

Joan put her arm around David.

"Hey, Dave," she said, "How are you feeling?"

"Fine, Mrs. Karasik," replied David, his glance moving rapidly around at the day, the lawn, the sun, the long striped tent and the picnic tables set up for the event, the figures roaming in their different ways through the light. "Just fine."

David had hurt his back falling down during a fire drill at the group house where he lived in Taylorville, a little town near the Brook Farm campus. When he had been home for his customary birthday vacation in late summer, it had been hard for him to sleep because of the pain.

I also was at Mom's house that week—since Monroe had died I tried to be at Joan's when David came home—and had watched Joan rub his back.

This was in Joan's new house. The move out of Lenox Street was done.

Dave sat on a dining room chair pushed away from the table, leaned back his head, his dark hair heathered with gray, and closed his eyes. Wrinkled folds ran from the edges of his eyes into creases across his cheeks. He breathed deeply. Joan worked the muscles in his shoulders, moving down his spine to the place where the hurt started. Strong hands, kneading, kneading.

We are all getting old.

Joan had called Rudolph Zarek. He'd been glad to hear from her, sorry to know that Dave's back was still giving him trouble. He apologized again and told her they had fixed the step David tripped on. The two of them commiserated about the endless maintenance needs of old houses.

In 1995, David had been at Brook Farm for fourteen years. The combination of the Zareks' warmth and their approach to behavior modification had been just the right thing for David. His outbursts were fewer and fewer. Although we felt that David hadn't been challenged much by the programming at Brook Farm for the past several years—the events in his life consisted mostly of field trips—Brook Farm's ability to change the violent behavior had made his life happier. Besides, we didn't know of any other programs we could afford that would be better for him, which meant that it was likely no such programs existed. Joan and Monroe had worked as volunteers on behalf of people with special needs for so long that if something opened up, people they respected and who respected them—and who owed them for the things they'd made happen—would let us know if the program might be good for David.

We liked Rudolph and Diane. We were proud that we'd been part of Brook Farm from early on. Rudolph Zarek was a friendly, funny man, a large man, a person who made friends easily, and watched out for them. Rudolph had a small airplane he'd use to help other people. Once he had offered to fly David to Martha's Vineyard, just as a favor to the family and for the fun of flying.

At the celebration Joan was in a chair up front so that the Zareks could thank her for being one of the people who had believed in Brook Farm before they'd really been established. David and I sat side by side in the middle of the crowd, David dressed formally, sitting stiffly, his injured back in a brace.

Parts of the ceremony were emotional. Diane broke down in tears when staff and residents described the sense of community that she and Rudolph had created at Brook Farm over the preceding twenty years.

David held my hand throughout the long program. Often, during the speeches, he nodded off, his eyelids gradually, gradually floating down over his eyes, his neck relaxing until, with the sudden fall forward of his head, he jerked awake. A great deal of the program was repetitive and boring, like many of these kinds of affairs, but David was also falling asleep because he was so heavily medicated to ease the pain in his back.

At the end of the ceremony, Rudolph and Diane invited everyone to make themselves comfortable at the picnic tables and help themselves to food.

The crowd dispersed from the shade of the tent into bright day.

I looked around. At the other tables, figures clustered in groups of three and five. Aging parents and middle-aged siblings like myself chatted with one another, but always, like plants leaning toward the light, either with the tilt of their head or the angle of their torso, they were watching the person they had come to visit, seeing if he or she had enough to eat, listening to pick up and connect with a shard of language, looking for opportunities, in act or in word, to share the day.

Two weeks later, I discovered I was pregnant.

I flew to Italy, where the man lived, to discuss the future. Steve Rosenfeld had become my sweetheart only in the past year, but he was someone I had known my whole life, the son of old family friends. We decided to make a future and raise our baby together.

So I was going to have a new set of responsibilities, I was going to move to Italy after the baby was born, and then Paul and Michael would have to watch out for Mom and Dave for the time being.

Mom called me at the office. It was the spring of 1996, just before the weekend David was to come home for Easter, and I was hugely pregnant.

"David's got a busted rib," she reported. "Another fall, they're guessing. The doctor is reducing his meds, maybe too much is causing these falls."

We worried about David's inner ear, his balance, something crazy in his central nervous system. Wiring zapped after all those years of meds.

My baby was born in July, a boy named Theo, and in September Steve, Theo, and I flew across the ocean to live together in Italy. In late November, however, my attention returned to my brother David. Michael sent me an e-mail message:

> Things are not good at Brook Farm.
>
> Things at this moment look very good for David.
>
> Brook Farm is losing its license to operate, rampant reported cases of abuse both physical & sexual. We were first contacted last Friday and have since learned that Brook Farm is in deep trouble. Many people are being taken back to Maryland for replacement within the next 48 hours. David will be taken care of by a very highly placed competent person (who is in

constant touch with us). While he is home this weekend, he will be shown
new places in Montgomery County to live. The situation is under control.

"Rampant reported cases of abuse both physical & sexual."

David's rib. David's head nodding because of his medication the day of the Open House. His bad back. A finger that had also been broken.

I imagined David being hit, thrown down. I didn't like thinking about sexual abuse. I imagined someone yelling at my brother.

I imagined David frightened. He calls out in his words that we understand but other people don't. My tall elegant awkward brother, crying as he falls: "You're Luke! Luke!" David confused and hurt and scared and falling down. Being hit.

Then something happened with enough force to break a rib. Was he hit with a fist or with a cane? Or was he kicked?

Was David violent? Was the person who hurt him someone who could not handle his violence except by being violent in return?

"Luke!" And no help. Nothing.

He was not able to tell us.

Doubtlessly I had met the person who hurt my brother; I had shaken the hand that had pulled back my brother's finger until the bone cracked. And I had smiled at the man and I had walked away and gotten into the car and left my brother with him.

I left David to be hit again and to be told, "This is because you are bad. And if you tell anyone—anyone—I'll get you worse next time."

I left my brother alone.

In the weeks after I got the e-mail from Michael and before I could come home, I spoke once or twice to Joan.

Mom was brief. She said things that terrified me, just in passing. For example, she said that five Brook Farm staff members were under arrest. So I asked, "Well, then, what's happening with the Zareks themselves?"

"Well," Mom replied calmly, "Rudolph's still in the hospital. Taped from head to toe."

"What is he doing *there?*" I asked.

"I didn't tell you?" Joan said.

The story, the way she had heard it, was that Rudolph Zarek had been flying a few sick children to a Shriner's hospital that was up in the northern part of the state. This was just as the scandal was beginning to break. He hit bad weather and the plane went down; two children were killed. Rudolph survived, but barely.

Joan added that the person who told her about Rudolph's airplane had commented, somewhat ironically, that God had saved Rudolph Zarek so that he would have to face the things he had allowed to happen at Brook Farm, things he had systematically covered up.

When I came back to the States in mid-December with Steve and Theo, I didn't ask David about what had happened.

We all talked among ourselves about Brook Farm, but not with David. We had been told that if David had experienced any abuse, he would not talk about it until he could be absolutely sure that he would never go back to the abusive situation. I said a few ridiculous and awkward sentences to him about what he had been through and where he was headed, and he just listened. He didn't say a word.

When David was interviewed for the new program, the psychologist, who had agreed with Joan to explore about possible abuse, said, "So tell me, David, who are the people you like at Brook Farm?"

David mentioned one of his recent house counselors, a large calm man from West Virginia who hadn't much impressed Joan when she talked to him.

"Who are the people you don't like there?" she then asked.

"I'd rather not say," replied my brother. .

And later, when the psychologist asked David how he broke his finger, he answered, "I'd rather not talk about it."

■   ■   ■

When the investigators from Adult Protective Services came onto the Brook Farm campus, in the first days of what would be a very long stay, they discovered a locked metal box.

Inside this box they found reports of abuse on clients. These were reports by staff of misconduct by other staff members. These were not included in the clients' files, where they would have been available in routine reviews by external inspectors.

Each contained a report of behavior that clearly should have been reported to authorities within twenty-four hours, according to the law. Nonetheless, on the front of each report were these words: "Investigation not warranted."

Here is what was in the locked reports:

A staff member twisted a client's arm and slammed him in the stomach three times, another hit a client for stealing iced tea, another hit a client with a clipboard, chipping a tooth. A staff member put both hands around a client's neck. A client was punched in the stomach and chest and threatened with a knife. A client was hit with a broom handle. A staff member slapped a client and pulled her hair.

A staff person withheld a hot dog from a resident and had the resident chase him for five minutes before giving him the food. A client received a swollen lip while "playing" with a staff person.

A staff member hit and dragged a client from the dining room, causing the client to lose a tooth; he called the client "a stupid ass." A staff member pushed a client to the floor, slamming the client's head on the floor eight to ten times.

In October 1994, six reports went into the metal box. In November, eight reports went into the metal box. In the spring of 1995, there were only a few reports, but they picked up again in the fall. Six in September, four in October, several scattered over December and January, four again in February and March 1996.

The staff had turned in these reports, even though they must have realized that what they reported was not investigated. I imagine they were discouraged, and for that reason I believe that these papers represent a small percentage of what could and should have been reported.

One person we heard from at the time, who had run many day programs, told us that, even after so many years, he would wake up in the middle of his sleep worrying about slipping. You have to watch the staff, he said, you have to watch yourself, all the time. Once you open the door to the wrong attitude, the wrong behavior, it is almost impossible to stop.

In March 1996, a client died at Brook Farm. The lawsuit that was later filed alleged that the man suffered leg cuts, a broken shoulder, and bruises on his face, chest, back, arms, and legs. The newspaper report said that the cause of death, according to an autopsy, was a head injury.

In September, a client was beaten for two to three hours.

In November, after a client appeared at the emergency room of the local hospital with marks that were inconsistent with the diagnosis of a fall, Adult Protective Services arrived at Brook Farm.

Joan believed that Rudolph lowered standards just when he should have been tightening them up. The work was getting tougher, not easier.

Times had changed. Brook Farm, a large facility in an isolated setting, was no longer considered an example of best practice by the state governments whose funds supported many of the residents. Places like Maryland were creating residences and jobs for their citizens with disabilities back home, in the communities where their families lived, sending fewer people out of state. The people they did send were often harder to handle.

To fill up their houses, Rudolph and Diane took on responsibility for people with severe behavioral or medical problems. They failed to give the staff the support they needed to work with and empathize with the residents who were already there, let alone the newcomers. There was no training in handling outbursts or how to intervene with strong, out-of-control men and women so that no one would be hurt.

In addition, some of the people they hired were the wrong people: people who could be deliberately cruel to residents, people who were not there out of a need to help, but out of a need to hide, who stayed at Brook Farm because there they found a place where, simply put, helpless people were at their mercy. The nonverbal clients at Brook Farm were especially vulnerable to these staff members.

Why David was beaten, which I believe to be true, we will never know. We will never know the circumstances. It doesn't really matter; David was hurt. I don't know what's worse, violence or the fear of violence, but my brother had both. He lived surrounded by the continual possibility of violence, days, nights, everywhere he was, no matter what he was doing.

Maybe worst of all was that he knew, just like everyone else knew, that it was all being lied about.

David knew what was going on at Brook Farm, and couldn't—or wouldn't—tell us. And what was going on at Brook Farm was physically and emotionally dangerous in ways that the rest of us are unlikely to ever experience in our far less "sheltered" lives.

I remembered the photo of David sitting on the widow's walk in his pajamas, back at the old house on Lenox Street, that spring day a year and a half back, smiling happily for the camera. Smiling in spite of the things he couldn't tell us about. Happy being with his family.

I remembered David's hand trembling later that day, as he sat next to me on the porch. Sitting quietly, before the plate fell from his hand and broke.

He wasn't upset about Michael. David's hand was trembling not because of what was happening on the porch, but because it reminded him of what he was headed back to when he left us.

I saw nothing, really, when I looked at David.

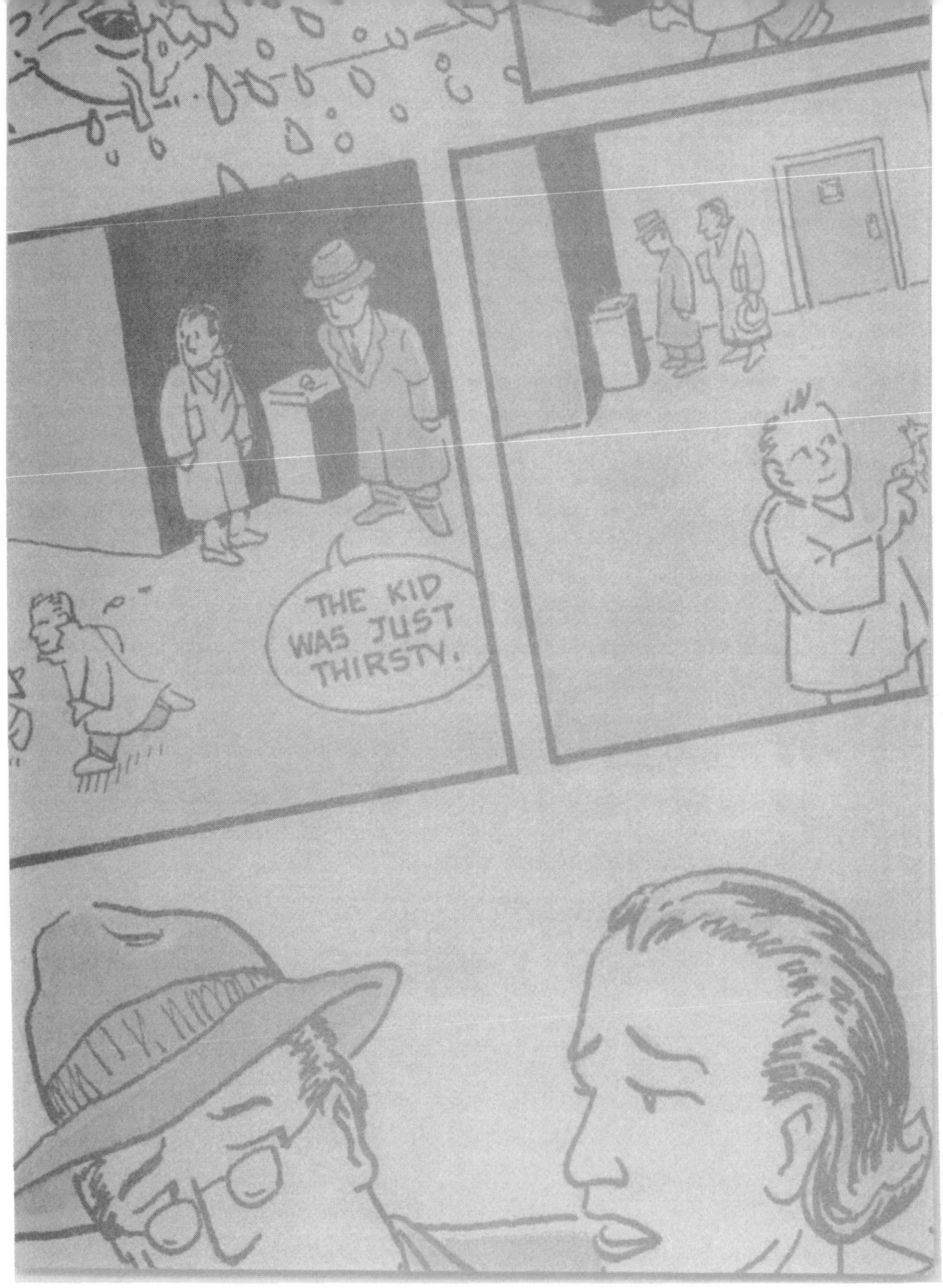
THE KID WAS JUST THIRSTY.

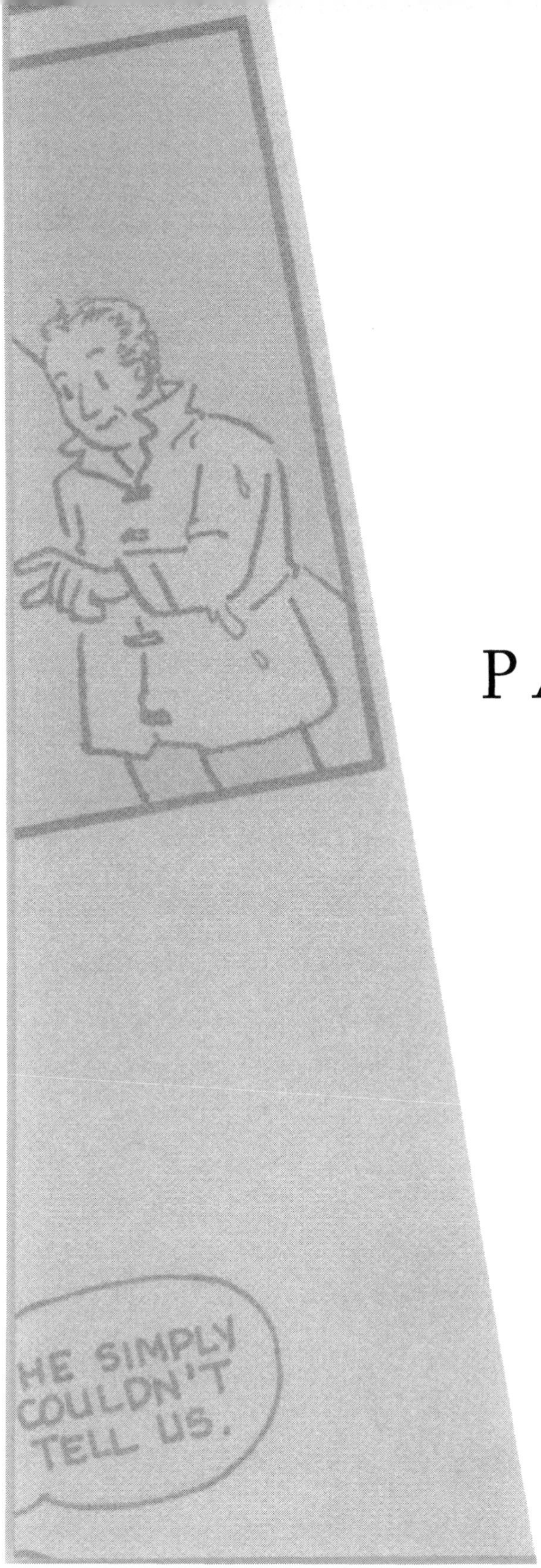
HE SIMPLY COULDN'T TELL US.

PART FIVE

2001

18 The Ride Together

The annual picnic is a green sunlit slice of human chaos in the middle of my gray workweek. When David, Paul, and I arrive it is in full swing, a crowd eating and talking along eight long rows of tables under a tent next to a big field. People are all ages, all sizes, white, black, and tan, and I hear foreign-born lilts to much of the language. These are David's fellow clients, counselors, program staff, and everyone's family, all mixed together so that you can't tell who is who and who is with whom.

David is now in a program located near Mom, a program for people with autism only, who live in the community and work at real jobs.

In this program, it is our family's hope that David can become engaged in life, just like anyone else who has a job. Just as Pop always said, a way to make a contribution. Everybody needs to be able to make a contribution.

Once we've eaten, Paul and David work the crowd. Paul jokes with someone, maybe a counselor, maybe an administrator. David moves along the tables, offering his hand to shake, touching people lightly with the tips of his fingers. He sits next to a white woman with short, dark hair, sprinkled with gray, a client.

David faces away from her, apparently staring toward the open field, his right hand stroking his forehead. His left shoulder brushes gently against her back. The woman chats energetically with her counselor. I try to talk with Dave but his thoughts are elsewhere.

This leaves me with a moment of nothing to do. If Theo were here, I would get out the frisbee, but Theo's in Italy. If I were at Mom's house, I would be excusing myself from the family weekend for an hour or so, borrowing her desk, trying to make Monday's deadline on top of the time with Paul and David, but there's no desk here. These times together are rare, and they are packed. Last night we were up at Michael and Ellen's for dinner and a family meeting. Today, while David, Paul, and I attend the picnic, Joan remains in Baltimore to work through her estate and finances with Michael, who understands, as his siblings do not, the wonderful things numbers can do in different combinations and disguises.

Tomorrow Paul heads back to his home and Dave to his residence. And this afternoon, Paul is going to show David the final draft of the book we've been writing about the family. I hope David finds a way to like it.

I walk out onto the field, past swings, two barbecue grills, a sturdy wooden climbing castle, and a slide, toward a long, wide playing field surrounded by woods. Figures are scattered across the landscape, kids kicking balls, a group at a remote picnic table, children on the castle jumping around adults, some of the adults sitting on platforms or swings, rocking back and forth—which, here, nobody thinks is strange. Two adults walk the perimeter of the playing field, an elderly man with his hand on the shoulder of a middle-aged man.

A counselor introduces himself with a smile; he is a short, fit, very dark black man. He's heard that I live abroad. He is also separated from his family for the sake of work and income, but his case is much more difficult than mine. My four-month job here, in its final hectic weeks, has paid well enough so that Theo has been able to bounce across the ocean several times between Italy and Joan's house, and Steve and I can talk daily, if briefly. This man sees his wife and children once a year, for the eight weeks permitted by limited visas; instead of phone calls, they send tape cassettes back and forth. Shoes, clothes, and money also arrive from America. He is cheerful; where he comes from, his life looks like opportunity.

I don't think that Steve and I will ever agree to try four months apart again, but once you have a family, you never know what the future will contain.

Except that some of it will contain the past. On his most recent visit Theo complained how unfair it was that David got to watch *his* show. I used Joan's words to explain, and, in a supernatural moment, my son interrupted me, saying exactly what I had said so many years earlier.

"Okay, Mom, I *get* it!" Off he stomped.

I can't see David from the field, but once I get back under the tent I find him, eating another hot dog.

"How's that, Dave?"

"Pretty good."

"You having a good time?"

"Yes, ma'am!" he replies.

Paul waves me over to where he sits with Daphne, the director of the program, a trim blond woman, and a client, a nicely dressed dark-haired white man in his early thirties. The client tells Daphne that he is making good progress driving and plans to get his own license soon.

"That's great," she says.

Then the conversation takes a turn, the way a laughing person can suddenly stop laughing.

"Daphne," he asks, "Daphne, what did you do when you came to Maplewood?"

I can tell she's answered this question before. Maplewood was a local facility which was closed down. I don't remember the specifics.

"I knocked on the door," she says, "and they let me in."

"Did you bring the police with you?"

"Yes," she replies, "I brought the police. You know that."

"Then what happened? What happened?" he asks, his voice rising with some urgency.

She is calm. "You know what happened," she replies, factually, gently.

"What happened at Maplewood?" he asks again.

"Now, you know what happened. I want you to take those thoughts and put them in a drawer."

"Put them in a drawer," he says.

"Now, are they in the drawer?" she asks. He nods. "Now shut the drawer," she says, making a pushing motion in the air with the flat of her hand. "And lock that drawer tight!"

"Lock it tight," he says. "Just lock it!"

She smiles, nods her head, then asks, "Can I go practice driving with you in the parking lot sometime soon?"

"Sure, Daphne," he says, and then turns and walks toward the light and the swings.

She looks at Paul and me. "That pain never goes away, does it?"

David has wandered off, I suddenly realize. I leave Daphne with Paul and find Dave, stroking the hair of the woman he had been sitting next to earlier.

He stands up and strokes my hair, too. "Judy?" he says, "you're nice."

"You're nice, too, Dave," I reply. This is what I always say.

Then Annie, one of Dave's house counselors, who is from Sierra Leone, calls from the end of the row of tables. "David, there's ice cream!" she says, her West African voice putting song into the English. Dave heads for the truck and Annie gives me a knowing smile. "He loves his ice cream," she says.

I follow my older brother, but slowly. As I pass the woman David has been getting close to, she says to her counselor, "I like the boys. I like that David Karasik." Then she smiles, wickedly and girlishly. "But I dump them fast, don't I? I don't keep any one of them for long!"

At the truck David needs no help. He's fine. The picnic is closing down. When he finishes the ice cream and we find a trash bag for the wrapping, I say, "Let's help clear up the tables, Dave." Paul reappears with a cup of coffee and the three of us pile plastic plates and cups and put them into big plastic bags.

I see Annie with Pete and Willie, Dave's housemates, getting into her car and I am glad that David is coming with Paul and me back to Joan's. As much as this weekend comes at a bad time in terms of my workload, and as little as I have to say to David and him to me, and as friendly and caring as everyone is who works for the program, still I don't like relinquishing my older brother. I don't like that moment when the door to his residence snaps shut behind him and David, inside his very busy mind, is inside that trim little house.

Through the wide asphalt lanes of suburban Maryland, we share the ride together. Paul suggests we drive down to Chevy Chase, past the old house on Lenox Street, but then we decide against it. It's too far out of the way.

The house, which has been greatly altered by its new owners, is now remarkable more for how it rejects our memories than in how it kindles them. When our eyes seek out the special places where, over the years, we trained one another to be human beings in this particular family, it is exactly in those spots that the building has been changed. The widow's walk is now a mere skylight; the slant in the driveway, where I stood that day yelling at Michael and Paul, is now covered with more house. The strange square turning central staircase has been replaced; the porch has been extended. Even the row house on Allison Street is no longer in our life; Dorothy and Ed have sold it and moved to Knoxville, where their son James lives with his wife and children.

Our old stage sets have vanished; we inhabit new scenery. Joan has made the long drive to Knoxville several times so far, once by herself, once with Paul, twice with me and Theo. The bungalow Joan bought in Silver Spring, another Maryland suburb, is long and low, not boxy and high—but it has a porch where we eat and drink, just as before, still rocking on the bentwood chairs from Mr. Dietz.

As the places have changed and our story has changed, so have the characters, or anyway so I hope. When I look back to that afternoon in April, and remember the question I asked my brothers in the driveway, I cringe a little. Make a plan, make your promises, and everything is settled and everyone will always love one another and nothing can harm any of us.

As if it were that simple.

At our final stoplight, I look over at David, sitting silently, his lips moving slightly. He is on to the next thing already, I can tell, he is thinking of the programs he has lined up for this afternoon, remembering where he left his papers, starting to envision new ways in which to shuffle them.

The light changes and we move ahead. We are all quiet in the car. Paul and me and David, words soundlessly cascading through our brains.

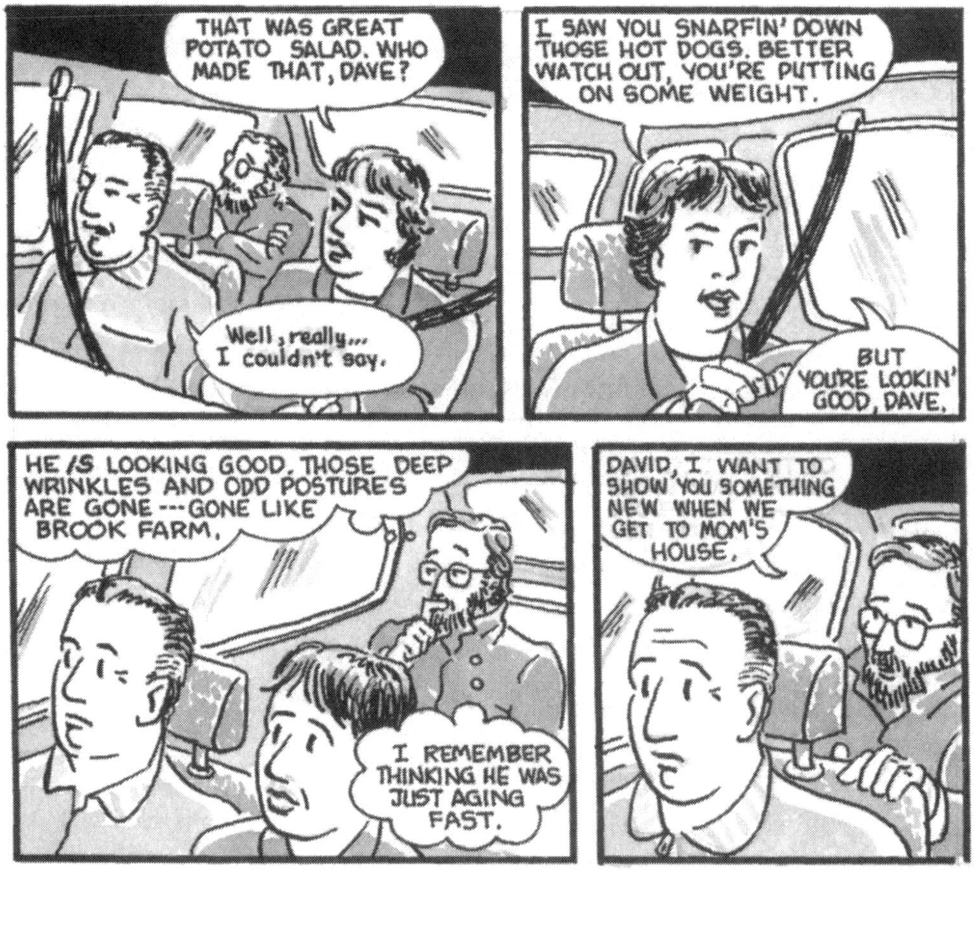
THAT WAS GREAT POTATO SALAD. WHO MADE THAT, DAVE?
Well, really... I couldn't say.
I SAW YOU SNARFIN' DOWN THOSE HOT DOGS. BETTER WATCH OUT, YOU'RE PUTTING ON SOME WEIGHT.
BUT YOU'RE LOOKIN' GOOD, DAVE.
HE IS LOOKING GOOD. THOSE DEEP WRINKLES AND ODD POSTURES ARE GONE---GONE LIKE BROOK FARM.
I REMEMBER THINKING HE WAS JUST AGING FAST.
DAVID, I WANT TO SHOW YOU SOMETHING NEW WHEN WE GET TO MOM'S HOUSE.

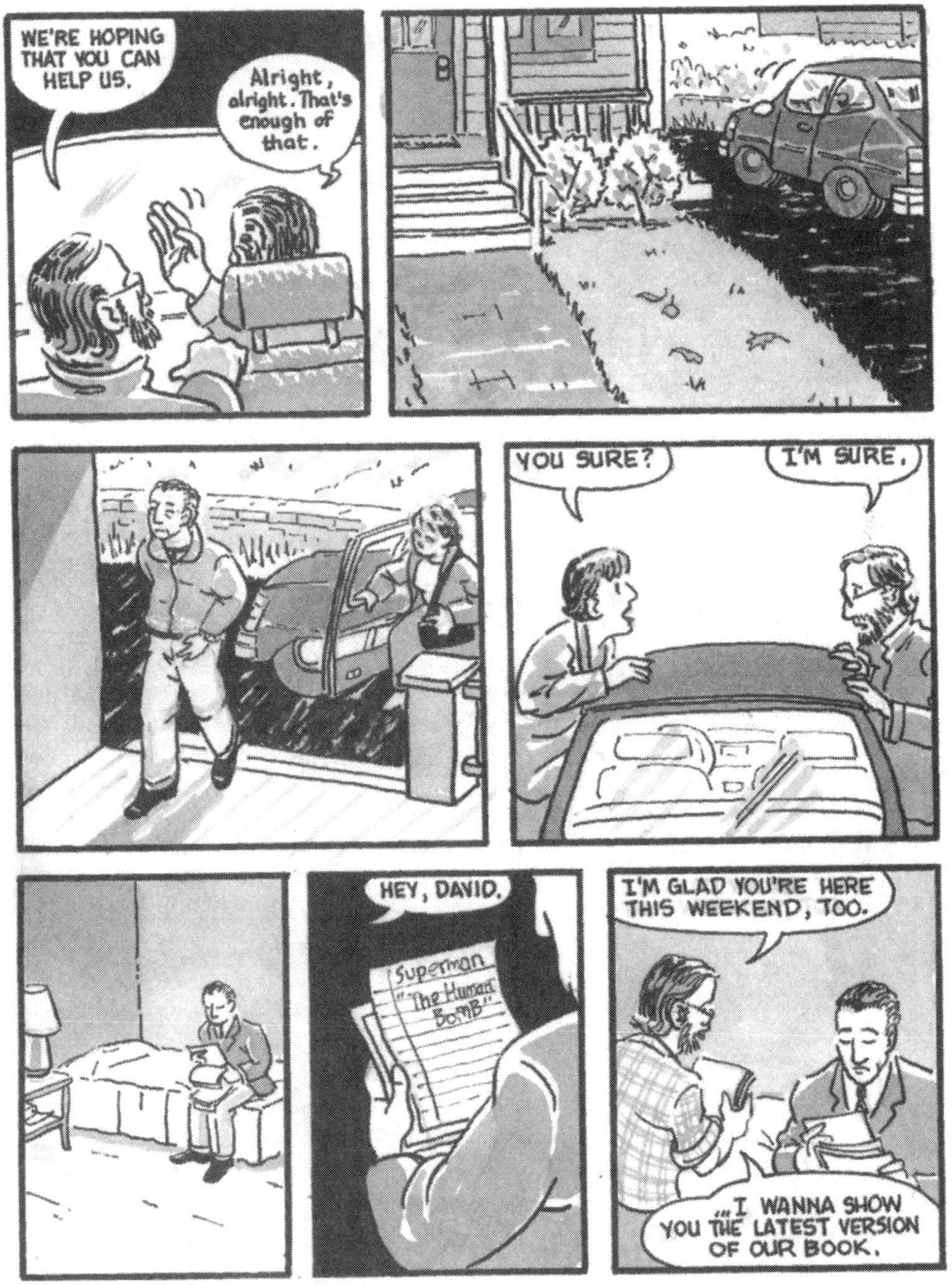
WE'RE HOPING THAT YOU CAN HELP US.
Alright, alright. That's enough of that.
YOU SURE?
I'M SURE.
HEY, DAVID.
Superman "The Human Bomb"
I'M GLAD YOU'RE HERE THIS WEEKEND, TOO.
...I WANNA SHOW YOU THE LATEST VERSION OF OUR BOOK.

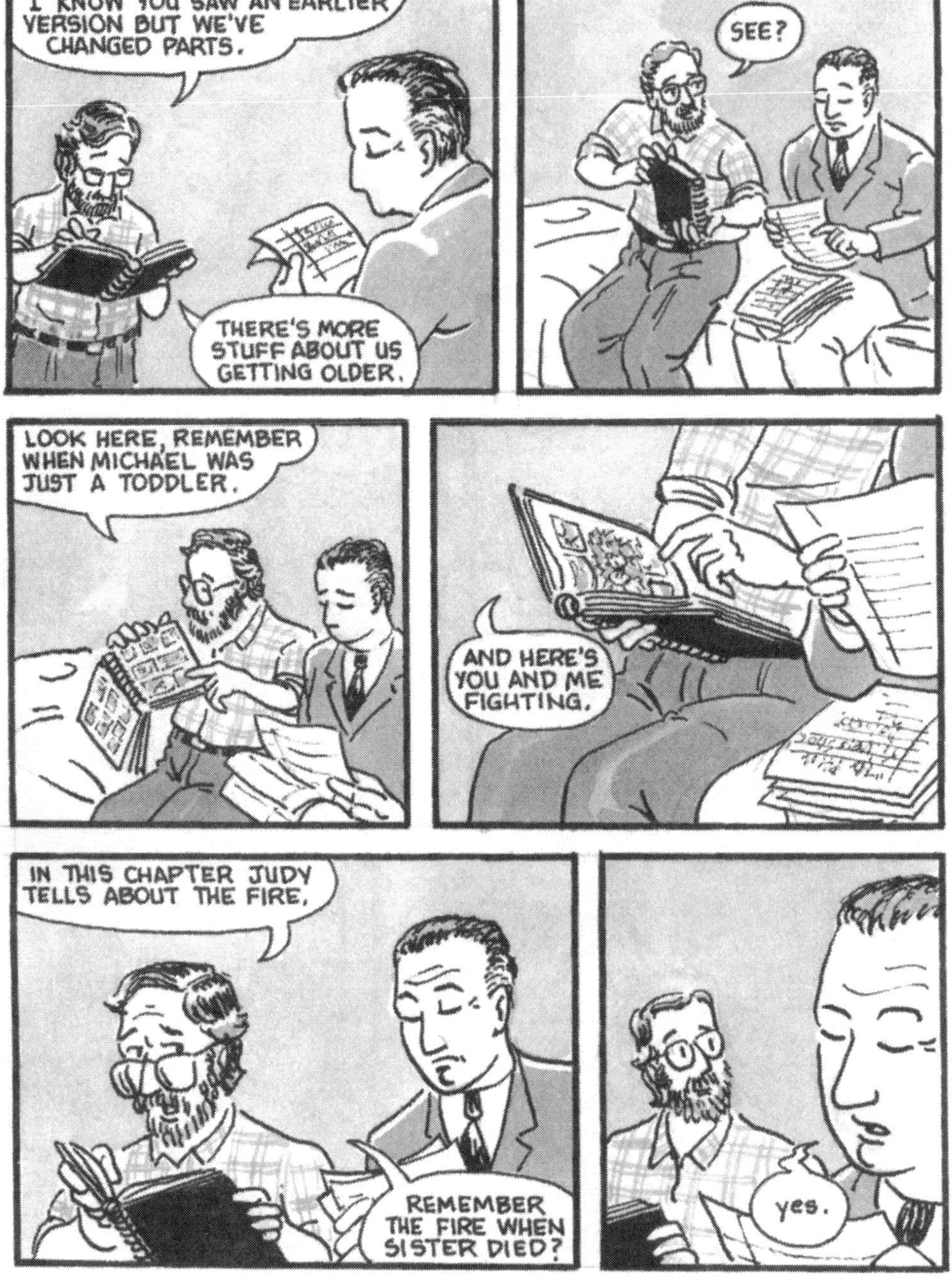
I KNOW YOU SAW AN EARLIER VERSION BUT WE'VE CHANGED PARTS.
THERE'S MORE STUFF ABOUT US GETTING OLDER.
SEE?
LOOK HERE, REMEMBER WHEN MICHAEL WAS JUST A TODDLER.
AND HERE'S YOU AND ME FIGHTING.
IN THIS CHAPTER JUDY TELLS ABOUT THE FIRE,
REMEMBER THE FIRE WHEN SISTER DIED?
yes.

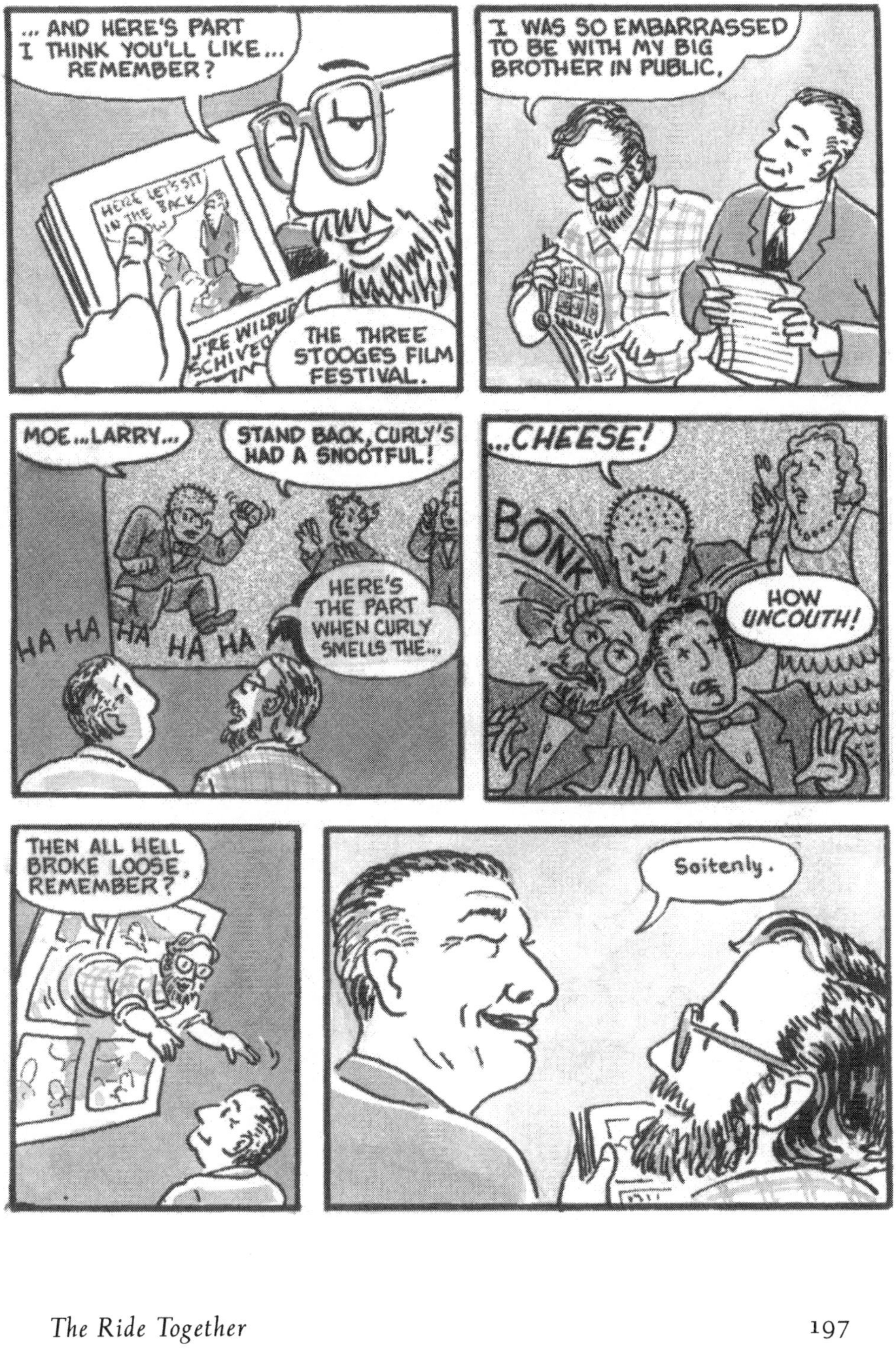
... AND HERE'S PART I THINK YOU'LL LIKE... REMEMBER?
THE THREE STOOGES FILM FESTIVAL.
I WAS SO EMBARRASSED TO BE WITH MY BIG BROTHER IN PUBLIC.
MOE...LARRY...
STAND BACK, CURLY'S HAD A SNOOTFUL!
HERE'S THE PART WHEN CURLY SMELLS THE...
HA HA HA HA HA
...CHEESE!
BONK
HOW UNCOUTH!
THEN ALL HELL BROKE LOOSE, REMEMBER?
Soitenly.

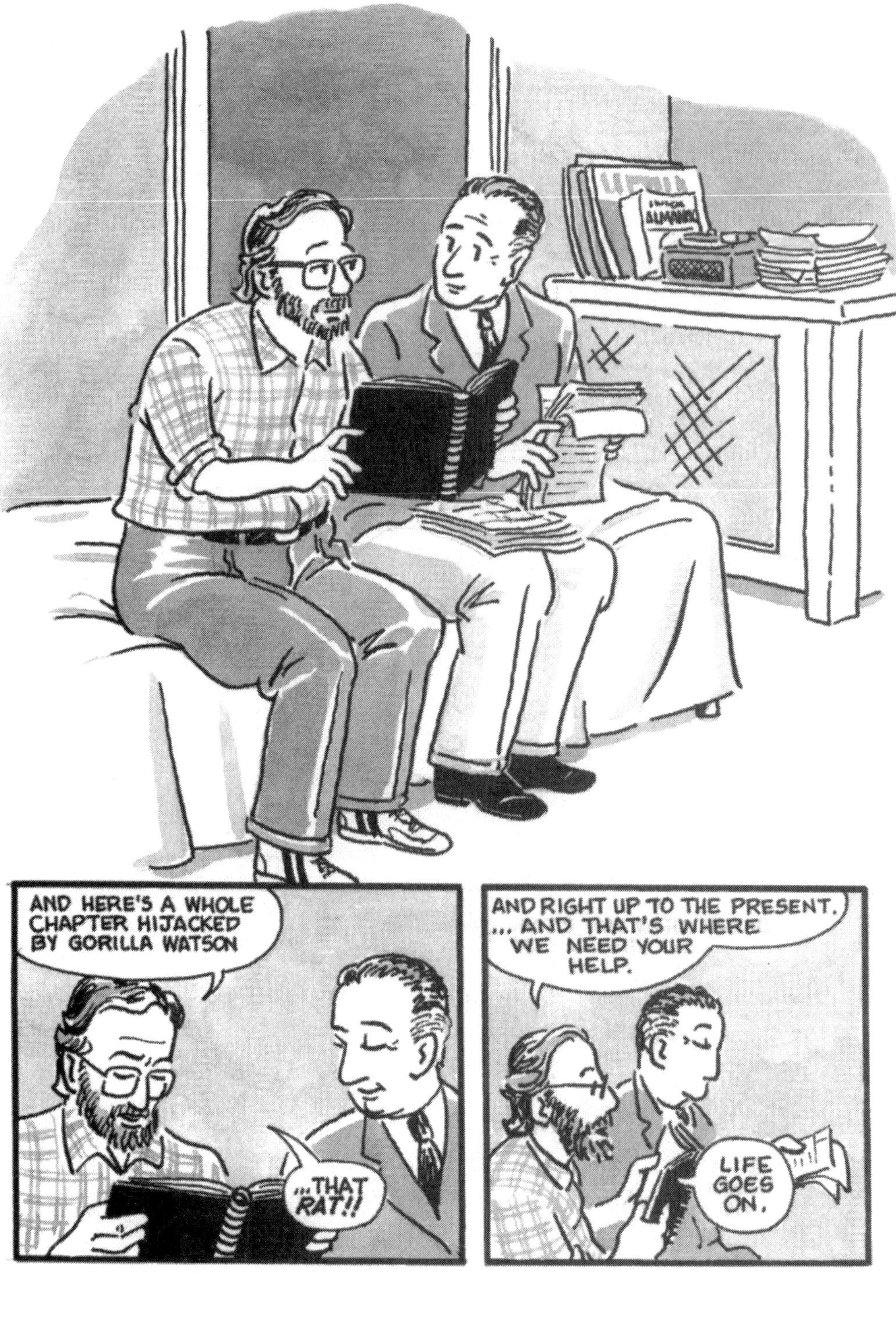

AND HERE'S A WHOLE CHAPTER HIJACKED BY GORILLA WATSON
...THAT RAT!!
AND RIGHT UP TO THE PRESENT. ... AND THAT'S WHERE WE NEED YOUR HELP.
LIFE GOES ON.

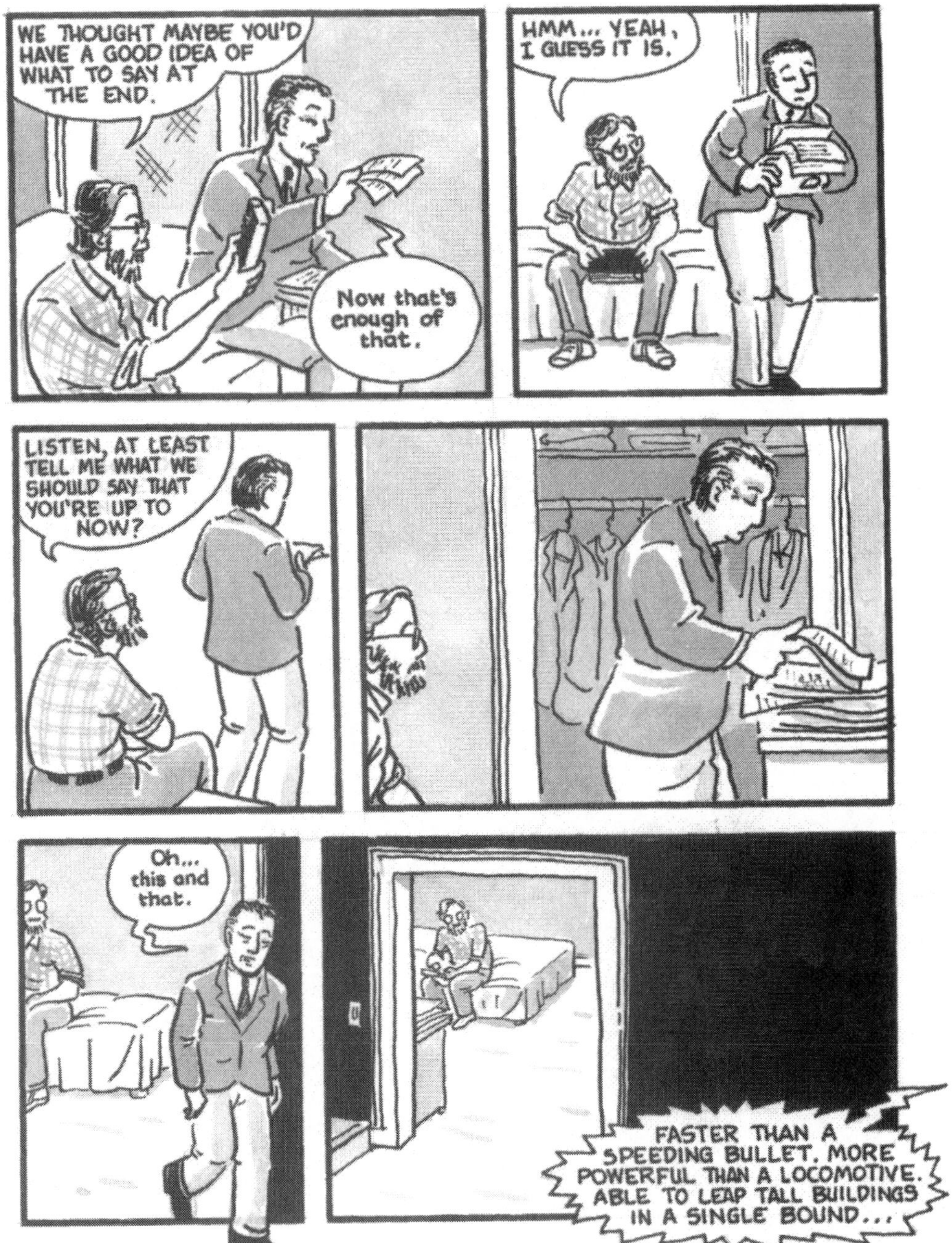
WE THOUGHT MAYBE YOU'D HAVE A GOOD IDEA OF WHAT TO SAY AT THE END.
Now that's enough of that.
HMM... YEAH, I GUESS IT IS.
LISTEN, AT LEAST TELL ME WHAT WE SHOULD SAY THAT YOU'RE UP TO NOW?
Oh... this and that.
FASTER THAN A SPEEDING BULLET. MORE POWERFUL THAN A LOCOMOTIVE. ABLE TO LEAP TALL BUILDINGS IN A SINGLE BOUND...

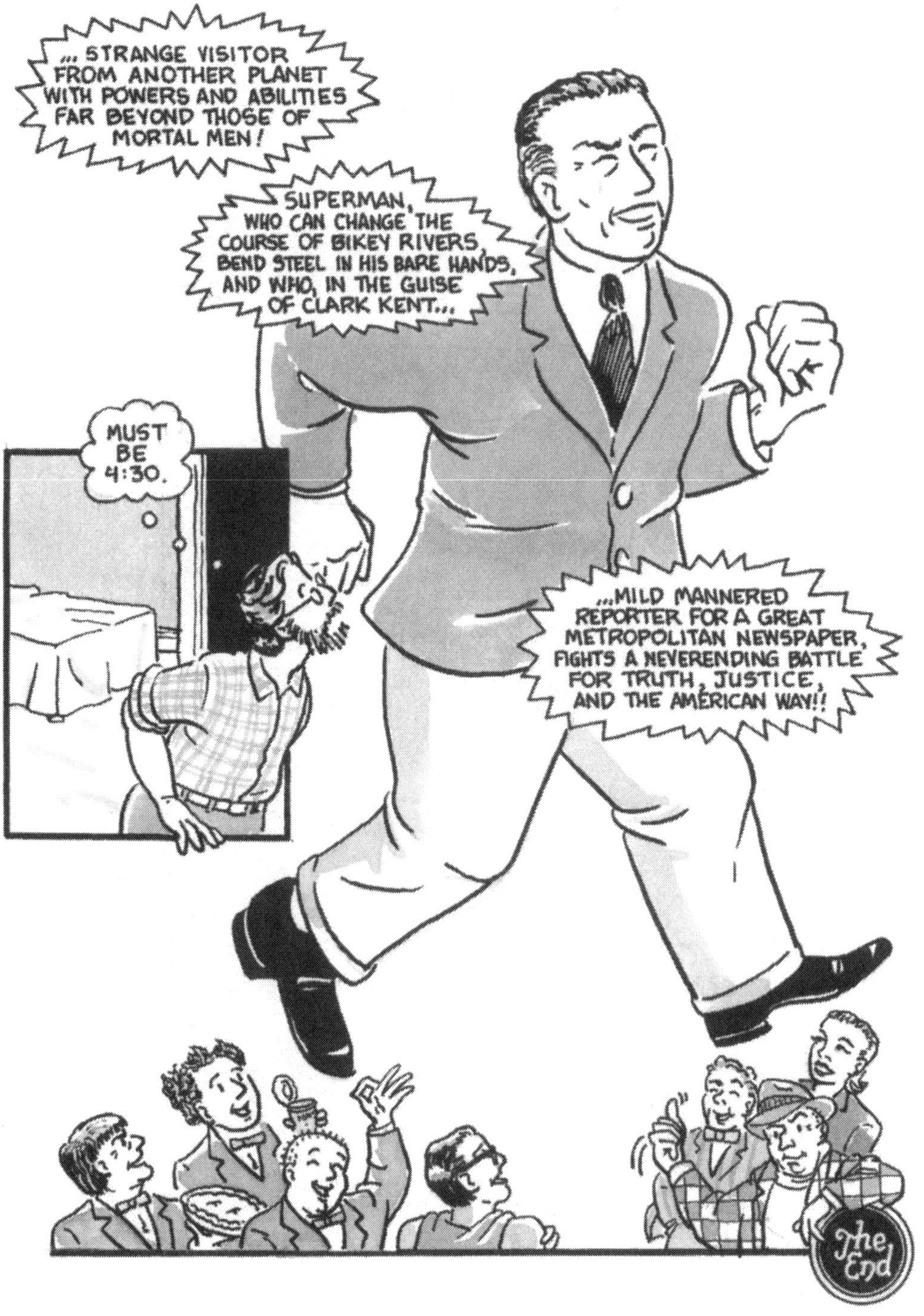
... STRANGE VISITOR FROM ANOTHER PLANET WITH POWERS AND ABILITIES FAR BEYOND THOSE OF MORTAL MEN!
SUPERMAN, WHO CAN CHANGE THE COURSE OF BIKEY RIVERS, BEND STEEL IN HIS BARE HANDS, AND WHO, IN THE GUISE OF CLARK KENT...
MUST BE 4:30.
...MILD MANNERED REPORTER FOR A GREAT METROPOLITAN NEWSPAPER, FIGHTS A NEVERENDING BATTLE FOR TRUTH, JUSTICE, AND THE AMERICAN WAY!!
The End